ROME

KEYS to the ANCIENT CITY
The ASTUTE TRAVELER'S Guide

1-TAKE
PUBLISHING, LLC

COPYRIGHT

1-TAKE Publishing, LLC
6216 Pacific Coast Hwy, #321
Long Beach, CA 90803
www.1Take.com
www.ItalyTravelBooks.com

Ordering Information:
Quantity sales. Special discounts are available for quantity purchases by corporations, associations, and others. For details, contact the publisher at the address above.
Orders by U.S., Canadian, and UK trade bookstores and wholesalers, please contact:
IPG
814 N. Franklin Street
Chicago, IL 60610
IPGBook.com

Printed in South Korea.

Publisher's Cataloging-in-Publication data Civalleri, Patty.
ROME: Keys to the Ancient City - The Astute Traveler's Guide / Patty Civalleri.
ISBN-10:1-7340602-0-4
ISBN-13:978-1-7340602-0-1

1. Travel.
2. Italy/Rome
3. European History.
4. Art History

First Edition
1 2 3 4 5 HPSK 24 23 22 21 20

To my son Jason, a man that has brought so much joy and pride to my life; my friend, my buddy, my partner in futility, my lawyer. You are a rare bird on this Earth, and it saddens me that there aren't more just like you.
Alas, poor world.

Acknowledgments

Many thanks to the **Italian National Tourist Board** in Los Angeles who has helped me with this series by pointing me in the right direction, to the right people, and for opening doors.

Darius, it was a pleasure getting to know you and the American Institute for Roman Culture, and to glean a proper perspective of Rome from you. Your ambition is contagious! Rob, I am amazed when I think of all you did for my research while I was in Rome. Indeed, friends for life! Professor Bernie Frischer, I love, love, love your **RomeReborn.com** project! It was great to find that we have something in common: our mutual love for Rome. Primo and Iris, thank you for showing me how to fall in love with Tivoli. Saluti!

Roger, how many girls can say that their husbands support them in their crazy endeavors as well as you do in mine? Florence, Venice, Rome. Time apart, time together. You are the other half of my brain, and I couldn't have done this without you in lock-step. You are stuck with me forever, baby!

*"Go where they don't go.
Do what they don't do.
Know what they don't know.
Travel."*

~ Patty Civalleri

TABLE OF CONTENTS

TABLE OF CONTENTS

Julius Caesar, 100bce - 44bce

The STUFF in the FRONT of the BOOK

INTRODUCTION

Everyone knows the Trevi Fountain. But did you know that 30 seconds away is a place where you can go under the ground, back 2,000 years in time, to see the ancient aquifers that still feed the Trevi today? And that it is refreshing and uncrowded down there?

Everyone knows the Colosseum. But did you know that within a 5-minute walk is Michelangelo's "Moses," the sculpture he considered to be his very best work - *ever?*

Everyone knows the Forum. But did you know that within steps of the Forum, you can visit the fantastic ancient, 2,000-year-old Marketplace of Trajan? And that you can climb through the whole place because the most of the structure still stands? And that it is uncrowded?

Everyone knows the Pantheon. But did you know that right behind it is a church with fabulous Michelangelo and Bernini sculptures that most don't even know are there? And it is relaxed and uncrowded?

The major travel sources boast the same half-dozen places in Rome. Those are the places that get the big marketing budgets, and they are the easiest places to write about - they don't require much research. So that is as far as most guides will take you, and why those places are so darned crowded!

Rome is over 2,500 years old. So you'd think they left behind more than a half-dozen places, right? As it turns out, they did, and all are within walking distance of where the crowds gather.

My name is Patty Civalleri, and this is the way I see Rome. With a 20-year background in archaeology and history, I dug deep *(no pun intended!),* and found a marvelous city that most never see when they visit: The Secret *(and growing!)* Underground Rome.

Perhaps you have already been to Rome, and you have already seen these famous places. But don't stop there. Because I can go on for days telling you about all of the recent archaeological discoveries, the places where you must don a hard hat to enter, and the sites with enough bone-chilling stories to inspire Hollywood.

Some of these sites are difficult to understand because they have been ravaged by the unkindness of time. A variety of new technologies are now available to make it easy for you to understand what you are seeing. 3D Virtual Reality is used in many of the ancient sites around the city. It has never been easier for you to jump into these places and come out truly understanding what the ancient Romans experienced.

At the end of each day, when you are hot and tired from walking the ancient cobblestones, I will take you in the opposite direction: instead of going down, I have skimmed the rooftops of Rome to find a whole host of places where you can rest, get the very best photos in the city, and cool down with a chilled glass of that incredible Italian Prosecco.

Let me show you my Rome. It will become your new favorite city in the world, as it has mine.
Ciao for now!

II

SEE IT YOUR WAY~FAQ'S

If you are not sure where to start in Rome, try this: Check off questions for which you would like to find the answers. These Frequently Asked Questions will point you in directions that will help you to see more of what's fun for you - without wasting your short visit on the fluff that everyone thinks you SHOULD see.

_____ Where should I stay in Rome? `14`

_____ Where should I eat in Rome? `15`

_____ Is it possible to escape the crowds and cool off *(with great views)*? `236`

_____ Which statue did Michelangelo hit with a hammer, hoping it would speak? `196`

_____ Where must I wear a hard hat to visit? `69`

_____ Under which Aqueduct can I play golf? `88`

_____ Where did they crucify 6,000 of Sparticus' men? `87`

_____ What place used thousands of human bones to decorate?? `85`

_____ Why are there so many baths? Why are they so big? `64`

_____ Which Emperor built the biggest Baths? `64`

_____ Is Ponte Sant'Angelo really haunted? `255`

_____ Which Emperor built the biggest Forum? `59`

_____ Who was the Pirate Pope? `206`

_____ Was there really a woman Pope?!? `216`

_____ Can I enter the WWII Bomb Shelter in Mussolini's former home? `150`

_____ Where are the most 'happening' areas of Rome? `14, 224, 227`

_____ Who were the Etruscans? `142`

_____ What did the Etruscans have to do with Rome? `142`

_____ Where are the quietest areas of Rome? `14, 229, 234`

_____ How is the Forum laid out? `46`

_____ Why is the ancient Port City of Ostia Antica so important? `280`

_____ What are some good ideas for Day Trips from Rome? `272`

_____ How do I get underneath Trevi Fountain? `81`

_____ Where did the Gladiators live and train? `75`

_____ What symbolized Rome's power to the rest of the world? `276`

_____ Why was Hercules so important to Rome? `70`

_____ Where in Rome can I stand to see 3 countries at once? `256`

_____ What's in the underground site of Domus Transitoria, and where is it? `68`

_____ Was Caesar really murdered in a Cat House? `76`

The STUFF in the FRONT of the BOOK

The STUFF in the FRONT of the BOOK

13

WHERE to STAY in ROME?

This is a frequently asked question. If you understand your personal interests, the answer is simple. Use this as a general guide when finding your own neighborhood in Rome.

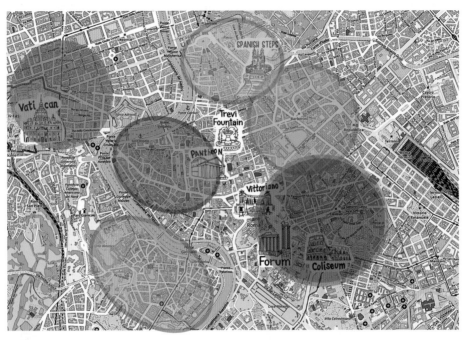

Ancient Sites
The oldest parts of Rome are near the Colosseum and Forum. If you want to step back to ancient Rome, this is your neighborhood!

Art
Rome has some of the greatest art galleries in the world. Some are in museums, some are in Palazzos (Palaces), some are in churches. They tend to be somewhat spread around the city. To see great art, you can stay anywhere in Rome!

Religion
Vatican City is an obvious choice. But GREAT churches are spread over the entire city.

Shopping
The international designer stores are mostly near the Spanish Steps. Local boutiques can be found everywhere.

Quiet
For a quiet, relaxing visit to Rome, you may want to stay in Trastevere, away from the main Piazza. You'll enjoy the romance of this area!

Happening
Fun! Bars! Festivals & Events! Dancing...! So much happens all around Rome, but if you love the late nights, the area surrounding Piazza Navona is your place!

The STUFF in the FRONT of the BOOK

WHERE to EAT in ROME?

After having traveled the world over, I have come to the realization that Italy is not a country where you should be concerned about food. On the contrary, go to Rome for its historical heart, and you'll quickly realize that the food will come naturally - all over the city! As long as you know the differences between the types of fooderies, you won't get surprised by the menu or the bill.

UNLESS... you eat at tourist-driven places. You will probably feel ripped-off when dining at the big shiny, bright restaurants that are near the big touristy sites. Look for smaller, darker restaurants, with few or no windows. They will be filled with Italians - not tourists. You cannot go wrong if you brave-up and walk in. The food will be out of this world, and the prices will be fair.

RISTORANTE = FORMAL, TABLECLOTHS, DRESS CODE, EXPENSIVE

TRATTORIA = FAMILY-OWNED, LARGE PORTIONS LESS EXPENSIVE

OSTERIA = DINING IN AN INN

INOTECA = WINE & SNACKS

BAR = BAR

TABERNAE = SHOPS, INDOOR MARKETS

Food Rules

Do you know how you hate it when someone belches in a restaurant? Or they try to order pancakes in a steak house? Well, we have dining rules, as does every other culture in the world. Visitors to your city may not realize that belching is not acceptable, or that asking for pancakes in a steakhouse just isn't done. Italy has their rules as well. Here are some guidelines (as silly as they may seem). But follow them, and you won't get flagged as a "turista stupido!" Oh yah, one more thing: I've heard newbie travelers complain because Italian food isn't as good as 'American' Italian food. Oftentimes, Italian food has been Americanized. That's correct! But in Italy, you are getting REAL Italian food, according to their regioni. Be open-minded when it comes to food, and learn to eat like an Italian. You won't be disappointed!

- Don't order Cappuccino after 11am
- Fettuccine Alfredo doesn't exist
- Spaghetti & Meatballs don't exist
- Pepperoni doesn't come on pizzas
- Pizzas: mostly vegs; salmon, prosciutto or eggs if you crave protein
- Drink wine or water with your meal
- Don't ask for salad dressing; reach for the olive oil & vinegar instead
- Dine slowly. Period.
- If you don't ask for your check, you won't get it. They assume you're just hanging out, enjoying yourself.
- Eat gelato any time, every day.

The STUFF in the FRONT of the BOOK

17

Where to Begin?

THE "WELCOME to ROME Museum"
CORSO VITTORIO EMANUELE II, 203

The STUFF in the FRONT of the BOOK

Away From the HEAT!

GREAT FIND!

UNCROWDED!

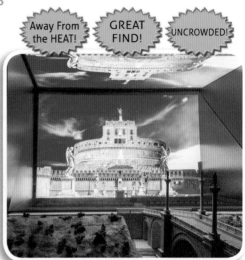

Rome is a big city, with an even bigger history. If you have never been here before and don't know where to start, try starting here.

Rome can be difficult to penetrate if you don't have a good idea about what you want before you get there. Sometimes, it can even be difficult to ask the right questions. So folks will often start with "Where does everyone else go?" or "What are the main sites?" **This is a sure way to become overwhelmed and lost in the sheer mass crowds.**

On the main boulevard of Corso Vittorio Emanuele II, you will find "Welcome to Rome," a museum that serves as a warm greeting to Rome. The presentations will last about one hour, and is a great way to begin your visit to Rome.

Since Rome is all about its ancientness, each room will present a different part of the city's past. You will start with the beginnings of the city, and progress chronologically through each room's immersive cinematic presentation.

Each presentation is created in a unique way, utilizing a variety of technologies. By the time you leave, you will have a good 'feel' about the stories of Rome's past, as well as some great ideas of what you would like to see in the city. *Benvenuti a Roma!*
(Welcome to Rome!)

ROMA PASS
Visit RomaPass.it

The Roma Pass is a good way to save some time and money. It will gain you discounts into as many as 80 museums, sites, exhibits, and events. Some of the venues will give you opportunities to cut ahead of the long lines. When you pick up your PASS, don't forget to get your free city map as well.

Additionally, you can use the ATAC transportation system in Rome, which includes the Metro *(subway)* system and some city buses. Just look for the ATAC logo on the sides of the buses.

To learn more about the Roma Pass, visit RomaPass.it.

ROMA PASS

48 or 72 hours

- Free entry to the first 1 museum or archaeological site.
- **Unlimited free access** to the ATAC urban public transport network.
- Reduced tickets to all other museums and/or archaeological sites visited thereafter.
- **Direct access to** Capitoline Museums and Castel Sant'Angelo. **Mandatory booking through dedicated channels** for Coliseum, Borghese Gallery **(temporarily suspended)** and Palazzo Valentini (Domus Romane).
- **Over 80 discounted tickets** for exhibitions, events and other collaborating operators and businesses.
- **Roma MAP:** a map featuring the most interesting site in Rome, all the Tourist Information Points, Metro and Buses to create your tourist itinerary!

The Keys to Rome aren't the shopping malls and restaurants. Those can be found anywhere in the world. They are the fantastic morsels of the past left from the Ancient Republic, the Roman Empire, the Renaissance, and the Baroque eras. Archaeologists in Rome are amongst the very best in the world, and the sites they have prepared for you will change the way you see the world. And they should! There are literally hundreds of sites around the city; we have gathered some of the most interesting of them for you to enjoy during your stay in Rome.

LUDUS MAGNUS

A BRIEF HISTORY OF ROME

ALL KINGS, RULERS & EMPERORS

It is clear that Rome has been through a lot! With all of the conquerers, winners, losers, and usurpers, how did this city last for 2,700 years? Look at year 238, for example. It looks to be a pretty difficult year for Rome's Ruling Class! And there were more just like it. Cheers to the stout heart of our Romans to see it through FOR OVER 1,000 YEARS!

Kings: Regal Period

Romulus • 753–716 BCE
Numa Pompilius • 715–673 BCE
Tullus Hostilius • 673–642 BCE
Ancus Marcius • 642–616 BCE
Tarquinius Priscus • 616–579 BCE
Servius Tullius • 578–535 BCE
Tarquinius Superbus • 535–509 BCE

Rulers: Roman Republic

Cato the Elder • 234–149 BCE
Tiberius Sempronius Graccus • 133BCE
Caius Sempronius Gracchus • 121 BCE
Caius Marius • 157–86 BCE
Lucius Cornelius Sulla • 138–78 BCE
Pompey, Julius Caesar & Crassus • 106–48BCE
Cato the Younger • 95–46 BCE
Julius Caesar • 100–44 BCE

Emperors: Roman Empire

Augustus • 27 BCE–14CE
Tiberius • 14–37
Caligula • 37–41
Claudius • 41–54
Nero • 54–68
Galba • 68–69
Otho • 69
Vitellius • 69
Vespasian • 69–79
Titus • 79–81

Domitian • 81–96
Nerva • 96-98
Trajan • 98–117
Hadrian • 117–138
Antoninus Pius • 138–161
Marcus Aurelius • 161–180
Lucius Verus • 161–169
Commodus • 180–192
Pertinax • 193
Didius Julianus • 193
Severus • 193–211
Caracalla • 211–217
Geta • 211–212
Macrinus • 217–18
Heliogabalus • 218–222
Alexander Severus • 222–235
Maximin • 235–238
Gordian I • 238
Gordian II • 238
Balbinus • 238
Pupienus Maximus • 238
Gordian III • 238–244
Philip the Arabian • 244–249
Decius • 249–251
Hostilianus • 251
Gallus • 251–253
Aemilianus • 253
Valerian • 253–260
Gallienus • 253–268
Claudius II • 268–270
Aurelian • 270–275
Tacitus • 275–276
Florianus • 276
Probus • 276–282
Carus • 282–283
Carinus • 283–285
Numerianus • 283–284
Diocletian • 284–305
Maximian • 286–305
Constantius I • 305–306
Galerius • 305–310
Maximin • 308–313

Licinius • 308–324
Maxentius • 306–312
Constantine I the Great • 306–337
Constantine II • 337–340
Constans • 337–350
Constantius II • 337–361
Magnentius • 350–353
Julian the Apostate • 361–363
Jovian • 363–364
Valentinian I • 364–375
Valens • 364–378
Gratian • 375–383
Maximus • 383–388
Valentinian II • 375–392
Eugenius • 393–394
Theodosius I • 379–395
Gratian • 394–395

Emperors in the East

Arcadius • 395–408
Theodosius II • 408–450
Marcian • 450–457
Leo I • 457–474
Leo II • 474
Zeno • 474–475
Basilicus • 475–476

Emperors in the West

Honorius • 395–423
Maximus • 409–411
Constantius III • 421
Valentinian III • 425–455
Petronius Maximus • 455
Avitus • 455–456
Majorian • 457–461
Libius Severus • 461–465
Anthemius • 467–472
Olybrius • 472–473
Glycerius • 473–474
Julius Nepos • 474–475
Romulus Augustulus • 474–476

HOW TO USE THIS BOOK

Don't read this like an ordinary book. Find your own interests on page **12**. *Thumb through it randomly, in any order that interests you.*

When you find little keys, pay attention to them; we're just letting you know about a rare treat or surprise that is not commonly known by the masses, and we've denoted it as one of our very favorite places.

The little red numbers **112** *simply refer to page numbers. They will appear everywhere, from maps to mid-paragraphs.*

BCE & CE
Scientists currently use these to demarcate dates.
BCE = Before Current Era *(Same as B.C.)*
CE = Current Era *(Same as A.D.)*

EERIE! | GREAT FIND! | Funky HISTORY | WORLD HERITAGE SITE
UNDERGROUND!
PHOTO OPS
Away From the HEAT!
3-D VIRTUAL REALITY Presentation

Watch for the dozens of little gold badges. They give quickie hints about things and places that should be noticed.

..at a glance

...AT A GLANCE

The "...at a glance" pages will give you a brief glance at what is coming up in the section, sort of a mini Table of Contents for that section only.

BUT not all "glances" will have a longer explanation or page reference. Some are simply tiny little finds that don't warrant a larger explanation, but we thought you might want to know about them anyway. Example: the Getting High section **236**.

Green Text are addresses. Simply show the taxi driver the green text and he/she will get you there post haste.

VIA QUATTRO NOVEMBRE, 94

Did You Know...
Blue boxes will share trivia, factoids, stories, and tales. These are great for picking up fast facts about the place or area you are visiting, like the one here...

"The word 'Italy' is a geographic expression, a description which is useful to shorthand, but has no political significance." ~ *in a letter from Austrian Statesman Klemens von Metternich c.1847*

A BRIEF HISTORY OF ROME

A BRIEF HISTORY OF ROME

Rome has an exceptionally long history. Because you are on vacation, we have significantly condensed Rome's past to just a few important points to help you get your bearings. We chose these points based on what you will see when you walk through the city. After all, when you are on vacation,

Republican Era begins 234bce.
Senators instead of Kings.
Hannibal & the Punic Wars.
Caesar became a powerful General.
Caesar became Emporor.
Rome tried to overpower Egypt.
Cleopatra & Caesar fell in love.
44BC Caesar was murdered.

Nero becomes Emperor.
Nero commits suicide-by-servant.
Mithraism gains momentum.
Christianity gains momentum.
Emperor Trajan defeats the Dacians.
Trajan grows the largest Empire.

Romulus founds Rome 753bce.
Mostly farmers.
Conquered other Hills.
Conquered the Sabines.
Mixed with Greeks & Etruscans.
Romulus = 1st of 7 early Kings.
Regal Period ends.

Octavian beats
Marc Antony & Cleopatra.
Octavian Augustus = 1st Emperor.
Pax Romana = 200 yrs of Peace.
Tiberius, Caligula: 2nd & 3rd Emperors.
Caligula was murdered 41ce.
Emperor Claudius beats Britain.

Christianity gathers strength.
Emperor Domitian persecutes Christians.
Domitian worships Greek Gods.
Rome is split into East & West.
Domitian is murdered by own staff.
Constantine I becomes Emperor.
Christianity declared offical religion.

100 bce	0	100 ce	200 ce	300 ce

Rome was founded 753bce.
Etruscan Huts on Palatine Hill.
Circus Maximus
Temple of Vesta, Temple of Castor & Pollux & Temple of Saturn were built.
The Rostra built in 338bce.
The Regia & Basilica Giulia were built.

Caesar updated Basilic Giulia.
Concrete was invented.
Old buildings were repaired.
Pompey's Theater.
Curia Giulia became Senate Building.
The Forum 29bce.
Ara Pacis
Augustus repaired/rebuilt 82 Temples.

Ludus Magnus
The Pantheon was built 126ce.
Domus Transitorius
2/3 of Rome burns in horrible fire.
Domus Aurea was built:
Nero's Golden Palace.
Colosseum
Castel Sant'Angelo
Catacombs

Baths of Diocletian
Aqueducts
Rome ruled by water.
Old St. Peter's Basilica
Basilica di San Giovanni in Late
Saint Paul's Outside the Wal

Baths of Trajan
Trajan's Forum & Marketplace
Baths of Caracalla
Trevi Fountain

A BRIEF HISTORY OF ROME

that is what really matters. *(That, and a little Prosecco!)* Enjoy this briefest of brief versions of an otherwise fabulous, dramatic, violent, beautiful, romantic, endearing and enduring history.

Borgia buys Papacy as Alexander VI.
High Renaissance dies with Raphael.
Church punished Galileo.
Martin Luther creates Protestant Reformation movement.
Caravaggio becomes Romes artistic Bad Boy.
Bernini becomes the new Michelangelo of Rome.
Pope Julius II beautifies Rome.

The Middle Ages settle in.
Rome is quiet while most
activity occurs in Constantinople.
Byzantines grow their empire.

Dante Alighieri standardized
modern Italian language.
Brunelleschi builds Florentine Duomo.
The Medici introduce Humanistic
concepts in thought and art.
Donatello, Leonardo da Vinci, Michelangelo,
Botticelli, Macchiavelli, Raphael, et al
create new artistic wave called
the Renaissance Era.

Constantine moves to Byzantium.
Gothic Wars.
Rome is sacked by Visigoths.
Roman rule in Britain ends.
Attila invades the north.
Rome is sacked by the Vandals.
Rome's final fall in 476ce.
Odoacer becomes King of Italy.

Italy becomes united in 1861.
Maria Monatessori creates her 1st school.
Italy defeats the Ottoman Empire.
Italy enters WWI.
Ferrari creates early sports car.
Italy is expelled from the League of Nations.
Italy enters into WWII.
Mussolini is assasinated.
Italy joins NATO.

400 ce	1000 ce	1300 ce	1600 ce	2000 ce

DARK AGES
ROME falls apart,
succombs to nature.
Cattle roams the Forum.
Goats take over Campidoglio.
Homeless encampments
take over the city.
Detritus and excrement
pile up everywhere.
Circus Maximus   Great buildings fall
rch of Constantine   to ruin.
nta Maria Maggiore

Renaissance
Great Beautification begins.
Santa Maria degli Angeli
Villa Farnesina
New St. Peter's Basilica
Villa Borghese
Vatican
Capitoline Museum
Palazzo Barbarini

Vittoriana: Altare della Patria
Vatican became City/State
EUR
Train Station
International Airport

A BRIEF HISTORY OF ROME

ARCHAIC Period 753 - 480 bce	REPUBLIC 509 - 27bce	EMPIRE 27bce - 476ce
Rome is founded by Romulus & Remus	509bce The Republic Begins	30bce Octavian defeats Marc Antony & Cleopatra VIII
Not yet a city, but a developing Village	450bce Twelve Tables, the basis of Roman Law are compiled	27ce Octavian becomes Augustus, and the Roman Empire begins
The Etruscans Dominate	264bce 1st Punic War	
Time-worn Greek Art and style evolves to a more naturalistic look and feel	218bce Hannibal Invades	Pax Romana = 200 Yrs of Peace under Augustus
	204bce 2nd Punic War	Run of bad Emperors: Tiberius, Caligula, Nero
7 Kings (Regal Period): • Romulus • Numa Pompilius • Tullus Hostilius • Ancus Marcius • Tarquinius Priscus • Servius Tullius • Tarquinius Superbus	73bce Spartacus Slave Uprising	Christianity builds
	60bce First Triumverate: Caesar, Pompey & Crassus	Trajan grows the Empire to its largest size
Persian Sack of Athens	49bce Caesar crosses the Rubicon. Civil War between Caesar & Pompey (Rome)	Domitian splits Rome into 2 halves
Development of Doric & Ionic forms of architecture	45bce Julius Caesar becomes a Dictator	Christianity declared official religion
	44bce Caesar is murdered by his own Senate members	Rome falls.
	The Republic ends.	

RENAISSANCE
1400 - 1600

Dante Alighieri standardized modern Italian Language. Wrote Divine Comedy.

Brunelleschi builds Florentine Duomo.

Medici introduce Humanism through art and literature.

Donatello, Leonardo da Vinci, Michelangelo, Botticelli, Macchiabelli, Raphael, et al create huge artistic wave called the Renaissance Era.

Great Beautification of Rome begins.

Inquisitions are in full swing.

Galileo gets imprisoned; dies.

Vasari pens first art history book.

BAROQUE
1600 - mid1700s

Popes maximize selfishness and greed.

Martin Luther rebels by starting the Protestant Reformation

Caravaggio becomes Romes dark darling of the canvas.

Bernini becomes the new Michelangelo of Rome.

The new St. Peter's Basilica is finished.

Villa Borghese is built by the family of Pope Paul V.

Piazza Barbarini is built by the family of Pope Urban VIII.

Palazzo Doria Pamphilj is beautified by the family of Pope Innocent X.

MODERN
1800 - PRESENT

Italy becomes united in 1861.

Victor Emanuel II becomes Italy's 1st King.

Altare della Patria is built.

The Vatican is built.

Italy enters WWI.

Ferrari creates early sports car.

Mussolini becomes Prime Minister of Italy.

Italy is expelled from the League of Nations.

Italy enters into WWII.

Mussolini is assasinated.

Italy joins NATO.

A BRIEF HISTORY OF ROME

HOW ROME GREW

As you try to determine where you would like to stay, bear in mind the way the city has developed over the millennia. As you can see below, the original city developed around the seven hills. They built the Servian Wall around the city, named after the sixth of the seven early Kings, Servius Tullius who ruled from 578-535bce.

In 271ce, Emperors Aurelius and Probus expanded the city limits with the Aurelian Walls. That is why the oldest sites in the city seem to be clustered around one area of the city.

For those of you who possess more than a passing interest in how Rome came together, I have assembled some stand-out points in Rome's history of 2,000 years in just a few pages. [No small task, indeed!]

Enjoy!

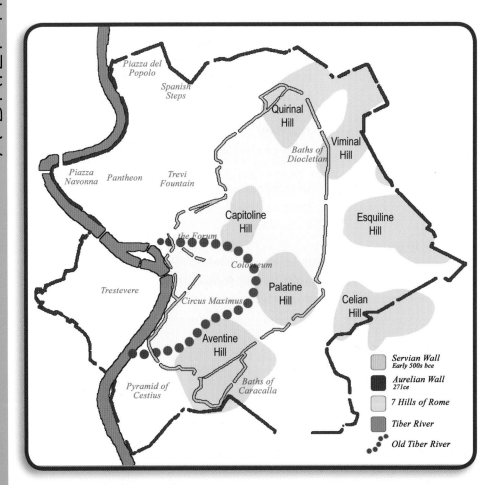

Servian Wall
Early 500s bce

Aurelian Wall
271ce

7 Hills of Rome

Tiber River

Old Tiber River

THE REGAL PERIOD 753 - 509BCE

The River Tiber ran a bit differently back then. Take a look at the map on the opposite page. The area of the Tiber river that borders Trastevere used to run much further east, closer to the three hills of Capitoline, Palatine, and Aventine.

It was then, legendarily speaking, that the twin boys, Romulus and Remus, were found in a basket washed up on the edge of the river near the Palatine Hill. They were discovered and adopted by a She-Wolf that nurtured them.

Palatine Hill was their home. It was there that as adults, they fought to the death. Remus died, and Romulus went on to found the village of Rome on Palatine Hill.

More villages existed on the tops of the six other hills as well. Between the seven hills, there existed various levels of wet marshy ground. Hills are great places to have a village. Because of their ability to spot intruders from afar, they are easy to defend.

Like some of the surrounding villages, the early Romans were farmers. They did not possess the ability to read nor write, so little to no official records have been left behind. Hence the legends.

A recreation of how Romulus' original hut may have looked.

They wanted control of more hills. So, being a conquering kind of a group, they overtook the other six hills. Over time, they learned non-farming skills from outsiders like the Sabines to the Northeast. They picked up high-order skills from the Etruscans in the North and the Greeks in the South. They traded with everyone.

According to Plutarch, the term 'lupa' in his tale, is not a 'She-Wolf' but was a slang term for Prostitute. So, was the legendary "She Wolf" that raised Romulus & Remus really a lady of the night?

Meanwhile, their village had grown to a city. The area was punctuated with Etruscan-style buildings. They decided they needed a King to rule. So Romulus became the first King of Rome. There were six other Kings after him during this period that lasted for the next 250 years, until the people decided they no longer wanted a single person to rule them. Most of the significant buildings in the Roman Forum were built during the Regal Period. This included the Temple of Vesta, the Temple of Castor & Pollux, and the Temple of Saturn. The Rostra was built in 338bce, the Regia and the Basilica Julia were also created in this Regal Period. When the people were finished with their Kings, it took a long while to decide what they wanted next. They eventually evolved into the 'People-run' King-free phase called the Republican Era.

THE ROMAN REPUBLIC 234 - 44BCE

During the next 200-year period, a body of Senators was chosen to lead the city. Rome had grown to a formidable size and power. A guy named Hannibal came up from a place called Carthage, a port city in the North African Country of Tunisia. He wanted - badly! - to disrupt the growing power of Rome, so, during the first two of three "Punic Wars," he tried. Hannibal even brought elephants around to attack Rome from the North, but alas, that too failed. Eventually, Rome had him cornered, So in 183bce, Hannibal committed suicide-by-poison, the womans' way out.

Familiar names populated the Republican Era, many of whom were hugely successful Generals. People like Scipio, Pompey, Marc Antony, Cleopatra *(the Queen of Egypt)*, and of course, the biggest Superstar of them all, Julius Caesar. *(Cheers to Hollywood for giving us a few bits of history.)*

The Republic saw the rebuilding of existing Forum buildings that were destroyed either by time or by fire. The Basilica of Sempronia was built, as was The Temple of Concord. Julius Caesar then made the Basilica Julia in the place of the old Sempronia, and he created the famous Rostra from which to give speeches. "Friends, Romans, Countrymen. Lend me your ears."

During the mid-first century bce, Caesar had convinced the Senate to let him lead Rome alone. As his power grew, he wanted not to be just a King, but he wanted to become a God while he was still alive. This incensed his fellow senate members who assembled a plot to end this.

During a fateful day of March 15 of 44bce *(known as the Ides of March)*, the most powerful man in Rome's history was stabbed 23 times by his own Senators. This led to the end of the Republican Era.

THE ROMAN EMPIRE 27BCE - 476CE

Angry that Caesar wanted to rule Rome by himself, the Senators murdered him. They then turned around and made Octavian, Caesar's adopted son, into the sole ruler of Rome called an Emperor. Thus, they established the official beginning of the Imperial Period of the Roman Empire.

This is where a whole list of military geniuses and crazy guys alike took the reins of Rome. Great guys like Octavian Augustus, Marcus Agrippa, Trajan, Hadrian, Marcus Aurelius, Diocletian, and Constantine the Great. Some not-so-great guys included a cast of Hollywood favs like Caligula, Agrippina, and Nero. Be it as it may, Rome continued to trudge forward and grow to become the robust and impassible force that ruled the Western world.

> "Caesar" is a popular salad dressing in the US. But it has nothing to do with our famous Roman ruler, Julius. It was named after its creator Caesar Cardini, an early 20th century chef who lived in Italy, Mexico, and Southern California.

In 165ce, the city - and all of Italy - was hit with the Plague of Galen. The city lost **2,000 of its citizens each day,** including Emperor Lucius Verus, and his famous co-regent/brother, Marcus Aurelius.

In the meantime, a quiet force was building in the background: Christianity. In its early days, it was considered to be a threat to the Empire, so various rulers attempted various things to thwart it. Things like persecutions that included harsh punishment or even death if one was caught practicing this new "Cult."

Size Mattered

By 117ce, Rome had grown to its height of physical size and power, through the genius leadership of Emperor Trajan **110**. By then, the Empire included France, Italy, Spain, southern Britain, Turkey, Israel, Egypt, and northern Africa.

The Roman Empire
in 117 AD, at its greatest extent

Christianity had also grown to achieve its own level of substantial size and power. Emperor Diocletian tried persecuting the Christians because he felt the official religion should continue to be the worship of the Greek Gods. Additionally, he felt the Empire should be split into two halves, the Eastern Empire and the Western Empire. Managing two Empires would be more comfortable and more efficient than maintaining a single huge one.

A year later, Emperor Constantine I, who against Diocletian's rules, decided to make Christianity the Official Religion of Rome instead of the traditional religion of the Greeks. This allowed Christianity to became a force of its own.

For the next Century, ethics and morals *(or lack thereof)* of the military and political rulers of Rome were losing ground to the hard-line growth of Christianity. Influential Christians were now leading the Eastern Empire. The Western side became disorganized, making way for a broad palette of unethical behaviors.

During the 400s, Rome was attacked from all sides. Her people were starving in the streets. Taxes were huge, with no ability to pay them. The Capital of the Western Empire moved to Milan for a short while, then to Ravenna. What a mess!

Rome was sacked by the Gauls in 390ce, and again in 410 by the Visigoths. Finally, in 476ce, Rome was sacked once more by Odoacer, a Roman soldier from Germany who had risen up through the ranks. He forced Emperor Romulus Augustulus to give up his crown, making Odoacer the first King of Italy. September 476 was the official End of the Roman Empire.

RIP
Roman Empire
27bce - 476ce

THE MIDDLE (DARK) AGES

Jesus on the Cross in the Medieval Basilica di San Clemente, Roma

With no official government, Rome fell into a long period of Barbarism that lasted nearly 1,000 years. Her people felt so battered and bruised by the last couple of centuries of brutality and mistreatment that they opted to turn back to the basics. Over the next centuries, books, poetry, and old philosophies were banned. Many documents were gathered and hid throughout the hills of Europe to protect them. In fact, reading and writing became illegal for most. The only acceptable art had to tell Biblical stories. Same with music. Walls sprung up around every city, town, and village to protect from invaders. People once again lived directly off the land, farming their own plots. When it came to politics, religion, and philosophy, citizens were forbidden to speak their own opinions. They only knew what they were told to know from their local city ruler and Church. Nothing else. Humanity had no value. Bullying rulers could throw away thousands of lives at any issue they felt was necessary, at any time. This went on for nearly 1,000 years, and this was why Plutarch later gave this period the moniker of the "Dark Ages."

To add to the darkness, 1347 saw another more severe bout of the Plague. Although there were no official record keepers back then, it is estimated that Rome lost approximately 30-40 thousand of its citizens to this Black Plague. But when a plague hits, the human death toll is not only the result. The living had it pretty bad as well. The crops rotted and had to be burned. Food shortages affected everyone, including the wealthiest. People were afraid to leave their homes and go to work, stopping all city, trade, and merchant services. The stench of burning rotten food and piles of dead bodies was always in the air. And the list went on.

THE RENAISSANCE ERA 1300 - 1600

As the Plague subsided during the second half of the 1300s, little bits of awakening began to occur. A guy named Dante started walking the streets of Florence, openly announcing his views of Free Thinking. A small family of wool growers grew into a wealthy banking family. This family was known as the Medici from Florence. They heard that non-religious paintings were being discovered under Rome; that ancient statues were being uncovered, that were not only non-religious but even nude! They learned that underneath Rome, wall paintings told stories of a time when people were publicly allowed to read, write, sing, and philosophize openly. Who knew?!?

So what would you do if you suddenly learned that a long time ago, a completely different culture lived under your city that could elevate objects, fly without machines, and turn invisible? This is akin to what it was like for the people of the middle ages to learn about the ancient Roman and Greek Empires initially. It started a fad. Which became an aphrodisiac which became a social explosion.

Back to our newly-educated Medici family. They became so enthralled with the old art that they paid mobs of people to dig up more of it. They learned that ancient books were hidden in remote monasteries throughout the hills of Europe, and they sent people to find those. It was as if they became addicted to this free and open world that had existed 1,000 years earlier!

The Medici family wanted their own art, just like the old stuff. They searched for the best artists and sculptures they could find to create them. Up until this point, early to mid-1400s, people were still not allowed to speak their own minds openly. This new and incredible art became their voice because, oddly, art was allowed to exist, where their personal views were still being squelched.

The fever for new art exploded in Rome and all over Europe. The themes for paintings and sculptures were vast and represented every aspect of life, instead of merely Christian life. People were waking up from a 1,000 year-long sleep. This period was later nicknamed The

Michelangelo's Renaissance "David"

A BRIEF HISTORY OF ROME

Roman Names

   People were named by various methods.
By birth order: Quintus, Sextus, Decimus (5th, 6th, or 10th child)
From a distinguishing physical feature: Balbi (bald), Verricosus (warts), or Rufus (red hair or beard).
From an ancestor: Uncle Caesar
From their disposition: Tarquinius Superbus (Tarquinius the Proud)
From their livelihood: Lucretius Vespillo (Lucretius the Undertaker)
   These extra names, or cognomina, were akin to nicknames that stuck.

Renaissance Period by a 16th-century artist named Giorgio Vasari. Renaissance is a French word meaning Rebirth.

Now we are in the 1400-1500s, and most of Europe was awake. And what a stir they created! The Church was weakening, and people were now being taught that they, as individuals, had value. People like Donatello, Michelangelo **156**, da Vinci, Botticelli, and Raphael **162** popped up in Florence to answer the mighty roar for creating great new works of art. A small middle class of people began to spring up where none could ever exist before. Power grabs and shifts were occurring all over Europe.

THE BAROQUE ERA 1600-1750

On the approach of the 1600s, the taste for art and architecture began to shift. People began to do away with the balanced, symmetrical Classical Renaissance style, and moved toward a style where life, drama, and excitement ruled the canvas and the stone. In Rome, fantastic artists like Bernini and Caravaggio popped up to answer that call.

Popes were regaining their footing through the leadership of their wealthy families, who raised children to become religious leaders. Money was flowing nicely through Rome again, and the ancient eyesores around the city were being broken down to reuse their materials for new construction. *(Alas.)*

Wealth flowed through the city, and people were no longer as concerned about the safety of their lives as they were in past centuries. But like always, when things are good, and people are no longer concerned with their immediate safety and survival, their dark sides have time to seep through. Gossip, nepotism, greed, and avarice once again haunted Rome's secret rooms, even in the Vatican.

On the outside, the beauty of art, architecture, and music permeated everyday life. Science was becoming an official 'thing.' People were discovering sides of themselves that were entirely inexpressible for 1,000 years. The sun shone, and the birds sang for several more centuries.

THE 20TH CENTURY

The experimental age of telephones and horseless carriages brought with it a new war that involved many countries. Italy became involved with WWI in 1915, a colossal event that cost them 600,000 of their own citizens.

Bernini's Baroque "David"

Like so much of the world, the Great Depression wreaked havoc at every level of personal, professional, and governmental lives. This was followed closely by the ravages of World War II.

Megatons of bombs were dropped on the city of Rome. The neutral Vatican was, for the most part, spared. Neighborhoods outside the walls were completely destroyed, but most of the major ancient sites were spared.

Mussolini's **150** bullying tactics and hard-lined fascist stance that grew him into

---

Arguing Justice

When wealthy people committed crimes, they were not typically sent to prison. Rather, they were usually given huge and exorbitant fines. These fines contributed significantly to the city's coffers.

There were no official prosecutors in ancient Rome. Anyone could be hired to defend a member of the elite community. They simply had to be good at arguing in order to win, and to be paid high fees.

Many self-made 'arguers' would make a good living by ensuring that there was always someone available to accuse rich people of one crime or another.

---

power was also a large part of his own demise. But as a huge fan of ancient Rome, Mussolini was actually responsible for much of the restored and rebuilt Rome that you can see today.

A giant fan of Octavian Augustus **100**, Mussolini wanted to recreate Rome to even greater heights than the Empire. The street that goes through the middle of the Forum, Via dei Fori Imperiali, was created. Circus Maximus **72**, which was a homeless haven at the time, was cleaned up, and new upbeat events and festivals were held in this space. He cleaned up the Mausoleum of Augustus, and the Colosseum **42**, opening both to public visits.

TODAY'S ROME

Since WWII, archaeologists have flooded into Rome to help with the discoveries and excavations of her ancient self. Global shopping brands now line the streets, as do restaurant chains and high-tech services. Modern architecture now punctuates the skyline. And automobile traffic gnarls every reasonable attempt to traverse the city.

But Rome has clearly not lost her soul. She knows who she is and where she has been. She is clear about her assets, as well as her flaws. Best of all, she is secure in the fact that she will always be... Eternal.

A BRIEF HISTORY OF ROME

ANCIENT & HISTORIC SITES

The image of Rome is constant. Or is it? We all know the Colosseum and the Forum, Vatican City and the Pantheon. But what about the rest of the gems that are hidden all throughout the city? Some are hiding in plain site, and many are underground. These are some of our most favorite, and we hope you enjoy them as well.

The key to Rome is not the shopping malls, bars & restaurants. We can get those anywhere in the world - including at home. The real key to Rome - the reason why people are so vastly interested in coming here - is its ancient history. A further secret: so much of ancient Rome is still underground. Which is cool. I mean, cold. Many of these sites are a welcome break from Rome's heat. Because most visitors don't think of Rome in terms of its historic heart, so many of these sites are uncrowded.

Caesar took his name from an ancestor that was reportedly born by what is known today as a C-Section, or Caesarian Section.
Julius Caesar was not born via C-Section.

The Tortellini was modelled after the belly button of a beautiful woman.

...AT A GLANCE

42 ## Colosseum

The games, the competition, the blood! Visit the most popular site in Rome. It is rated the #1 site in the world. How did it come to be? Who built it and why? Did it get its name from its massive size? No, but who would have guessed?

46 ## Roman Forum

Allow me to un-confuse you when it comes to the Forum. Easily see how it is laid out, and learn the difference between the Roman Forum and the Imperial Forums (Forae?). Everything will now fall in place as you walk through this fantastic archaeological site.

Temple of Vesta & its Virgins 52

The house of the Eternal Flame. Its demise would mean eminent danger for the city of Rome. Learn the jobs of the six Vestal Virgins who were charged with the life of the flame. If the flame were to extinguish, punishment was severe!

House of Vesta 53

This 50-room palace is where the six Vestal Virgins lived. Fully staffed including a robust team of guards to prevent men from entering and stealing their chastity. The punishment for losing their chastity was brutal!

Arch of Constantine 54

Triumphal Arches, whose concept has long been attributed to the Romans, are a distinctive monument to honor war victories, the completion of important construction, or even the death of an important family member.

Basilica of Maxentius 55

We might think of a Basilica as a church. But in Ancient Rome, a Basilica was a large building with a raised ceiling, and a variety of apses. Our rendering of the interior space is both beautiful as well as academically correct.

Palatine Hill 56

The Beverly Hills of Ancient Rome, but even better. They were the Palaces of the Emperors, and Rome's ultra wealthy. Even the "White House" of Rome - where the Emperors lived - was on the Hill overlooking the Forum. Smashing views of their workplace!

ANCIENT & HISTORIC SITES

ANCIENT & HISTORIC SITES, Cont'd.

ANCIENT & HISTORIC SITES *(vertical, left margin)*

...AT A GLANCE

58 · Trajan's Marketplace

Right across from Caesar's Forum is one of the greatest sites in Rome, and it is nearly empty! Walk through all of the levels of Emperor Trajan's marketplace as you imagine it bustling with ancient vendors selling their wares.

59 · Trajan's Forum

Trajan was the Emperor that grew the Empire to its largest size ever! He built this Forum with a huge marketplace, libraries, and a giant public bath. Romans loved Trajan. He was one of the good ones!

61 · Trajan's Column

Emperor Trajan fought the 3rd battle against the Dacians and finally won. Trajan's column was created to tell the whole story of the battle. Take a close look at it: you'll see every part of the battle told in stone. Incredible!

62 · Baths of Caracalla

The largest baths at that time, they could accommodate thousands of bathers per day. Why were public baths so popular? Go underground to learn how they kept them running 24/7. Why did the Emperors not use the baths?

64 · Baths of Diocletian

Emperor Diocletian ruled Rome from the Eastern Capital. But once near the end of his reign, he visited Rome and left this fabulous gift to the Romans: the largest and most beautiful public baths that the Romans had ever seen.

...AT A GLANCE

Castel Sant'Angelo 66

Castel Sant'Angelo has a storied past that adheres to Rome's history tighter than most sites: The Popes that hid from war. The Bodies that are buried here. This is a rare opportunity to visit a true fortified castle.

Domus Transitoria 68

Emperor Nero's first palace. It was destroyed during the Great Fire of 64ce. Found on Palatine Hill, go underground to see the 3DVR presentation of Nero's first dream house, before it burned.

Domus Aurea 69

Don a hard hat and descend into the cold depths of Nero's Golden Palace. A 3DVR presentation will help to visualize the sheer opulence of Nero's dream. But why was he so hated?

Forum Boarium 70

Hercules. A big-muscled, strong guy. They built this Temple to him, and Temples are for worshipping Gods. Why was he so important to Rome? What did he do to deserve such gratification? Great question!

San Crisogono 71

San Crisogono is a a dark ancient site under a Parish Church and minor Basilica from the 1100s. 12 feet underground lies the remains of several much older structures.

Circus Maximus 72

Hollywood's "Ben Hur" made famous this race track that lies in the valley between the Palatine and Aventine Hills. Able to seat up to 250,000 spectators, it was used mostly for Chariot Racing...

ANCIENT & HISTORIC SITES

ANCIENT & HISTORIC SITES, Cont'd.

ANCIENT & HISTORIC SITES

74 ## Circus Agonalus
Did you know that you can go underneath Piazza Navona **224** *to see the ancient circus, or Sports Arena? The best athletes competed here, just like they did in the Greek Olympics. This is a fun find!*

75 ## Ludus Magnus
Right across the street from the Colosseum is the Gladitorial College,dorms, and a practice arena where the Gladiators trained every day. When it was show time...

76 ## Largo Argentina
Was Caesar murdered in a cat house? What does this mean? Why is this part of the forum so far from the Forum you know today? Nestled in the middle of Rome's modern bustling streets lies this ancient archaeological site.

78 ## Domus Romane
Tucked quietly underneath Palazzo Valentini (across the street from Vittoriano), the remains of ancient Patrician homes will come to life with the help of 3DVR. An eerie experience as you walk on suspended glass floors -- in the dark!

79 ## Crypta Balbi
The 'Lasagne' of Rome! Learn how one square block of Rome has been settled by many, and its uses have been transformed over the past 2,000 years. The excellent museum upstairs beautifully explains the underground.

...AT A GLANCE

TREVI FOUNTAIN `80`

Why is Trevi Fountain so popular? Perhaps it is because of the spectacular sculptures that make it up. Perhaps it is because of the Legend of the Coins?

TREVI UNDERGROUND `81`

Everyone sees the Trevi Fountain in Rome. But very few people know that you can go UNDER Trevi to visit the ancient aquifers that still supply the water to the fountain...

Basilica di San Clemente `82`

Street level: you've gone back 1,000 years. Down a level: you've gone back 1,700 years. Down another level: you are now back 2,000 years! Visit the secret Mithrea, and an ancient neighborhood!

Capucchin Crypts `85`

The Capucchin Monks used the bones of thousands of deceased people, including children, to decorate their crypts. Why would they do this? Read on, dear traveler, this is one for your journals!

Roman Catacombs `86`

For 300 years, Rome buried their dead in a wide open field. What did they do before that? And what did they do after that? Why did the use of the Catacombs only last 300 years? Visit the Popes' tomb and...

Appian Way `87`

This road saw parades, festivals, processions, and crucifixions. Everyone traversed Via Appia to get to and from Rome. Look closely to see the ancient wheel ruts. You can almost...

ANCIENT & HISTORIC SITES

ANCIENT & HISTORIC SITES, Cont'd.

...AT A GLANCE

88 Roman Aqueducts

In the ancient times, if you could control water, you had power. These aqueducts made Rome was the most powerful controller of water in the ancient world. Today you can even play golf next to these picturesque aqueducts!

89 Case Romane del Celio

Hiding under the Basilica of Saints Peter and Paul is a superb surprise! These ancient Roman houses in the Celio district are superior examples of life from the 3rd century ce...

90 Mausoleum of Cecilia Metella

As you walk down the Appian Way, the Mausoleum of Cecilia quickly rises to dominate your view. Built in the late first century bce for the daughter of the Roman Consul, Crassus...

91 Villa dei Quintilli

The Quintilli brothers were known for their exquisite taste. Their palazzo was so beautiful and admired that Emperor Comodus killed the Quintilli brothers so he could take their home for himself! Photo ops abound.

92 Mithraea

Before there was Christianity, there were cults. Hundreds of them. One of the more successful cults was Mithraism, going back over 2,000 years. Where did they come from and where did they go?

93 Mausoleum of Augustus

Once described as "a hill with a golden Augustus on top," the Mausoleum of Augustus had become a disappointing jumble of rubble. But having now been under vast renovations for several years, Rome has revamped this amazing structure.

ROMAN AQUEDUCTS

88

280

56

PALATINE HILL

68

DOMUS TRANSITORIA

OSTIA ANTICA

58

TRAJAN'S MARKETPLACE

76

LARGO ARGENTINA

79

CRYPTA BALBI

ANCIENT & HISTORIC SITES

COLOSSEUM
NO ADDRESS REQUIRED!

COOL ARCHAEOLOGY!

Near the ROMAN FORUM!

PHOTO OPS

TRULY STUNNING!

POPULAR

UNDERGROUND!

Completed in 80ce, the Roman Colosseum is today, the single most visited tourist site in the entire world! Built to help the Romans to forget about that nasty Nero guy that used to live in this space, it is fabulous to look at, and it comes with a colossal bag of great stories, most of which include blood. The Colosseum has enough content to supply artists and writers for the past 2,000 years. Today, it is still a true Hollywood favorite!

Blood Lust
When you look at the Colosseum, you will see its maze of walls, tunnels, rooms, and passageways that are open to the sky. In the ancient heyday of the Colosseum, those walls were underneath 44 a ceiling that made up the performance floor or 'arena' of the Amphitheater.

The amount of blood was staggering! Yes from people, but more blood was spilled from animals. Scouts were sent to Africa to trap every sort of wild beast that they could find. The more exotic and unknown, the more excited the crowd would become. These animals included lions, tigers, elephants, giraffes, bears, wolves, jaguars, and hippopotamuses. Every sort of crazy competition that could lead to the possible death of the athlete, and the certain death of the animal, took place. And the crowds roared their love!

ANCIENT & HISTORIC SITES

Both the animals and men, albeit athletes or slaves, stayed in the underground chambers until it was their turn to 'play.' They were then led through the tunnels to opposing wooden elevators where other slaves would toil to begin the lifting process of raising them. A trap door would open above their heads, and they would each appear on the arena floor. The elevator cages *(previous page)* would open, the captive competitors would exit. Then the elevator would reverse direction heading back below the surface, and the trap door would close. Let the games begin!

In 2015, a replica of an elevator was carefully designed, built, and lowered into the Colosseum by a 200-foot-tall crane. Today, you can tour below the ground to have a look at how all of this came together seamlessly and precariously to create some of the most blood-rendering competitions in human history.

• •

It's huge. It's gigantic. It's colossal! Hmm... is that where this massive pile of stone got its name? Oddly enough, no.

Have you ever heard the story about how there was a great fire in 64ce that charred 2/3 of Rome and was started by Emperor Nero who just sat around playing his fiddle while his city burned? *(Even though he wasn't even around during the fire, he was never-the-less blamed for it.)*

The fire burned down his magnificent home, his sanctuary that is known today as Domus Transitoria **68**. So he decided to do a giant land-grab *(since there was sud-*

denly a bunch of newly vacated land available) and built the biggest, most awesome palace ever built: Domus Aurea, his Golden Palace. **69**

Never mind the fact that 2/3 of the city was rendered homeless and hungry. Our Nero was going to create the coolest palace ever made because he knew that would make everyone joyful. *(Yah, right.)*

To sweeten the pot, he was going to have a statue of himself created in the likeness of the Sun God, Sol, to put on the front porch because folks everywhere would be happy about this too.

The statue was 121 feet tall and placed on a 20-foot pedestal, making the figure taller than our Statue of Liberty! And there it stood, right on his porch to greet his guests.

> Covered in sand to soak up the blood, the Colosseum arena floor was easy to keep clean. The word *'Sand'* in Latin is *'harenae'* and is pronounced *'arena.'* Now you know where the word 'arena' came from.

After Nero's death a new Emperor named Flavius, plowed Nero's Golden Palace into the ground. He wanted to find a way to return this land to the people, so he built a new huge grand amphitheater that everyone could be proud of.

But what of that huge COLOSSAL statue? Officially named the **Flavian Amphitheater,** after himself, of course, he used 24 elephants to drag Nero's colossal statue to stand it in front of his Amphitheater.

And that, my happy travelers, is how the Colosseum got its name: not from its size, but because of the size of Nero's colossal statue that stood next to it.

P.S. The Statue has long since vanished from our Colosseum, leaving behind only fragments of its pedestal. But the name stuck, and we will forever know this incredible structure as The Roman Colosseum, rather than the Flavian Amphitheater.

The Colossal statue of the Sun God Sol might have looked similar to this if it had survived the millennia. But alas, only bits of the pedestal remain.

THE FORUM

COOL ARCHAEOLOGY!   PHOTO OPS   POPULAR

The trials, the tribulations. The verbal wars. The masterful coups. The walls of the Forums are inlaid with endless stories of sadness, madness, power, and greed.

The Forum area that you can visit today is a mash-up of individual forums built by a variety of leaders that wanted an area from which to lead, and one which was greater than the one before him. They consist of the Roman Forum, the Forum of Caesar, the Forum of Augustus, the Forum of Vespasian, Nerva's Forum, and Trajan's Forum. They are laid out on pages 48-49. The Roman Forum is considered to be the most important because of the existence of the Senate Building.

This land was once a wet marshland, so the Romans created the first-known sewage system to drain it. That system was called the Cloaca Maxima.

As you can see, the Forum was a complex series of buildings and Temples, some of which were erected to the ancient Gods. The Roman Emperors also believed that if you built a Temple and dedicated it to yourself, you too would become a God.

Excellent tools exist today to help you to visualize the Forum as it was in its heyday during the fourth century. One such tool is a 3d virtual reality app called "**Rome Reborn.**" It was expertly designed and is academically correct. With it, you can visit many parts of the forum as it existed 1,700 years ago. *[The app is available in the Apple app store and the Google Play store.]*

This photograph was taken as you look down from the back side of Piazza Campidoglio.

THE FORUMS

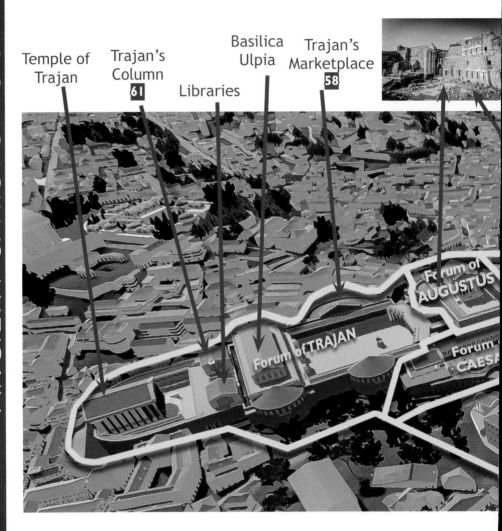

Temple of Trajan · Trajan's Column **61** · Libraries · Basilica Ulpia · Trajan's Marketplace **58**

The Forum was originally created during the Republic as the central site of civic administration. When Caesar came into power, he had his own forum created, just for him. Clearly, that started a ball rolling, because many Emperors after that had to have their own forum. These were added as each of the others fell apart.

The largest forum belonged to that of Emperor Trajan, who was loved by his people for defeating the Dacians and taking all their riches. This newfound wealth enabled him to not only build this great monument to himself, but he also created a huge bath facility on top of Nero's ex-Golden Palace, Domus Aurea **69**.

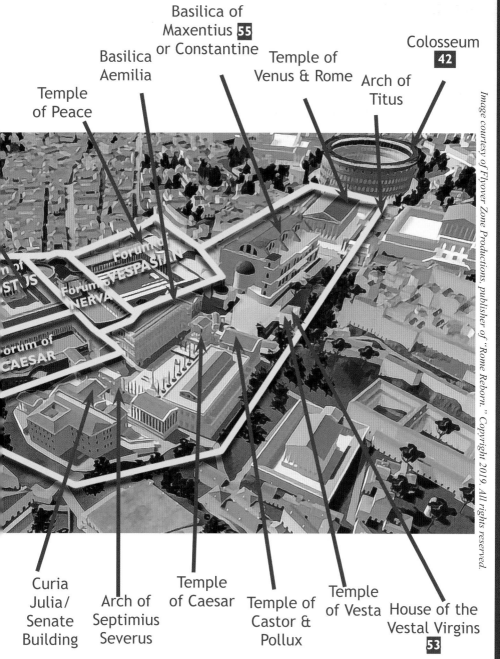

Temple
of Peace

Basilica
Aemilia

Basilica of
Maxentius **55**
or Constantine

Temple of
Venus & Rome

Arch of
Titus

Colosseum
42

Curia
Julia/
Senate
Building

Arch of
Septimius
Severus

Temple
of Caesar

Temple of
Castor &
Pollux

Temple
of Vesta

House of the
Vestal Virgins
53

ANCIENT & HISTORIC SITES

Using an image from the **Rome Reborn project 296**, you can see how the forum is laid out. Now as you walk through the rubble of the Forum, much of the broken bits and pieces begin to make sense. The arrows above depict a few points of reference as you pass through each area.

THE FORUM

TEMPLE OF VESTA - Then & Now

Inside the Temple of Vesta, six Vestal Virgins kept an eternal flame lit. The flame represented the eternity of the city of Rome. If the flame was extinguished, the city would certainly die. The six virgins were chosen between the ages of six and ten, when each would take a vow of servitude and chastity to last for 30 years. If they were found to have broken their vow, they would be buried alive as punishment. The fire was to be relit in an annual ceremony on the 1st of March. Inside the Temple the sacred cake (mola salsa) and the sacred water, both used for the re-lighting ceremony, were kept.

ARCH OF SEPTIMIUS SEVERUS - Then & Now

This triple-arched monument was erected in 203ce to celebrate the victories of Septimius Severus and his defeat over Parthia, which today make up parts of Iran and Iraq. On the top marched a team of bronze horses. Additionally, the top section was reserved to honor his sons Caracalla and Geta with statues of both. However, when Caracalla **62** *later murdered his brother, he had Geta removed from the Arch. The Arch itself stands approximately 75 feet high, by 82 feet wide. The large central arch once contained a stairway but was later converted into a road.*

THE FORUM

TEMPLE OF CASTOR & POLLUX - Then & Now

Castor & Pollux were the twin sons of Jupiter (Zeus in Greek) and Leda. Jupiter, the God of all Gods, was also the God of Lightning and Thunder. Built during the Regal period **27** *in the early 5th century bce, it has been used as a Senate building, an office of records, weights & measures, and the treasury. As the legend goes, Castor & Pollux appeared on the field of battle to assist the Republic. After the battle ended, they entered at this spot to water their horses. The Temple was built in their honor.*

CURIA JULIA - Then & Now

This is the third structure that has occupied this space. Originally, it was an Etrucsan Temple during the Regal period **26***. The word 'Curia' simply means 'Meeting Place.' It was eventually used as the Senate House. It was once believed that Caesar was stabbed on the steps of this building. But because it was under construction on that fateful Ides of March, the Senate met in Pompey's Theater down the road. (See Largo Argentina on page* **76***.) It was there that Caesar was murdered by his own Senators. This iteration of the building is one of the few in the Forum that has retained its ancient appearance over many versions of reconstruction.*

ANCIENT & HISTORIC SITES

THE FORUM
TEMPLE OF VESTA

The Temple of Vesta struggles for attention in the Roman Forum. You will easily recognize it from its round footprint.
See 3D rendering on page **50**.

The Temple of Vesta, recognizable by its circular base, was where an eternal flame was kept lit by the Vestal Virgins. The extinguishing of the flame would portend destruction of Rome. *(See below.)* The Temple was the storage facility for sacred documents, contracts, and wills of the wealthy.

The exact date of the construction of the Temple is not known, but it has been verified that the ancient cult of Vesta was practiced in this location as far back as 700bce!

The Temple has been built, destroyed, and rebuilt several times throughout history. Its first known destruction occurred by the Gauls in 390bce. The most recent construction took place in 191ce by Emperor Septimius Severus, with Greek architecture for the main design, using marble, Corinthian columns, and a cella - a small inner chamber.

This last iteration stood tall for 1,400 years until the Renaissance period. In the late 1400s - early 1500s, the Forum was seen as a big trash heap of old structures. So the Popes, during a century-long city-wide renewal, gave orders to their architects and engineers to rape the Forum of its usable marble, bricks, and metals to use for new construction projects around the city.

The remains that you see today, are all that is left of Severus' version, nearly 2,000 years ago.

THE JOB OF A VESTAL VIRGIN

Six Virgins were required to guard the Eternal Flame within the Temple. This was taken VERY seriously. In exchange for at least 30 years of service, she enjoyed a long list of freedoms and luxuries. Because if the flame were to go out, it would portend doom for the city of Rome. A Virgin's job would begin between ages 6-10, and was chosen according to her Paternal background, family standing in the community, and proof of chastity. Once chosen, she would train for ten years to tend the fire. Her job could last as long as 30 years. The Virgins were considered

THE FORUM
HOUSE OF VESTA

Although little remains of the House of the Vestal Virgins, you will know you are there when you see this line-up of female statues.

The Home of the six Vestal Virgins was a fifty-room, three-storied palace. It surrounded a long rectangular-shaped courtyard around two long pools and an elegantly lush garden.

It was guarded 24/7 by a team of sentries who assured the city that no outsider could enter and risk usurping the virginity of one of the women. The Vestal Virgins were allowed to roam the markets and the city, guarded, of course.

Once in a great while, a man would find a way to win the affections of one of the Virgins, which would undoubtedly end with his torture and her live burial. *(See below.)*

to be Priestesses, who were dedicated to the Goddess Vesta who watched over the City. If the flame were to become extinguished, a trial would be held, and one of the Virgins would be found guilty of breaking her vows of chastity - whether or not it was true. It was believed that the loss of chastity is what caused the flame to extinguish. In this case, the guilty party would be lowered into an underground room and given a candle and a blanket. The chamber would be sealed, and she would never be seen again.

THE FORUM
ARCH OF CONSTANTINE

ANCIENT & HISTORIC SITES

Triumphal Arches, whose concept has long been attributed to the Romans, are a distinctive monument to honor war victories, the completion of important construction, or even the death in an important family member.

In Rome, there were as many as 36 arches, of which only three survive into the present day: The Arch of Constantine, The Arch of Titus, and the Arch of Septimius Severus **50**.

This diagram depicts the various eras of construction as follows:

Emperor Trajan - 98ce

Emperor Hadrian - 117ce

Emperor Aurelius - 161ce

Emperor Constantine I - 306ce

These great men loved to display symbols of their victories on this glorious arch.

The very best view of the Arch of Constantine is from the top level of the Colosseum. It's easy to get a lay of the land from way up there. The ancient road went through both sides of the arch, although there is now a green patch in front of it. Try to imagine pageants and parades with horses, soldiers, and banners streaming through this magnificent arch. Both sides of the great road were lined with solid throngs of people. A majestic site this must have been!

THE FORUM
BASILICA of MAXENTIUS

We might think of a Basilica as a church. But in Ancient Rome, a Basilica was a large building with a raised ceiling, and a variety of apses. The Basilica was used for an array of social activities that required a space big enough to hold a large number of people.

Construction was started by Emperor Maxentius in 308ce, and was completed in 312ce by Emperor Constantine I. It housed an assortment of statues of the ancient Roman Gods in the wall-embedded nooks and niches around the inside of the building.

The Basilica of Maxentius used to house a gigantic statue of Constantine 1, but that sculpture has long since been broken down; some of its pieces can be seen today in the Capitoline Museum **130**.

*The way the inside of the Basilica probably looked in 320ce.
From the ROME REBORN.com project.*

The beautiful marble used in the original decoration was removed over the centuries to create decorations in other buildings and churches. Some of it has been used, sadly, as the stall floor for cattle, or even ground up to be used in the mortar that lines bricks in other construction projects.

A stunning view of the Basilica of Maxentius from a ledge on Palatine Hill.

PALATINE HILL

COOL ARCHAEOLOGY! · Near the ROMAN FORUM! · PHOTO OPS · POPULAR

Forum
Palais de Tibère
Septizodium (hors champ)
Domus Flavia
Domus Augustana
Stadium
Domus Augusti
Area Apollinis
Domus Severiana
Domus Praeconum (non représentée)
Paedagogium
Circus Maximus

Palatine Hill is where many of the Emperors and the very wealthy elite folks lived in Ancient Rome. Their homes ranged from merely lavish to highly ostentatious. The word 'Palace' came from these homes on Palatine Hill.

Palatine Hill is the Beverly Hills of the Roman Empire. Rome's wealthiest Emperors and community leaders built their homes on the bluff that is the Palatine. It is strategically located for many reasons:

*This is a reproduction of what is believed to be the original hut of the founder of Rome and her first King, Romulus (the surviving suckled twin). It was found on the sloping side of Palatine Hill, an area known as the Steps of Cacus **70**. Its waddle-and-daub construction was burned and reconstructed several times over the past 2,700 years. The wealthiest leaders of Rome built their elaborate palatial neighborhood on the Hill to be near to their original King.*

1. *It was originally near to the Home of Romulus, the first King of Rome (left)*

2. *The whole neighborhood has a stunning view that looks down upon their workplace: the Roman Forum*

3. *The cliff side looks down over the Circus Maximus. During the events at the Circus, the leaders and their friends could gather in their palaces to get a front-row, bird's eye view of the games.*

4. *Because of its position on the hill, it was easy to defend.*

Today's visitors can enter two of the ancient residences: the House of the first Emperor Augustus *(above-left)*, and the house of his wife Livia. They are important because of the lush frescoes that still remain within.

A whole room was removed from the House of Livia and moved to the Palazzo Massimo **139** awaiting your visit.

The garden courtyard of Domus Augustana, the domestic wing of the Palace of Domitian on Palatine Hill.

This was the private stadium for the wealthy. Neighbors could gather here on the Palatine Hill to witness their own races, and contests. Being situated in the middle of this neighborhood of only the super wealthy meant they didn't have to go far to enjoy exclusive events with their friends.

The Imperial Palace, or the White House of ancient Rome, enjoyed this view where the Emperor could keep a watchful eye on the Forum below from Palatine Hill above.

TRAJAN'S MARKETPLACE ♥
VIA QUATTRO NOVEMBRE, 94

ANCIENT & HISTORIC SITES

COOL ARCHAEOLOGY!

Near the ROMAN FORUM!

UNCROWDED!

Lying quietly directly across the street from Caesar's Forum, rests Trajan's Forum. This site sadly, is nearly always uncrowded. But do not believe that it is because this site is of a low quality or uninteresting. It is because it is not on the city's list of top 5 sites, it gets little support, and so, few visitors know about it. If you are looking to get away from the crowds and want to visit one of the most interesting sites in Rome,

THIS SITE IS HIGHLY RECOMMENDED!

Visitors can freely walk into, through and on top of this incredible historical site. Enter through the Museum of Trajan (Museo Traiano) around the corner at the address at the top left of this page.

Trajan, aka Traiano **110**, was the 13th Emperor of the Roman Empire. He is best remembered for winning a years-long battle with the Dacians, a people that occupied an area north of the Danube, known today as Romania. He took the spoils from that war, namely the Dacian Gold & Silver, added them to Rome's city coffers, and used these vast sums to build this magnificent and majestic center for all citizens to enjoy. He also built the huge baths of Trajan that plowed through a part of Nero's former Golden Palace *(Domus Aurea **69**)* to make room.

It is easy to imagine this semi-circular marketplace filled with a variety of shops and vendors all shouting for attention. Musicians played and sang in the middle, and people filled every space that you can see.

TRAJAN'S FORUM

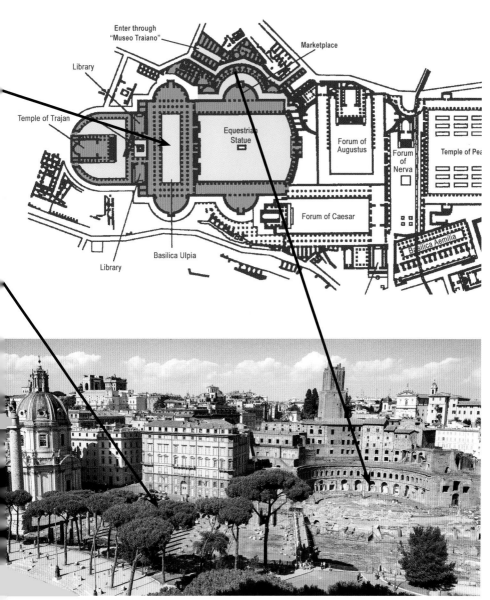

Trajan's magnificent Forum is nearly the size of the Forums of Caesar, Augustus, and Nerva - combined! Currently an active archaeological dig site, new information and treasures are being discovered and excavated every day.

Trajan's Column, which stands imposingly next to his Marketplace, used to be surrounded by his Forum building *(top right)*. The Forum, called the *Basilica Ulpia,* was filled with monuments, paintings, and sculptures that honored the heroes of Romes past. Additionally, it is where the city Courthouse resided during Trajan's rule.

Trajan, cont'd.

Archaeologists have taken years to uncover this wondrous site. So much of its pieces were removed during the Roman Beautification projects, that it is difficult to reassemble all of the remaining crumbs. The the marketplace as a whole is largely intact, making it a fun adventure for you to wander in, on, and through. Everywhere you look, you will find historical treasures just laying around: chunks of ancient columns, statuary, decorative trim, etc. A walk through all of the levels will reward you, as the museum uses some of the ancient vendor stalls to display interesting excavated pieces. Trajan's Forum is the largest of all of the other Roman forums.

TRAJAN'S COLUMN

The long curved arch-filled hallway inside the Market-place will treat you to an abundance of won-derfully-framed views. This is looking out at Trajan's column, which, during his time, would have been hidden from view by his own Forum building.

This beehive-domed room is an adjunct to the Marketplace. Today it exhibits a variety of statu-ary and architectural relics from the period.

TRAJAN'S COLUMN

The column was constructed of white Carrara marble, with 17 monolithic drums stacked upon one another. Each drum weighs around 32 tons each. The center of the column is hollow, allowing for a spiral staircase of 185 steps which lead to the square viewing platform near the top. This inner staircase was added after the full height of the column had been completed.

Spanning approximately 656 feet, the scroll is in high relief, and spirals around the column 23 times. It tells the story of the two wars that Trajan fought against the Dacians: in years 101-102, and 105-106 when finally he defeated the Dacians. The scroll contains 2,500 characters, of which 59 are of Trajan himself. The Dacians were a race of people that occupied the area that we now know as Romania.

The statue at the top is not Trajan, but Saint Peter, the Patron Saint of the city of Rome. However, when the column was created, a bronze Trajan stood majestically at its top. The statue disappeared some time during the medieval period.

The column was hidden from the sight of the Roman Forum by the creation of the Basilica Ulpia, the main building in which the courthouse was located. Balconies in the Basilica were created at different levels to make the viewing of the storied scroll easier.

The museum exhibits an interesting display of amphorae that were used to transport wine, vinegar, and oils from all over the world during ancient times.

BATHS OF CARACALLA
VIALE DELLE TERME DI CARACALLA

3-D VIRTUAL REALITY Presentation   COOL ARCHAEOLOGY!   PHOTO OPS   UNDERGROUND!   TRULY STUNNING!

The Baths of Caracalla were created between 211 and 216ce, by Emperor Septimius Severus, and finished by his son Caracalla *(known at the time as Antoninus)*. Caracalla co-ruled with his dad for a couple of years. When his father was too old to rule, Caracalla co-ruled with his brother Geta as per their father's wishes. However, once dad died, Caracalla murdered Geta, leaving himself as the sole ruler of the family, and of Rome.

Bust of Caracalla, aka **Marcus Aurelius Severus Antoninus Augustus**. *Emperor from 211-217ce.*

The architectural style of these Baths was later used to design the Baths of Diocletian and other structures around the world. Traffic flow through the building was both practical as well as efficient. Bathers would enter the building *(photo right)*, go directly into the dressing rooms, then to the *Palestra (gyms)* for a workout, later on to the *Natatio (pool)* for a swim. After, they would move into the *Laconium* for the steam bath that would prep them for the hot temperatures of the *Caldarium*. Next, they would enjoy the transitional cool-down of the *Tepidarium*. Lastly, they would move into the *Frigidarium* for the ultimate cold water shock back to real life.

Handling the needs of 1,600 simultaneous bathers, and as many as 8,000 per day, required a massive crowd of people to keep it all going. The above-ground staff was well-dressed and mannered. Below ground, however, thousands of slaves were needed to burn tons of wood per hour in the 50 ovens located throughout the two miles of tunnels. They moved 18.5 gallons of water per second - that is equivalent to the rate of water used today in the city of Siena!

Periodic concerts and performances are held in the ruins of the Baths of Caracalla. In this instance, a performance of Verde's "Aida" is preparing for an eager audience.

Why Were Public Baths So Important to the Romans?

The Romans were a nice-smelling bunch. They valued cleanliness, good hygiene and grooming. Homes did not have their own showers or baths inside, so public bathing was their only option. Public bathing became a dominant part of their daily culture, where they would meet up with friends, and socialize on a very regular basis.

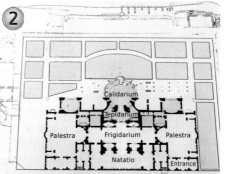

A visit through the underground tunnels will enable you to enjoy the cool subterranean environment, while providing you with a rare insight as to the operations of these ancient Bath complexes. Your 3DVR goggles will fill in the visual blanks so that when you leave, you will possess full knowledge of the running of the Baths.

The Baths of Caracalla is a monumentally cool site! Archaeologists have done an excellent job with site excavation, preservation, and signage, and should be congratulated.

1: an artist's rendering of the way the Baths looked during their heyday.
2: Floor map of the most important rooms in the facility.
3: The ruins as they look today; some of the areas retain vestiges of the original mosaic floor tiles.
4: A journey underground will show you the areas where 50 ovens kept the fires burning to heat the water for the baths.

ANCIENT & HISTORIC SITES

BATHS OF DIOCLETIAN
Via delle Terme di Diocleziano

NATIONAL ROMAN MUSEUM

ANCIENT & HISTORIC SITES

Located directly across the street from the Termini Train Station, the Baths of Diocletian are a fantastic surprise!

Built to honor the African return of Emperor Diocletian **112** *(298-305ce)*, these were the largest public baths in Rome at that time. Similar in structure to the Baths of Caracalla, these baths remain in better condition after nearly 2,000 years.

During the Imperial Period, there were upwards of 900 baths in Rome. This was due to the fact that people had neither baths nor showers in their homes.

The BIGGEST EVER
These Baths were the largest thermal complex in all of Ancient Rome. They were built by Emperor Diocletian in 305ce with capacity for more than 3,000 people. Emperor Diocletian visited Rome only once.

Romans were a clean lot, and the baths were a main social activity. People would gather in the baths regularly with their friends and neighbors to chat, play ball, read, listen to music, and every other form of social intercourse imaginable.

Top: the floor of the Swimming Pool was once covered in artistic mosaics, and lined with a beautiful white marble.
Center: The Main Entrance was a large foyer where a variety of things could be enjoyed: art shows, performances, etc.
Bottom: We have added an aqua blue to the Swimming Pool to make it easy to imagine it filled with water.

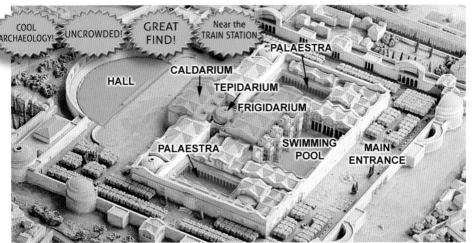

COOL ARCHAEOLOGY! UNCROWDED! GREAT FIND! Near the TRAIN STATION

PALAESTRA
CALDARIUM
HALL
TEPIDARIUM
FRIGIDARIUM
PALAESTRA
SWIMMING POOL
MAIN ENTRANCE

The Baths of Diocletian was a huge facility that may have held as many as 3,000 people. The Caldarium was akin to a giant hot tub where the pores of the skin would cleanse. The Tepidarium was kept slightly warm. The Frigidarium, or Cold Bath, became popular because after so many years of use, the hot tub room (Caldarium) required so much energy (wood) to keep it hot that the surrounding forests became thin. The Palaestra were used for a variety of activities. This included indoor ball games and competitions, changing areas, storage areas, social gathering places, etc. The Baths of Diocletian also included other areas such as a Library, Gardens, Eateries, Bathrooms, and beautiful meeting Halls.

One of the four National Roman Museums, it is one of the best in the city, and holds beautifully-preserved objects that were discovered in the area. Over the centuries, parts of the Baths have been covered by other structures. In the early 1500s, Michelangelo was commissioned to design a Church **198** and Cloister that covers a portion of the Baths. While you are visiting the Baths, taking the extra time to visit the Cloister and the Church will be worth your time, as they are both excellent examples of Michelangelo's architectural prowess.

Today, the Baths of Diocletian contain an excellent museum to showcase many of the items that were found during the excavation. This room-sized mosaic is a stunning site to behold!

Who Turned Off the Water?!?

The Baths of Diocletian were operational until the Barbarians cut off their water supply in 537ce.

CASTEL SANT'ANGELO
LUNGOTEVERE CASTELLO, 50

Castel Sant'Angelo has a storied past that adheres to Rome's history tighter than most sites. Many places around Rome had their heyday for short periods once upon a time, but Castel Sant'Angelo's story has been continuously active since its construction 2,000 years ago.

It was first built for Emperor Hadrian during his reign (117-138ce) as a mausoleum to house the remains of him and his descendants. Taking the round shape of the Augustian Mausoleum, it ultimately housed the remains of the Emperors through Caracalla (217ce).

During Hadrian's time, it was illegal to bury a person within the Aurelian Walls, so a popular spot for burials was on the other side of the river. He built the bridge as the grand entrance to his burial place.

Over the next 1,500 years, the building was in a constant state of remodeling as its use changed with every passing Emperor and Pope. *(See next page.)*

What to Look for in Castel Sant'Angelo
- 5 Floors, all reachable by a long spiral ramp
- Chamber of Ashes, Prison & Torture Chamber
- Papal Residence - Gorgeous Renaissance frescoes
- The Vatican Treasures and Archives
- Excellent display of Medieval Weaponry
- Complicated maze of rooms, chambers, staircases, passageways, and courtyards
- Upper Restaurant & Bar with city view
- Top Deck with magnificent views of the city

- **139** - *Hadrian's Mausoleum*
- **271** - *Fortified Outpost*
- **403** - *The Aurelian Walls were expanded to include it; defensive military fortifications were added*
- **400's** - *The Visigoths sacked Rome, and converted it to a Fortress*
- **590** - *Pope Gregory dreamed that Saint Michael the Archangel announced the end of the Plague, so a statue was erected in his honor*
- **14th Century** - *Orsini Pope (Nicolo III) created a tunnel to connect it to the Vatican*
- **1492** - *The Borgia Pope (Alexander VI) converted it into a lavish residential Palace*
- **1494** - *Pope Alexander VI turned parts of the building into a prison and torture chamber*
- **1514** - *Michelangelo designed the side chapel dedicated to the Saints*
- **1527** - *Pope Clement VII (Medici) fled the Vatican through the tunnel only to be trapped in Castel Sant'Angelo for 7 months during the invasion of Spain's Charles V*
- **1901** - *Castel Sant'Angelo was turned into a Museum*

Most of the in-between years saw massive remodels to suit every Pope that came into power. Until today, this facility has been shrouded in construction scaffolding for nearly its entire long life. Now, it poses beautifully for tourist photos in all of its grand historic glory.

ANCIENT & HISTORIC SITES

ANCIENT & HISTORIC SITES

PALLATINE HILL
DOMUS TRANSITORIA

3-D VIRTUAL REALITY Presentation · **UNDERGROUND!** · **Near the ROMAN FORUM!** · **COOL ARCHAEOLOGY!** · **UNCROWDED!**

Domus Transitoria
was Emperor Nero's
first, or transitional, palace. It was destroyed during the Great Fire of 64ce.
Located on Palatine Hill, this is a fun discovery for under-grounders.
(Domus Transitoria = Transitional House)

Built in the 1st century, Nero grabbed a large swath
of land that extended from the Capitoline Hill to the
far side of today's Colosseum. He wanted the palace
to reflect his position as an absolute ruler. He wanted
shiny marble everywhere, gold-gilded everything,
and rare gems to trim that gold. Fountains in every room, both inside and out. But of course, many
people were not impressed. They felt he was too
opulent, too showy, and was spending far too much
of their tax money to create it.

Then the Great Fire of 64ce raged through the city, destroying over 75% of
Rome, including Nero's palace. To add pressure to his pain, he was blamed
for starting the fire. For nearly 2,000 years, people believed these rumors.
But recent evidence proves otherwise: Nero did not actually fiddle while
Rome burned. It now appears that he was not even in Rome when the fire
was started.

Once you descend below ground under the ruins of Domitians Palace, you will
be asked to take a seat and don a pair of 3DVR glasses. Suddenly, the badly
broken room around you will come to life: marble walls, frescoed ceilings,
and fountains will spring up all around you. This is a fantastic way to see
these ruins as it will enable you to get a clear idea of the true beauty of Nero's Palace. As you walk through the little site, note the details of the elegant
mosaics, and the shadows of frescoes that remain on the walls and ceilings.

The site entrance is under- neath Domitians palace.

Stunning mosaics remain in some of the rooms.

The ruins will come to life with the help of 3DVR.

DOMUS AUREA

VIA DELLA DOMUS AUREA 1
(Inside Parco del Colle Oppio)

3-D VIRTUAL REALITY Presentation

Away From the HEAT!

UNDERGROUND!

Near the COLOSSEUM!

COOL ARCHAEOLOGY!

After the Great Fire in 64ce destroyed the city, Emperor Nero further enraged his citizens by usurping a large chunk of land on which to build his new Golden Palace. As opulent as his first palace was, Domus Aurea topped even that - by magnitudes! The enormity of the palace, and the sheer decadence of its decor was enough to feed the already huge pot of negative rumors about Nero. The citizens of Rome grew to hate Nero beyond reason.

Today however, a visit to Domus Aurea is a very pleasant experience. Once you don a hard hat *(right)*, you will see the unique-ness of the architecture. Nero's favorite architects, Severus & Celer, managed to create an entire tower that rotated! We still can't figure out how they did it, and alas, not much is left today. This site re-tains the cool temperature of the under-ground earth, making this visit a welcome break from the exhausting heat of Rome.

Halfway through your tour, you will be treated to a **3DVR** break that will instantly propel you back in time 2,000 years ago, when this palace was at its height. You will see the luxurious lengths to which Nero went to create an environment that he hoped would please his citizens. But alas, it had the opposite effect on them.

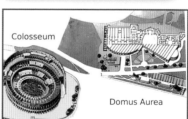

Colosseum

Domus Aurea

Note the massive size of Domus Aurea in relation to the Colosseum. Nero wanted his Golden House to be the most impressive building in history. And it was!

ANCIENT & HISTORIC SITES

FORUM BOARIUM The Cattle Market
VIA DELLA GRECA

COOL ARCHAEOLOGY!   **FREE!**   GREAT FIND!   Near the ROMAN FORUM!   PHOTO OPS   Quick & EASY!

Not much remains from the original Cattle Market Forum, except the two Temples here, and the Bocca della Verita across the street.

The round structure (1) is the Temple of Hercules. According to legend, Cacus was an ogre of a man, that could repeat only one word "Cacus. Cacus." He ate people, and animals alike, instilling fear and loathing into our villagers. One day, a strong cattleman arrived in town herding his cattle along the river. He heard about the dangerous ogre that lived in a cave next to the river. So he fought Cacus, won the fight, and became a hero for all time henceforth. His name was Hercules.

The place where the Temple sits is the place where Hercules first spotted Cacus. Legendarily speaking, of course.

Forum Boarium (bo-AR-ee-um) was a large cattle market during the Roman Republic. Cattle barges would land on the docks, and the cattle would be sold in the marketplace here.

The square structure (2), the Temple of Portunus *(right)*, was possibly dedicated to watch over the cattle barges and the port itself.

Both structures have been restored at various points in history. Example, the tile roof on the round structure was added recently. They think the original roof was a dome, but they don't really know for sure.

ANCIENT & HISTORIC SITES

SAN CRISOGONO
PIAZZA SIDNEY SONNINO, 44

UNCROWDED! EERIE! COOL ARCHAEOLOGY!
UNDERGROUND! GREAT FIND! Away From the HEAT!

San Crisogono is currently a Parish Church and minor Basilica from the 1100s. However, approximately 12 feet underground lies the remains of several much older structures. Archaeologists have not yet come to agreement on the original use of the main building. Some say it was an ancient church built in the 300s. While others feel that there was no Christian activity here during that period, and that it could have been anything from a school to a die factory. Regardless, the structure eventually came to be used as a church. As you pass through, you will see a mash-up of items from differing periods that include a variety of sarcophagi - some ornate, an ancient altar, something that might have been a baptismal font, brick and stone work from a range of ages, and worn frescoes from the middle ages. Signage is poor, so this may be the only write-up you might find about San Crisogono.

ANCIENT & HISTORIC SITES

CIRCUS MAXIMUS
VIA DEL CIRCO MASSIMO

Circus Maximus fills the lush valley area between the Palatine Hill and the Aventine Hill. Used primarily for horse and chariot racing, the citizens of Rome also enjoyed watching the animal hunts that took place here. For the Rulers of Rome, Circus Maximus seemed an ideal place to carry out public executions as well.

A vast 2,000-feet long and 460 feet wide, it was able to accommodate 250,000 spectators making it the largest sports and entertainment venue of all time!

Besides the sporting events, the Circus Maximus is quite famous for a few other reasons. In 64ce, it is believed that the great fire that destroyed two-thirds of the city *(during Nero's rule)*, started in one of the vendors' booths here in the Circus and spread quickly throughout Rome.

Further back in history is the story of the Rape of the Sabine women. As

the legend goes, Romulus' army, all men, were concerned about their legacies, as there were not enough women in the village of Rome with which to create families. So Romulus held a festival in the Circus Maxi-

mus and invited the virgin women from the neighboring town of Sabine. At the moment of a prearranged signal from Romulus, the men in the audience were to jump up and grab a young woman to keep. The men of Sabine were so shocked that their women were abducted, they started a war with Rome. But the women, many of whom were happy to find husbands, stood up and took the blame for the war. This caused both sides to back down and create a peace treaty among the two towns.

UNCROWDED!

COOL ARCHAEOLOGY

3-D VIRTUAL REALITY Presentation

PHOTO OPS

Near the COLOSSEUM!

Near the ROMAN FORUM!

3DVR

Today, a visit to the Circus Maximus is a fun activity for the whole family. The venue provides 3DVR *(3-Dimensional Virtual Reality)* glasses which, after putting them on, you can walk around a predetermined area of the Circus to learn about its construction and operations.

(**1**) *A view from the Paliatine Hill side of the Circus Maximus, looking down from the side where the Emperor's Balcony sits.* (**2**) *A 3D model of Circus Maximus during ancient times.* (**3**) *A visitor wears 3DVR goggles as he tours his way through the Circus Maximus.*

CIRCUS AGONALIS
VIA DI TOR SANGUIGNA, 3

UNDERGROUND!   COOL ARCHAEOLOGY!   Away From the HEAT

GREAT FIND!   Quick & EASY!

Stadium of Domitian underneath Piazza Navona

If you are already hanging out in Piazza Navona, here is a treat that very few know about. You can actually go underneath Piazza Navona to visit this ancient sports venue.

After the great fire of 64ce destroyed much of Rome, this sports arena was built to fill part of an area known as Campus Martius.

Seating as many as 20,000 spectators, it was created entirely for athletic competitions. Much smaller than the Circus Maximus across town, it was an appropriate size for foot races, and other track and field events.

An audio recording will walk you through this underground museum that contains ruins from the original stadium. Pieces of walls and arches have been placed here in museum fashion.

Once you understand that Piazza Navona sits in a space above an ancient stadium, you will see from where it derived its shape.

The visual boards discuss the types of games and competitions that were once held here. Very similar to the Olympic games of Greek origin, the stadium was a popular venue that separated the pros from the amateurs.

While you are down there, look for one of our "FUN FINDS," Serpens Ultor, the Avenger Serpent **264**

This activity will take around one hour, making it an easy stop while you're in the neighborhood.

These walls and archways have been placed here from their original underground location in the stadium.

ANCIENT & HISTORIC SITES

Near the COLOSSEUM! · PHOTO OPS · Quick & EASY!

LUDUS MAGNUS
Gladatorial College

Ludus Magnus was created as a dormitory and training arena for gladiators that came from a variety of countries. Here, they would eat, sleep and train. It was built by Emperor Domitian, along with three other practice arenas in the city.

When a gladiator arrived, they were segregated according to their specialty. A 'doctor' of that specialty was brought in to help them sharpen their skills.

A tunnel connected Ludus Magnus to the Colosseo across the street, giving the gladiators an unencumbered access to the stadium without exposure to the public.

 Easy to find, Ludus Magnus is on the east side of the Colosseum.

The arena area has been cut off by the modern development of the city. The remainder of the original practice arena lies beneath the new buildings, awaiting excavation.

ANCIENT & HISTORIC SITES

75

LARGO di TORRE ARGENTINA

COOL ARCHAEOLOGY!   FREE!   PHOTO OPS   Quick & EASY!

Although Largo di Torre Argentina is several blocks away from the Roman Forum, it was possibly an extension of the original Forum complex. As it happens, this is the place where Caesar was murdered by his Roman Senators in 44bce. The plan was to kill him after a Senate meeting, which was usually held in the Curia Julia located in the Forum. But because the Curia Julia was under construction, meetings were temporarily held in the Curia Pompey. Recent excavations at Largo di Torre Argentina unearthed a plaque placed by Augustus *(Caesar's adopted son)* to remember the spot where his father was stabbed on that fateful Ides of March.

Largo di Argentina contains the remains of four buildings left over from the Republic:

A. The Temple of Juturna was built in the 3rd-century bce. It was this area that later became the Curia Pompey, the place where Caesar was murdered.

B. The round temple with six standing columns is the youngest of the four structures and was built around 101bce.

C. This is the oldest of the four buildings, dating back to 4th or 3rd-century

ANCIENT & HISTORIC SITES

bc, and was probably devoted to Feronia, an ancient goddess of fertility. After the fire of 80ce, this temple was restored, and the white and black mosaic of the inner temple cella dates back to this restoration.

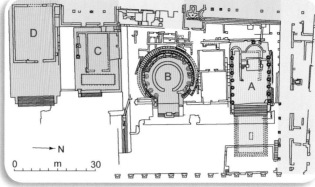

D. This is the largest of these temples and goes back to the 2nd-century bc.

The name of this site has nothing to do with the country of Argentina. The Torre *(tower)* was named after Johannes Burckardt, the Master of Ceremonies for five Popes. He was born in Strasburg, which in Latin, translates to "Argentoratum."

A Cat House?

Today, the site is a legal Cat Sanctuary. A small area has been reserved for the person that tends to the kitties. At one time, as many as 220 cats lived here in Largo di Torre Argentina.

DOMUS ROMANE di PALAZZO VALENTINI
VIA FORO TRAIANO 85

Near the ROMAN FORUM! | COOL ARCHAEOLOGY! | 3-D VIRTUAL REALITY Presentation | UNDERGROUND!

Tucked quietly underneath **Palazzo Valentini**, lies **Domus Romane**, the remains of a few ancient Patrician homes that come to life within this excellent excavation.

Domus Romane is a conglomeration of ruins consisting of an area of land where many families have lived, grown, and changed the structures through the years.

As you progress through this site, you will see how families have moved in, remodeled, removed walls, and added new walls to accommodate their lifestyles.

These homes hardly seem like ruins, as they come to life when the multimedia begins in each room. Ceiling frescoes above you, marbled walls all around you, and beautiful tiled mosaics beneath your feet give you the feeling that you are walking through the homes of ancient wealthy Romans.

Ancient kitchens, bathrooms, and furnishings all come to light as each room is awash in videos that cover most surfaces. You will easily be able to visualize these homes from the deep Roman past.

The site is dark or dimly lit throughout. For some, the glass floors might be disorienting to step on in the dark. Be prepared to be spatially disoriented.

But beneath the glass floors are the ancient ruins of each room in the site. Dishes, jewelery, even ancient trash was found in these spaces.

A treat at the end of your tour will give you a gopher's-eye view of the bottom of Trajan's Column that sits just outside of this site.

ANCIENT & HISTORIC SITES

CRYPTA BALBI

Via delle Botteghe Oscure, 31

NATIONAL ROMAN MUSEUM

UNCROWDED!   COOL ARCHAEOLOGY!   Near the ROMAN FORUM!   UNDERGROUND!

ANCIENT & HISTORIC SITES

Archaeologists love trash heaps! This is where so much historical treasure is found. Being an archaeological aficionado for many years, I have visited many trash dumps around the world. The fascinating site of Crypta Balbi is the oldest continuous-ly-used garbage heap in Rome.

This site is a deep diary of a block of land that was occupied for 2,000 years. The archaeol-ogists did a great job of at-tempting to separate the untidy layers of history. It reminded me, appropriately, of a lasagna!

So what happened in this little city block over 2,000 years? Basically, everything! Who lived and/or worked here? Pretty much everyone from cultures all over the world.

Walking through the site is quite cool, but can be a bit confusing as you see a partial room tucked underneath another, or the floor of one room jutting from the middle of another. But hang in there. Once you are finished going through the underground portion, head upstairs to the museum. This 4-lay-er eye-feast takes it all apart and explains the various layers of mixed up archaeology below. Be sure to visit all four floors of this little museum, be-cause the curators and archaeologists did a mighty good job of peeling apart the underground layers for you.

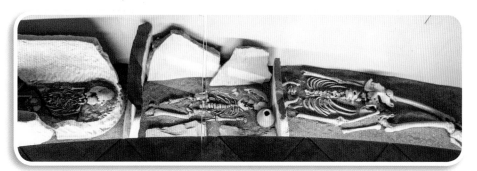

TREVI FOUNTAIN
PIAZZA DI TREVI

POPULAR   PHOTO OPS

Trevi Fountain *(Fontana di Trevi)* is a visitor favorite. It is the largest Baroque fountain in the world, and undoubtedly the most famous. In the 1600s Pope Urban VIII **214** had initially asked Gian Lorenzo Bernini **170** to design a new fountain to replace an existing one, but the Pope died before the project began. Holding a contest, a sculptor named Alessandro Galilei won the bid to create the new fountain. The locals created a mad kerfuffle because they felt that a Florentine shouldn't be allowed to create such an import-ant Roman project. So they gave the job to the second-place winner, a local named Nicola Salvi. He too died before its completion, and 4 other sculptors took up the conclusion of the project. Even though it seems that many hands have contributed to the design of the fountain, the Trevi still maintains strong echoes of Bernini's original design and style. The striking sculpture of Oceanus in the clam shell creates a stunning centerpiece to the fountain. • • •

The Legend of Trevi Fountain

Tossing 1 coin will lead to romance, 2 coins mean that you will return to Rome, and 3 coins will lead to marriage! Whatever you choose, one thing is for certain: the more money you toss, the more will be collected from the fountain, come cleaning day. Approximately 25 thousand euros are gathered each week. This totals around 1.3 million euros each year, which is donated to a food program to help the needy.

So keep on tossing and making those wishes because the magic of the Trevi will make the dreams of many hungry people come true.

ANCIENT & HISTORIC SITES

TREVI UNDERGROUND
VICOLO DEL PUTTARELLO, 25

Away From the HEAT! · GREAT FIND! · UNDERGROUND! · COOL ARCHAEOLOGY!

As famous as the Trevi Fountain is, her underground is equally un-famous. As thousands of people gather around the fountain to snap a photo, toss a coin, and suffer the heat, you will be enjoying the relaxed and secret passageways of the underground archaeological site located just a few steps away. Called **Vicus Caprarius**, it was once the crossroads where three water channels met to supply ancient Rome with water. Legend has it that the original aqueduct, aptly named the Acqua Vergine, was where a Vestal Virgin 53 led the Romans to find the water. Houses and buildings were built on top of it over the next two thousand years.

Note the herringbone pattern on the floor: during the second century ce, this pattern was popular because of its hardiness, ease of installation, and affordability. When you see floors like this around Rome, you will know that you have descended nearly 2,000 years into the past! The archaeological site is also an excellent museum that tells stories of the items that were discovered here during their excavations.

Water still flows through the ancient part of the city (now underground) that was the water source for the Ancient Romans. Today, this water is still tied to the water that feeds the fountain in Piazza Navona. 224

Sixteen amphorae (jars) were found during the excavations. These came from Africa and were used to transport oils.

ANCIENT & HISTORIC SITES

BASILICA di SAN CLEMENTE
Via Labicana, 95

COOL ARCHAEOLOGY! *GREAT FIND!* *Near the COLOSSEUM!* *UNDERGROUND!*

1

San Clemente is a 3-Layer Cake filled with sweet treasures throughout! Upon entering this Basilica, you will have gone back nearly 1,000 years in time, to the year 1099. But not completely, as its interior is a mash-up of art and architecture of later centuries. The golden Byzantine mosaics and frescoes over and behind the altar rise above the tomb and relics of Saint Clement. Note that the columns are unmatched in both size and style; they were borrowed from a variety of ancient sites. The side naves have been decorated in the Baroque style. The stones in that magnificent floor were brought from other countries, and/or borrowed from older sites. They were cut and placed during the construction of this top story. Each section of the floor is unique to each other. To descend into the lower layers, enter the shop, to purchase a ticket, and go down from there.

2

The middle layer was once the home of a first-century nobleman. It was converted into a church in the late third century. Note that the walls have been filled with stone and rubble to support the building above. This gives each nave a feeling of seperate long slender rooms. Before they were filled, the 3 pillared naves were of one great room. Notice in the fresco of "The St. Clement Mass," where many of the heads of people have been cut off by the ceiling, which is the floor of the newer Basilica upstairs. This level contains the best collection of early Christian art in the city. The church was dedicated to Saint Clement, who according to legend, was drowned in the Black Sea with a rock tied to him.

3

The bottom and oldest of the three layers of the Basilica was used as a place of worship for the Pagan cult of Mithra, a Zoroastrian sect from Persia. Several rooms are available to see, including the Banquet Room (right) where rituals were held. As you walk through this nearly 2,000-year-old facility, note the columns and arches, where some have been severed by the odd placement of newer walls, which were placed later to support the Basilica above. The room at the far end was used as a classroom to spread the teachings of Mithra. In the early 300's, the advent of the Edict of Milan (313ce) ended Christian persecution, giving rise to Christianity, and ending Mithraism.

ANCIENT & HISTORIC SITES

3

When you exit the underground Mithraeum, you will pass across this long hall. But it's not a hall at all; it used to be the alleyway between the Mithraeum and the building next door. Picture it not covered with a narrow vaulted ceiling, but open to the sky. You are entering the surrounding neighborhood from 2,000 years ago!

Approximately 120 years after the creation of this building, the original floors were replaced with this herringbone style of flooring. This kind of flooring was laid throughout Rome during this period, as they found it to be both rugged and inexpensive. Whenever you see it around Rome, you'll know you are looking back approximately 2000 years.

As you pass through the many rooms of this ancient building, you can still hear the water running through it! This is the original source of water that took care of these people long ago. You'll see a latrine, and a marvelous variety of other rooms. This building seemingly goes on forever, room after room, until you ascend back up to the 21st century.

By now, you are deep within the Earth. You can hear the sounds of the running ancient waters that today, still connect San Clemente to the Colosseum. Because of its proximity to the Colosseum **42**, the underground building next door to the Mithraeum was identified as a Mint, even though there is no physical evidence to bear this out: no minting equipment, no caches of coins, etc. Current theories include a warehouse, a manufacturer of 'something unknown,' or some other type of industrial facility.

ANCIENT & HISTORIC SITES

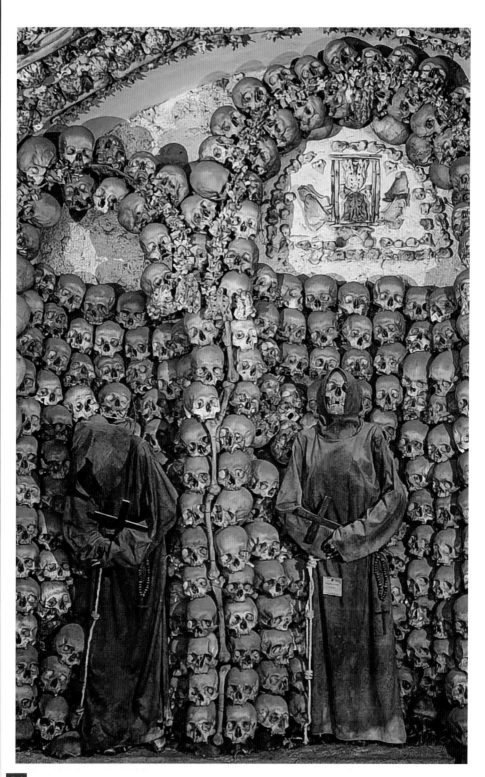

CAPUCHIN CRYPTS
VIA VITTORIO VENETO, 27

EERIE!   UNCROWDED!   GREAT FIND!

The Capuchin Friars are an off-shoot of the Franciscan order. They follow the same basic tenets of Saint Francis, but they choose to live a more basic lifestyle. They wear sandals with no socks, and a long brown coffee-colored robe, hence the name 'Capuchin.'

Located next to the church of Santa Maria della Concezione dei Cappuccini, the Crypt consists of several small chapels that have been thoughtfully decorated with yes, human bones. The bones of over 3,700 people are the dominant decorative feature.

When Monks passed away, they were buried in the ground for 30 years to allow their bodies to decompose. After 30 years, they were dug up, and a newly-deceased Monk would fill that space in the ground. The bones of that dug-up Monk were cleaned and used to decorate these crypts. While alive, the Monks considered it a privilege if their bones would end up as part of the decor.

The rooms in the Crypt include the Crypt of the Skulls, the Crypt of the Pelvises, the Crypt of the Leg & Thigh bones, etc. After seeing this, I had a little difficulty getting to sleep for a while.

ANCIENT & HISTORIC SITES

CATACOMBS

UNDERGROUND!   Away From the HEAT!   EERIE!

The Roman Catacombs consist of the underground tunnels where the dead are buried. They began with a large empty piece of land, then dug long trenches around six feet deep. They would dig body-sized holes in the walls of the trenches where the bodies were each placed, then the hole was closed with plaster to contain the odors. When the field became full, they would dig down another six feet, and create holes underneath the original bodies, and place another layer of bodies. When full, they would dig down again, and so forth. This explains why the oldest bodies are nearest the surface, and the newer bodies are further below. Everyone could be interred here, regardless of Religion or wealth. The catacombs were in use from around 150 - 400ce.

Catacombs in Rome

- Catacombs of Marcellinus and Peter
- Catacombs of Domitilla
- Catacombs of Commodilla
- Catacombs of Generosa
- Catacombs of Praetextatus
- Catacombs of Priscilla
- Catacombs of San Callisto (Callixtus)
- Catacombs of San Lorenzo
- Catacombs of San Pancrazio
- Catacombs of San Sebastiano
- Catacombs of San Valentino
- Catacombs of Sant'Agnese
- Catacombs of via Anapo
- Jewish Catacombs

The Popes' burial chamber, located in the Catacombs of Domitilla, held the bodies of many of the early Popes. Although the bodies have been removed, the tomb still retains interesting frescoes and sculptures. ▼

The tomb of Santa Cecilia, the Patron Saint of Music. The Catacombs can be quite complex; without a guide, you are guaranteed to get lost, as some of them my contain as many as 12 miles of tunnels! ▼

APPIAN WAY

PHOTO OPS　UNCROWDED!

The Appian Way is the ancient Roman road that was built in antiquity and still remains, although discontiguous, today.

One of the more gruesome events that occurred on the Appian Way was in 71 bce when the slave, Spartacus, lost his battle against the Roman Army. The Romans set up crucifixes and proceeded to crucify over 6,000 of Spartacus' men on those crosses. The crucifixions spanned a 120-mile expanse of the Appian Way!

The road begins around the Colosseum (1) and heads south. Much of the road

passes through the beautiful and scenic countryside where walking and bicycle-riding are popular activities. Many of the sites along the way are underground, because this is the area where the Roman Catacombs are located.

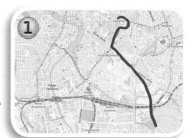

In some places along the road, you can find the ruts (2) where the ancient wagons have carved their form into the stones. Over the centuries, the old Roman roads have withstood modifications and repairs. This process included the lifting out and re-placment of the stones making the wagon wheel ruts discontiguous.

It is recommended to stop at the Visitors' Center to get descriptions of these stops *(below)* along the way.

Stops Along the Appian Way:

- Appian Way Visitors' Center
- Circus Maxentius (3)
- Catacombs of Callixtus
- Catacombs of Priscilla
- Tomb of Romulus
- Mausoleum of Caecilia Metella
  (4) *(the only woman in ancient times to get her own mausoleum)*
- Catacombs of San Sebastiano
- Chapel of Reginald Pole
- Church of Domine Quo Vadis

ANCIENT & HISTORIC SITES

ROMAN AQUEDUCTS

ANCIENT & HISTORIC SITES

PHOTO OPS · **UNCROWDED!** · **COOL ARCHAEOLOGY!**

Aqueducts have been around for nearly 10,000 years. Early evidence has been found in India, Assyria, and Egypt to bear this out. It wasn't until 312bce that Rome caught on to the art of the aqueduct. But when she did, she nailed it! Rome vastly improved on this ancient way of moving water making it possible for a population to exist as far as 50 miles away from its water source!

Did Someone say Golf?

Something I'll bet they didn't do here in the ancient times was to play golf. But today, that beautiful green meadowy area is actually a picturesque golf course. Have you ever known anyone that got to play golf under the Roman Aqueducts? Reserve your time by contacting the Parco degli Acquedotti.

Becoming the Kings *(or should I say 'Emperors')* of aqueducts, Rome built them all over the Empire. Today, remnants of the Roman aqueducts can still be seen in France, Greece, Spain, Turkey, and North Africa. And some of them still work today. For example, the Acqua Vergine still provides water to the fountain in Piazza Navona **224** and the Trevi Fountain **80** to this day. The iconic arches can be seen for miles around. Some of these waterways run across picturesque bridges, some run over-ground, and some traverse through subterranea. But however it flows, Rome has owned the Aqueduct bragging rights for nearly 1,700 years!

CASE ROMANE del CELIO

CLIVO DI SCAURO

COOL ARCHAEOLOGY! · Away From the HEAT! · GREAT FIND! · Must-See ART!

Near the COLOSSEUM! · PHOTO OPS · UNDERGROUND!

Hiding under the 1939 Basilica of Saints Peter and Paul is a superb surprise! The ancient Roman houses in the Celio district are superior examples of life from the 3rd century ce through the middle ages - nearly 1,000 years.

The underground site was once many separate houses. In the third century, they were connected to make a larger building. One of the houses is, according to legend, where the brothers John and Paul lived before they were martyred.

Room after room of frescoed vaulted ceilings are mesmerizing. Besides the maze of rooms in houses, you will find shops, streets, and a bath house. At one point, you can look down to see more levels that have not yet been excavated.

To reach the site, you must pass through a deliciously arched ancient street. This in itself is a wonderfully picturesque experience!

The exquisitely preserved fresco in Prosperpina's Nymphaeum.

ANCIENT & HISTORIC SITES

MAUSOLEUM of CECILIA METELLA
VIA APPIA ANTICA, 161 (ON THE OLD APPIAN WAY)

As you walk down the Appian Way, the Mausoleum of Cecilia quickly rises to dominate your view. Built in the late first century bce for the daughter of the Roman Consul, Crassus, it has been used and reused over the centuries by many for political, religious, and private events.

Behind the tower, a castle is attached which housed the families of Popes and paupers alike. During the 1300s, the place was used as a military fortification, and the crenelations *(great word!)* were added to meet that end.

In non-war times, the tower was used as a toll-booth which was known to charge unreasonably high rates for passage on the road.

 A visit inside the Mausoleum of Caecilia boasts an excellent study of the variety of building materials that were used over the course of 1,300 years. Many kinds of bricks, stone, marble, mortar, and more can be seen in various layers as patches, and as add-ons.

COOL ARCHAEOLOGY!

GREAT FIND!

PHOTO OPS

Must-See GEM!

VILLA dei QUINTILI

(on the New Appian Way) **VIA APPIA NUOVA, 1092**

These beautiful ruins are the remains of one of the most beautiful countryside villas left over from antiquity.

These picturesque ruins were once a fabulous villa built by and for the three Quintili brothers, mid-second century Roman Consuls. Their taste was said to have been exquisite, and the Villa was loved by its visitors.

> Villa Quintili was loved so much by Emperor Comodus that he killed the Quintili brothers so that he could take this gorgeous villa for himself!

The grounds were so massive that early excavators believed this to be an ancient town, only later to discover that all of this was the property of a single villa.

Levels and layers have been added over the centuries, making this an adventurous walk for today's visitors.

The property was fed by its own private aqueduct, and contained a hippodrome, a place to hold horse and chariot races. Additionally, you can visit the ancient baths, a tepidarium and a nympheum. The Grand Terrazza will give you a fine view of the countryside.

ANCIENT & HISTORIC SITES

MITHRAEA

UNDERGROUND | Must-See GEM! | EERIE! | Check CoopCulture.it for tickets.

Galleri

Mithraism, aka the Mithraic Mysteries, is an ancient cult religion that still has offshoots today. Originally based on the ancient Persian god Mithra, it was practiced in Rome in the first through the fourth centuries.

Part of the initiation included a hand-shake and an oath of secrecy. Members would typically meet in secret underground locations called Mithraea.

Mithraism focuses on the ancient Iranian god Mithras, and was popular among young military men because it promised them redemption in the afterlife. *(Sound familiar?)*

A serious competitor to the rise of Catholicism, Mithraists were persecuted toward the end of the fourth century, ultimately ending the practice, or at least sending it further underground.

The sacrifice of cattle is linked directly with Mithraism. Carvings of this sacrifice are present in most mithrea, as can be seen in this image (right).

SAN CLEMENTE Mithraeum

A 5-minute walk from the Colosseum, the Mithraeum under the Basilica di San Clemente is the easiest Mithraeum to visit, as it does not require special reservations like most of the others. Additionally, the overall experience of going down 3 levels into the Earth to visit adds to the intrigue. Seeing it in the context of an ancient neighborhood tops the cake. The whole experience is outlined on page 82

A spin-off *(no pun intended!)* of Mithraism that is still practiced today is the cult of the Dancing Dervishes, more commonly known as the Whirling Dervishes.

Here, a man is seen holding the snout of a bull, holding him down with his foot, and stabbing him with a knife. This kind of imagery is found inside most mithrea.

Historians reports that there were as many as 680 of these locations around the Empire. Archaeologists have located over 420 of these sites scattered about the Roman Empire. Today, at least 35 Mithraea are known, a few of which may be open to the public.

Catholics felt that building a church on top of a Mithraeum would cancel out the ancient cult. This explains why you will often find them hiding under churches.

MAUSOLEUM of AUGUSTUS

The Mausoleum of Augustus was created after Augustus' victory at the Battle of Actium in 31bce. He wanted a place of glory to house his family's remains.

Once described as "a hill with a golden Augustus on top," the Mausoleum of Augustus has become a disappointing jumble of rubble. But having now been under vast renovations for several years, Rome has revamped this amazing structure that Augustus built for his family's remains.

Built in 31bce, it was the second largest known Mausoleum in its day. It was originally made of bricks and covered with a gleaming white travertine marble. Its design was of alternating concentric circles of walls and dirt.

Over the 2,000 years since Augustus died, the structure has barely withstood cannon fire, looting, and many renovations including being turned into a castle. Time has not been kind to the structure, which would make our first Emperor Augustus roll over in his... Mausoleum.

A bit of mowing and weeding, fresh archaeological digs, clean paths, and bright lighting is bringing this circular gift from the past back to its former Roman glory.

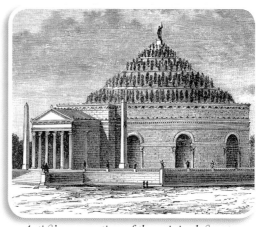

Artist's conception of the original structure.

RULERS & INFLUENCERS

This is a brief background of a few notable folks from Rome's illustrious past. Some are known for their stout bravery or great leadership skills. Some are remembered for their ultra bad behavior. In either case, these are the names that you will hear most often as you travel through the layers of Rome's great history. Sure, there are more, way more. But how long is your trip? Enjoy!

...AT A GLANCE

96 Julius Caesar

One of the greatest Generals of all time! His death toppled the stuttering Republic of Rome, only to launch the soon-to-be Roman Empire. He took Egypt's Queen Cleopatra as his lover.

100 Emperor Octavian Augustus Caesar

An adopted son of Julius Caesar, he was a shrewd and great leader that became the first Emperor of the new Roman Empire, which began after the death of his father Julius.

102 Agrippa

A warrior of spirit with a fierce loyalty to the safety and well-being of his lifelong friend Octavius Augustus Caesar, Agrippa was the best friend a Caesar could ever have.

103 Emperor Tiberius

He was remembered as a quiet man, but a very competent military General. Alternately, he was known as 'Tiberius the Monster,' a man with an ill mind, a downright crazy guy. So which accounts are true?

104 Emperor Caligula

Means 'Little Boots." Was he really as insane as Hollywood would lead you to believe? Was he ill? Or was he simply misunderstood?

...AT A GLANCE

Agrippina the Younger `106`

Nero's mother, Agrippina wasn't really a bad woman. Well ok, she really was. We're not just talking about 'stage mother' control here, we're talking truly unthinkable!

Emperor Nero `108`

TRUE OR FALSE: "Nero fiddled while Rome burned." False, as he wasn't even in the city when the Great Fire of 64ce began. So why did Romans have so much disdain for Nero?

Emperor Trajan `110`

Trajan grew the Roman Empire to its greatest size of all time. But he felt it was time to put an end to all of the Dacian's nonsense, and reclaim all of that land back for the Romans. So what did he do?

Emperor Hadrian `111`

A great guy, but slightly paranoid. So, non-traditionally, he built his palace outside of Rome: down in the beautiful resort city of Tivoli. He was the first bearded Emperor!

Emperor Diocletian `112`

Did so many great things for the Romans. He also chose the Ancient Greek Gods as the official religion, persecuting Christians. Bad move. Additionally, he split Rome into two halves: the West & the East.

Emperor Constantine I `114`

He ruled from the Eastern Empire (instead of from Rome). He chose Christianity as the official religion of Rome, persecuting all others. This changed the fate of Rome - and the world - forever!

JULIUS CAESAR
100bce - 44bce

Born Gaius Julius Caesar in 100bce, he is considered to be one of the greatest military generals of all time. He demonstrated a strong grasp of military strategy at an early age by providing excellent advice to his superiors until he gained enough rank to become a leader on his own.

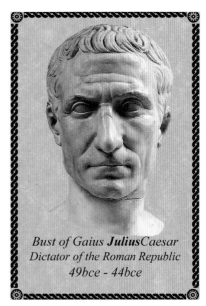

With Marc Antony at his side, Caesar moved through France, then Gaul, then on to Britain. In a single year, he was known to have slaughtered as many as one million people. An onslaught of this massive size left enough blood and bones in the soil to create a bumper crop in France that lasted several years.

*Bust of Gaius **Julius**Caesar*
Dictator of the Roman Republic
49bce - 44bce

Back in Rome, he partnered with his friend Crassus, a man of tremendous wealth, and Pompey, a very successful Roman General. Together the three of them were so popular with the people that they had enough power to run roughshod over the Roman Senate.

After Pompey was killed in Egypt *(see the blue box "The Fate of the Triumvirate")*, Caesar approached the Egyptian Co-Pharoah, a young Ptolemy XIII, Cleopatra's little brother. Julius was seeking support in the form of money and troops to overthrow the Senate and become the King of Rome.

This was the opportunity that Cleopatra needed to gain access and to warm up to Caesar. And did she ever! They became an international couple of the year and produced a son, Caesarian.

Caesar became the Dictator of Rome, he enacted a series of social and government reforms, and he changed the Calendar to the Julian Calendar that would henceforth include the month of 'July.' *(Guess why.)*

Meanwhile, back in Rome, the Senate, knowing that Caesar wanted to be named as King, devised a plan of their own to get rid of him, once and for all. They felt that without him, the Republic would return. But alas... Their plan was to gang up on him and stab him after a Senate meeting. They chose the 15th of March, the Ides, the day when debts should be settled, as the day they would resolve this little issue of their own.

After the Senate meeting at the Curia Pompey (in Largo Argentina 76), the

Senate members, including his nephew Brutus, stabbed Caesar 23 times. In his play entitled "The Tragedy of Julius Caesar," Shakespeare wrote that before dying, Caesar uttered the last words "Et tu, Brute?" *("Even you, Brutus?")* There is no documentation that this ever occurred, but it does tend to create a nice closure to the story.

The Fate of the Triumvirate

Caesar formed an alliance with Pompey, a celebrated military General, and Crassus, a man of legendary wealth in Rome. Together the three of them formed an elite group that had more power than the Senate and were able to get their way when they wanted it.

This partnership lasted several years until Crassus was killed during a battle with the Parthians *(Iran-Iraq)*. There are many legends about the specifics of his death including the story that molten gold was poured down his throat as a symbol of his greed. But this has never been proven.

After that, Caesar and Pompey were at odds. Pompey's army moved all over Italy with a relentless Caesar catching up behind them. After crossing the Rubicon River, their armies clashed. Pompey was defeated and fled to Egypt where he was murdered.

Caesar was the reigning victor - and sole survivor - of the Triumvirate.

The citizens, who dearly loved their Caesar, had a temple built in his honor in the Forum. Today, not much remains, but still Romans leave flowers in his temple in remembrance.

RULERS & INFLUENCERS

Roman Military Life

Proving their obsessiveness with order, each night the Roman army would pitch perfectly aligned tents, dig a trench around the encampment, and lash together pointed posts completing an enclosing wall. They erected these encampment cities every single night. In the morning, they would pack everything onto their backs and march again.

An encampment may house as many as 2,000 men. Each tent might sleep 8-10 men. Each tent cluster (below) is called a 'Cohort' and would sleep 480 men. 10 Cohorts made up a Legion.

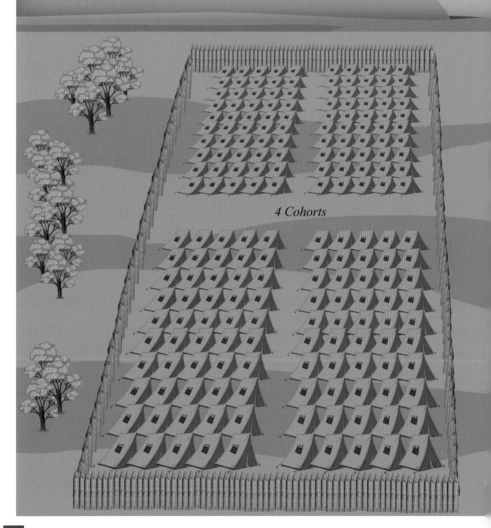

4 Cohorts

RULERS & INFLUENCERS

The Short Straw

One form of punishment for desertion, mutiny, or cowardice among the troops was to use the Short Straw method. And it worked. They would use this method to select one in every 10 soldiers. That guy would be clubbed to death by his own men. This kept the fear and obedience levels high.

The term decimation means the removal of a tenth.

A Cohort = 500 men
10 Cohorts = a Legion = 5,000 men

Life Marches On

The military troops were trained to march over 20 miles per day with a 50lb pack on their back.

They practiced fighting tactics every morning after breakfast, before their daily march began.

How Expense Management Can Lead to Power

The management of huge armies was an expensive undertaking. Imagine having to pay and provide food for a couple hundred thousand hungry men, every single day. Not to mention their horses. And to feed the livestock that travelled with them to later become food. The expense was staggering!

Generals knew that when they conquered new cities and/or countries, they would get to keep their wealth. This helped to pay for the maintenance of the legions, while growing their territories and the loyalty of their men.

Caesar was great at this tactic. Instead of paying his legions, he would promise that his men could split the goodies from their conquests among themselves. This kept them loyal to Caesar - instead of to Rome. Their greed kept them conquering. And the conquests gave a growing amount of power and fame to Caesar back in Rome.

As a result of his conquests, he made himself Governor of Northern Italy and Southern France, which in turn gave him more power and prestige in Rome.

RULERS & INFLUENCERS

Emperor OCTAVIAN AUGUSTUS
63bce - 14ce

RULERS & INFLUENCERS

Born on Palatine Hill, Gaius Octavius was the first Emperor of Rome. His great uncle on his mother's side was Julius Caesar, who adopted Octavian making the lad an official Caesar. After the tragic murder of Caesar, Marc Antony, Julius' best friend, gave a heart-felt eulogy that turned the tides of popular opinion against Caesar's killers. Octavian formed a new Triumvirate to avenge the death of his great uncle by seeking out and punishing the people responsible for Caesar's assassination. This second Triumvirate consisted of himself, Marc Antony, and General Marcus Lepidus.

Octavian's wife Scribonia produced his only natural child, a daughter named Julia. However, it was widely known that Octavian's relationship with his lover Livia *(Tiberius' mother)*, was growing closer. On the day that Scribonia gave birth to Julia, Octavian divorced her to wed Livia.

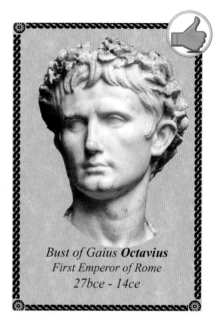

*Bust of Gaius **Octavius***
First Emperor of Rome
27bce - 14ce

"Falling on your sword," a term for a method of suicide, was an accepted and expected practice among Roman Generals. Marc Antony may be the most famous General that committed suicide this way, after losing the Battle of Actium to Augustus. Still alive, his men took him to Alexandria, Egypt, where he died in Cleopatra's arms. Soon after, she too committed suicide.

His Triumvirate dissolved after Marcus Lepidus' later exile, and Marc Antony's suicide in 30bce at the end of the war of Actium.

He and his most trusted military General Marcus Agrippa were elected as dual consuls by the Senate.

In 26bce, the Senate gave Octavius the titles of 'Augustus' and 'Princeps.' Augustus means 'the Illustrious One' and Princeps means 'First in Charge.' By this time, Julius Caesar had been deified. Augustus, to accentuate his closeness to Caesar, evolved his own image to match that of his Uncle Julius.

Under the leadership of Augustus, the Romans attained a nearly 200-year period of virtual peace known as the **Pax Romana**. Although Rome continued to conquer other lands to grow its overall empire, including the Middle East and Northern Africa, Rome avoided internal strife and invasion during this period of peace.

Upon his death at the age of 75 years, he was succeeded by Livia's son - Augustus' adopted son - Tiberius, the grandfather of the infamous Caligula.

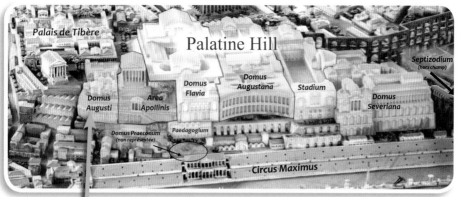

Domus Augusti was the formal home of Augustus.

The Mausoleum of Augustus **93** can be found at Piazza Augusto Imperatore.

The complicated ruins of the Forum of Augustus lie next to the Forum of Caesar on Palatine Hill.

Delicate but ornate frescoes still remain inside the Domus Augusti.

RULERS & INFLUENCERS

AGRIPPA
63bce - 12bce

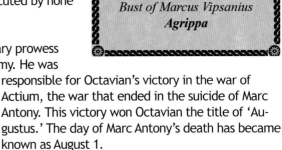

With close ties to the Caesar family, Agrippa grew up friends with Octavian *(Augustus)* since they were children, and ultimately married Julia, the daughter of Augustus.

A warrior of spirit with a fierce loyalty to the safety and well-being of his lifelong friend Octavius Augustus Caesar, Agrippa was the best friend a Caesar could ever have! His ability to shift between his veritable skills was dizzying. From commanding vast armies, to overseeing the building of significant architectural projects, to negotiating peace was a juggling act that could be so effectively executed by none other than Agrippa.

Bust of Marcus Vipsanius
Agrippa

He was most noted for his military prowess as lead General in Octavian's army. He was

responsible for Octavian's victory in the war of Actium, the war that ended in the suicide of Marc Antony. This victory won Octavian the title of 'Augustus.' The day of Marc Antony's death has became known as August 1.

But the talents and abilities of Agrippa did not end there. As the best friend of Augustus, he was entrusted with considerable responsibilities in Rome. When Augustus was away, Agrippa oversaw the business of Rome.

Agrippa, a gifted architect, held a pact with Augustus to turn Rome into a "city of marble." He oversaw the repair of roads, the growth of the aqueduct systems, and the erection of new buildings, baths, and porticoes. Agrippa built a Pantheon in Rome. Although it did not survive, Emperor Hadrian later built another Pantheon, keeping Agrippa's original dedication on the building, as you see it today (**1**).

Throughout his lifetime, he was awarded many state titles, allowing him to enter the Senate - even before he met the minimum age requirement. This included the prestigious honor of Tribunicia Potestas, or tribune of the Plebs. This gave him veto power, even over other Senators. **A sacred position, he was not allowed to be touched by another person without the penalty of death.**

Although Agrippa had built a tomb for himself, Augustus had Agrippa's remains placed in the Mausoleum of Augustus **93**, where they remain today.

EMPEROR TIBERIUS
42bce - 37ce

*Bust of **Tiberius** Claudius Nero*
Emperor from
14ce - 37 ce

Tiberius' reputation has been significantly altered throughout history, depending on who wrote the accounts of his life. He was remembered as a quiet, even sullen man, and a very competent military General. Alternately, he was known as 'Tiberius the Monster,' a man with an ill mind, a down-right crazy guy. So which accounts are real? Probably all of them.

His mother, Livia, married Octavius *(who later became Augustus)* to become Empress. Eventually, when Augustus was concerned about an heir, he officially adopted Tiberi-us, adding him to the Julian line. This made Tiberius ripe for the throne.

He married the love of his life Vipsania Agrippina. However, Augustus required that he divorce her to marry Augustus' daughter Julia. Julia, with an open distaste for her new husband, garnered an equally distasteful reputation as she wandered the streets openly with other men. Tiberius carried a torch for his first wife until his death.

Upon Augustus' death, Tiberius reluctantly accepted all appropriate titles and became the second Emperor of the Roman Empire in 14ce.

His contemporaries thought of Tiberius as a dark and sullen man. In his writings, Pliny the Elder referred to Tiberius as "the gloomiest of men." The death of his son Drusus only compounded his depression, making him unable to deal with the daily workings of running an Empire. So in 26ce, he left the day-to-day responsibilities to his trusted friend, and Praetorian Prefect, Sejanus, and he moved to the Isle of Capri.

But Sejanus wasn't as trusted as Tiberius believed. Possessing ambitions of himself becoming Ruler, Sejanus set about to make it happen. He purged members from the Senate that were in favor of Tiberius rather than himself, in a continued effort to shift the scales of power to his own favor. Tiberius, tired of hearing of these misdeeds, wrote a scathing letter to the Senate outlining an extensive list of power-grabbing moves made by Sejanus. Infuriating the Senate, they held a quick trial of Sejanus, with his swift execution occurring at the end of the week.

Tiberius lived to 78 years of age. His adopted grandson Gaius "Caligula" be-came his heir and the third Emperor of Rome.

EMPEROR CALIGULA
12 - 41ce

Rome's craziest Emperor? Mad? Bad? Sad? The most notorious ruler in Roman history? Wow! What did this guy do to deserve that kind of PR? To simplify for you, dear traveler, we will briefly outline his Rise & Demise, then let you decide for yourself.

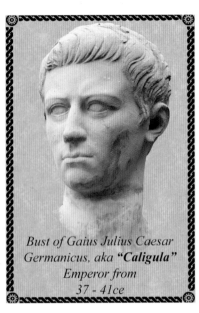

Bust of Gaius Julius Caesar Germanicus, aka "Caligula" Emperor from 37 - 41ce

Caligula, continuing the Julian-Claudian Dynasty, became the third Emperor of the Roman Empire, ruling only four years before his assassination. People were so afraid of their leader because somewhere during these four short years, he turned into a crazed lunatic. But was he?

As a young man in the custody of his grandfather Tiberius, Caligula had both a bright side and a dark side. Tiberius encouraged Caligula's darker side, stating that he was "nurturing a viper in the bosom of Rome."

When Tiberius died, Caligula and Tiberius' grandson Gemellus were made co-heirs to the Rulership. So, Caligula had Gemellus murdered, creating a swift fix to that situation.

Caligula also had a bright, ambitious side that truly loved Rome. He wanted nothing but the best for Rome - and himself while he was at it. He was fascinated with the lavishness with which the Egyptian Ptolemeys treated their leaders and wanted no less for himself.

As a moderate leader, he built two much-needed Aqueducts, new baths, buildings, and roads. He annexed Mauretania as a Province, expanding Rome's official reach. However, after two years of behaving like a good leader, he fell quite ill to fevers. Upon his recovery, his personality had noticeably changed.

He spent less time attending his civic duties and more time indulging his growing crazy and demented whims. It is difficult to separate myths and rumors from facts, as there is little official documentation from this period. But when fear lurks in the hearts and minds of people, rumors tend to run amok.

Little Boot

When he was a little boy, Gaius' mother enjoyed dressing him in military clothes that she had downsized to fit him. She had special little military boots made to fit him as well. Hence his lifelong nickname of "Caligula" meaning "Little Boot" or "Soldier's Boot."

RULERS & INFLUENCERS

Caligula is believed to have been guilty of everything from hosting lavish sexually-based parties, to immersing himself in unconstrained luxuries, to enjoying a regular variety of tortures. These stories were passed on through the 20th century by way of Hollywood movies about Caligula. But current archaeologists are reluctant to assign these episodes to Caligula without actual proof.

Nevertheless, people feared him. The Praetorian Guard, together with members of the Senate and other influentials, created a successful conspiracy to assassinate Caligula and his entire immediate family. He died at 37.

> Caligula is known for his overly unorthodox cruelty and boundless indulgences: He appointed his horse as a Consul. As a God, he waged a war with the Sea. Most people around him were eventually found dead, especially his senate members. His sexual indulgences were unrivalled. But there is little to no real evidence of the endless list of atrocities attributed to him. What is truth, and what is fiction?

Called a 'Round Ship,' this is one of Caligula's huge boats. It was discovered during the excavation of Rome's Fiumicino Airport. This area was once part of an ancient port city, located at the mouth of the River Tiber. The ship was between 312-340 feet in length, six levels high, and carried a robust crew of 700 people. NOTE: Learn about a Day Trip to the scenic Lake Nemi **294** *to see the excavations of Caligula's other personal Party Boats that were discovered in that beautiful Lake Resort town.*

Above Image: English. An 18th-century print of a royal barge as used by Caligula. Copied from a work by Nicolaes Witsen, his Aeloude en Hedendaegsche Scheepsbouw en Bestier; Nicolaes Witsen, Amsterdam, 1671

AGRIPPINA the YOUNGER

15 - 59ce Nero's Rather Colorful Mother

RULERS & INFLUENCERS

The odds are good that you have not heard of Agrippina. A beautiful woman with an iron will. She was Caligula's little sister. *(This explains a lot.)* And her outlandish misdeeds will earn her a place in your travel diary.

Agrippina wasn't really a bad woman. Well ok, she was. But her real vulnerability was her obsession with the success of her son Nero, followed by her combativeness against him. We're not just talking about 'stage mother' control here, we're talking truly unthinkable.

*Bust of **Agrippina** the Younger*
Empress from 49 - 54ce
Nero's Mother

Time Line of Agrippina's Life

◇ **At 13, she was married off to Gnaeus Domitius Ahenobarbus**
◇ **Nero, her only son was born**
◇ **Her brother Caligula becameEmperor**
◇ **Caligula exiled her**
◇ **Her husband died** *(mysteriously)*
◇ **Caligula was murdered, Claudius became Emperor**
◇ **Agrippa returned to Rome**
◇ **She married rich guy Crispus**
◇ **She murdered Crispus with poison**
◇ **She murdered Lollia Paulina who wanted to marry Claudius**
◇ **She married her Uncle, the Emperor Claudius**
◇ **She became Empress, the most powerful woman in Rome**
◇ **She convinced Claudius to adopt her son Nero**
◇ **She murdered Claudius' ex-mother-in-law**
◇ **She murdered Britanicus' tutor for plotting against Nero**
◇ **She murdered Calpurnia because Claudius thought she was pretty**
◇ **Nero murdered Britanicus, Claudius' only real son** *(competition)*
◇ **She murdered Statilius Taurus because she wanted his gardens**
◇ **She poisoned hubby Emperor Claudius with mushrooms**
◇ **Her son Nero became Emperor; She & Nero were at odds**
◇ **Nero had her power stripped**
◇ **Nero made several unsuccessful attempts to have her murdered**
◇ **Nero sunk her boat in the ocean, but she swam to shore**
◇ **Nero had her stabbed the next day. She died.**

> "I don't think anything produced by me and Agrippina could possibly be good for the state or the people."
> ~ *Gnaeus Domitius Ahenobarbus said of Nero.*
> *(Agrippina's first husband, Nero's father)*

C-Section

A common belief is that the 'Caesarian Section' was named after a technique used to give birth to Julius Caesar. However, it wasn't Julius that was wrenched from his mother's belly; it was his uncle Caesar.

Crossing the Rubicon

This expression is used to refer to crossing and a point (or line) of no return. It came from the time when Caesar and his massive troops crossed the Rubicon River, initiating a civil war against his own Senate. According to some historians, Caesar uttered the words "alea iacta est" (the die is cast) as he crossed the river.

Mens Sana In Corpore Sano
A Healthy mind in a Healthy Body.

In Vino Veritas
Truth in Wine

Exitus Acta Probat
The result justifies the deed.

Caveat Emptor
Let the buyer beware.

When in Rome, Do As the Romans Do

This familiar expression has roots dating back to the mid-300s. Saint Augustine, a Roman African Christian, travelled to Milan to teach. He was appalled when he found out that the local clergy did not fast on Saturdays, as was customary in Rome. He was advised by Saint Ambrose that when visiting a foreign culture, it is considered wise to practice as they practice.

RULERS & INFLUENCERS

EMPEROR NERO
37 - 68ce

The 'Monster.' The 'Mad Man.' The 'Tyrant.' *Many more nicknames have been applied to Nero, the 'Bad Boy' of the Julio-Claudio line of Roman Emperors. But was he really so bad? Or was his biography written by a guy that lived in a different generation, and whose political position differed so radically from Nero's that he wrote with a biased pen? Was Nero, like most leaders, just a multi-faceted man with a complex nature? Was he the result of an over-achieving, overly-controlling mother? Was he simply too young to begin his rule at 16 years of age? As it turns out, he was all of these things. And more!*

Last of the Julio-Claudio Line

Born in the year 37ce, Nero was a shy boy who learned early to follow his mother's rules. His mom, Agrippina the Younger, had soaring ambitions of ruling the Roman Empire. But because a woman was never allowed to do so, her second best option was to see that her son Nero became ruler.

*Bust of **Nero** Claudius Caesar Augustus Germanicus. Emperor from 54 - 68ce.*

Agrippina married Emperor Claudius, whom she insisted should adopt her son. This made Nero a direct descendant of the "rulership" upon the future death of Claudius. *(Of course, Claudius' eldest son, Claudius Drusus, would have to die as well in order to make this so. And so he did, at Nero's hand.)*

When Emperor Claudius died prematurely *(at Agrippina's hand)*, Agrippina cleared the path of dissenters within the Senate in order for Nero to rise to the position of Emperor. He was 16 years old.

BAD THINGS
- Murdered his Mother + 2 wives
- Murdered his step brother
- Built an Expensive Palace after the Great Fire of 64ce *(instead of helping the 1000s of people displaced by the fire)*
- Forced a man to commit suicide so he could marry the man's wife
- Castrated a slave, then married him
- Went to Greece for a year on a theatric tour *(thus ignoring his own country)*
- Blamed the fire on Christians, creating the first Christian Persecution
- Committed Suicide-by-Slave at age 30

(not so) BAD THINGS
- Ended closed-door political trials
- Banned Capital Punishment
- Outlawed bloodshed in the Games & Contests
- Allowed slaves to file formal complaints against abusive masters
- Provided aide to the Jews
- A Poet, Singer, and Actor
- Reduced taxes
- Competed in the Olympics
- Looked down on luxury *(at least in the early years)*
- Devout supporter of the Arts

The Great Fire & Human Torches

July 9th, 64ce. An event was being held at Circus Maximus. The bleachers were full, and cheers could be heard for miles. Suddenly, in one of the vendor stalls, a fire started. It quickly raged out of control, catching all of the other booths, and igniting all surrounding wooden structures. A wind blew the ash and cinders, creating fires all around the city. The flames stormed Rome for nine days before submitting to control.

When it was over, two-thirds of Rome was charred. Of Rome's 14 districts, only 4 remained intact. Rumors multiplied as quickly as the fire itself. People said that Nero caused the fire; that he played his violin as it burned; that he wanted to claim all that land for himself. People were furious with Nero!

But historians had since learned that Nero was not even in the city when the fire started and when he learned that his own beautiful home had been destroyed, he was genuinely distraught.

But the newly homeless people's rage grew. So Nero did the next best thing: he found someone else to blame for the fire: his scapegoat would be the Christians. He made a lavish public effort to denigrate them, then had them arrested. He had poles raised around the perimeter of his property. Then he ordered his men to tie the Christians to those poles. Come nightfall, they were to light them on fire.

Each night, hundreds of human torches were ignited *(above)*, creating the first-known official Christian Persecution.

Nero rebuilt much of the city in the Greek's image. This included his own new colossal palace, Domus Aurea. **69**

RULERS & INFLUENCERS

EMPEROR TRAJAN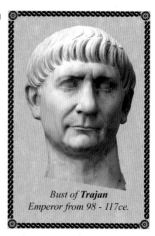
53 - 117ce

Born Marcus Ulpius Traianus in Spain, he rose through the ranks of the Roman Army, earning a reputation of patience, fairness, and bravery. Because Emperor Nerva died a mere 15 months after entering office, Trajan, his only heir, was promoted to Emperor with no contest in 98ce.

One of Emperor Trajan's first tasks was to tour the city to assess issues that needed addressing. Pleasing the people of Rome, he set about to mend badly-damaged roads, he built the last aqueducts, and he designed a massive public bath for the citizens. Romans were thrilled with their new leader!

*Bust of **Trajan** Emperor from 98 - 117ce.*

The Dacian War

By 101ce, Trajan was tired of dealing with the troublesome Dacians *(in modern-day Romania)*, so he marched with 100 thousand troops, only to return unfinished. Then in 105ce, he gathered 200 thousand soldiers to again march against the Dacians. But this time, he was victorious. Dacian leader Decebalus fled into the forest with his family, then ultimately committed suicide when the Romans found his hideout.

Trajan was heralded as a hero to the entire Roman Empire. To chronicle his most significant victory, the city erected the Triumphal Column of Trajan **61**, which pictorially tells the long story of his war with the Dacians. This 115-foot tall pillar tells the story in 155 scenes that illustrate the tactics, planning, sniveling, conniving, killing, and hiding that took place throughout the war.

Trajan grew the Roman Empire to its most extensive geography of all time. *(See the Roman Empire Map on page* **26***.)*

He went on to build the largest Forum the city had ever seen, including a *(SuperMall)* Marketplace, which is available to visitors today **59**. Additionally, he returned stolen lands to their rightful owners, property that was less-than-politely acquired by previous Emperors. Trajan started programs that provided the care and feeding of orphans. He used some of the money to make city-wide repairs of buildings, bridges, and canals. He built aqueducts and expanded the Port of Ostia **280**.

Trajan's rule was a prosperous time for Rome, prosperous mainly because of his expansions throughout the empire.

He was thought to be a fair-minded man that possessed a deep love for the Roman Empire. He died in 117ce after a stroke aboard a ship. Since he had formally adopted his cousin Hadrian, whom Trajan had helped to raise, the next person to claim the Emperor's throne was a mystery to no one.

RULERS & INFLUENCERS

Emperor HADRIAN
76 - 138ce

The third of what Pliny the Elder wrote as the "Five Good Emperors," Hadrian inherited a Roman Empire that was at its apex in terms of size. His cousin Trajan grew the Empire, and now Hadrian must manage it.

*Bust of **Hadrian***
Emperor from 117 - 138ce

His first order of business was to execute 4 members of the Senate because they opposed his taking of the throne. The next item on his list was to build a new house for himself and 1,000 of his closest friends. He wanted a place to live, to work, to conduct important meetings, and to host parties. It had to be outside of Rome, possibly because he was concerned that after murdering four senators, he might not be very safe in Rome. He selected Tivoli **274** *(15 miles east of Rome)* as his new home.

5 Good Emperors

Nerva
Trajan
Hadrian
Antoninus Pius
Marcus Aurelius

According to Pliny the Elder, these 5 men were considered to be fair, honest, with a true love for Rome and a desire to protect Rome above themselves.

He chose to grow a beard, an unusual choice for any Emperor. But as an ardent fan of all things Greece, he knew that all good philosophers were known to sport beards. This started a fashion trend among leaders all throughout Europe, for all time to come.

His biggest task at hand was how to control this huge diverse Empire that was created by Trajan. And the most difficult part of the management was how to keep all of these areas safe.

To meet this end, Hadrian built walls throughout Britain, along the Danube, and many other places where he deemed them to be viable protection for his new Roman territories. In all, he had erected 80 miles of walls. A few outlying areas were released from the Empire because they were difficult to protect.

An architect at heart, he built structures throughout the Empire. And being a devout lover of art, he erected statues all around the Empire as well.

He did not experience a happy marriage, but remained married to meet his political ends. Hadrian died in 138ce of congestive heart failure, but not before appointing Antoninus Pius as his successor.

RULERS & INFLUENCERS

EMPEROR DIOCLETIAN
244 - 311

Diocletian had the unfortunate honor of being Emperor during the Crisis of the Third Century, a period of empire-wide violence and chaos. But he put forth a valiant effort to calm the unrest.

Born to a humble, low-status family in Dalmatia *(Croatia)*, Diocletian quickly rose through military ranks as a calvary commander and a quick-thinking leader.

When Emperor Carus died, Diocletian beat out his son Carinus, becoming the Emperor in the East. He never had much of a fondness for Rome, preferring to run things from the East.

*Bust of **Diocletian** Emperor from 284 - 305ce*

A common problem as he saw it, was that the Roman Empire was simply too large for one man to manage. So he came up with the concept of the Tetrarchy, a plan that worked well toward lasting peace, at least for awhile.

The Tetrarchy
The plan was to formalize the splitting of the Empire into two, the East and the West. Each half would be led by an 'Augustus.' Each half would then be split in two, and the two new quarters would each be led by a 'Caesar.' In addition to the efficiency of local management, it also solved the age-old problem of throne inheritance. This rule by four people was called the Tetrarchy.

Now, if an Emperor were to be murdered, his Caesar would automatically become the new Emperor. This kept military Generals from deciding to instantly promote themselves to Emperor by murdering the existing one, a problem plaguing Emperors for centuries.

Managing an Empire
After winning battles in Egypt and Persia, a calm crawled over the Empire, enabling Diocletian to focus on domestic administration. He avoided nepotism by hiring people that were best qualified for jobs, rather than automatically hiring family members. Over time, power shifted away from Rome toward the East, where Diocletian resided.

Christianity
Christianity had grown steadily for the past 200 years because it appealed to the rich and the poor alike. It also had a unique concept that was widely appealing to everyone at every level: the concept of Forgiveness of one's sins. But because Christians were a disorganized, and unpredictable group for the

RULERS & INFLUENCERS

past couple of centuries, they were considered to be a pain in the neck for many Emperors.

Diocletian felt that a clear focus on the Greek Gods would return peace, but the fast-growing Christian population would have none of this. So he tried the age-old methods of Christian persecution, punishment, and torture. However, the Christians held fast, only serving to grow massive amounts of followers.

The problem with Diocletian at this juncture was that he felt HE was God. He didn't make the connection that people wouldn't agree with his wanting to be self-deified.

One day, he went to Rome *(the only time he had actually stepped-foot in Rome!)*, and became so ill that he was forced to abdicate, to retire. He convinced the other Augustus to retire, automatically promoting the two Caesars to become Augustuses, and bringing in two new Caesars.

Diocletian retired to his massive home in Split, Croatia, spending the remainder of his days growing cabbages.

P.S. In 306, the new Emperor Constantine I **114** unraveled the Tetrarchy, becoming sole ruler of the Empire, as well as adopting Christianity as the official religion of the Roman Empire.

Although Diocletian traveled to Rome only once, as their Emperor, he left them the gift of the largest Roman Baths ever created. As one of the 4 parts of the National Museums of Rome, the Baths of Diocletian **64** *is an uncrowded archaeological site waiting for your visit.*

RULERS & INFLUENCERS

RULERS & INFLUENCERS

Emperor CONSTANTINE I 👍
272 - 337

Constantine I was treated as a 'paragon of vir-
tue' during his lifetime.

Born in what is now known as Serbia, Constantine was the son of Emperor Constantius I. He
was sent to the east when he was 21 years of
age to be trained in the military. His intelligence and creativity led him to rise quickly
through its ranks. When he was thirty, he was
sent to Britain to campaign under his father.

When his father Constantius died in 306, Constantine became an Emperor. He battled with
Emperors Maxentius and Licinius, to become
the sole Emperor of the Roman Empire, east
and west.

*Bust of **Constantine I**
Emperor from
306 - 337ce*

He dismantled Diocletians **112** Tetrarchy, but kept the East/West separation
of Rome intact. Additionally, he separated military power from civil power to
prevent the military from turning Generals into Emperors. That practice had
gone on for centuries, and had caused clashes and murders within the ruling
class, so Constantine felt that taking the power out of the hands of the military was a good decision.

Constantine I came up with a new gold coin that would become the first
standardized currency in both the East and the West.

Although raised as a pagan, he became partial to the Christians during his
rule because of his Christian mother. He made it legal to be a Christian in
the Roman Empire, and created the first **Council of Nicaea** to organize the
philosophies - and the management of the Bishops - of Christianity. With
Licinius, he made Christianity the official religion of the Roman Empire. Out
of respect for his mother, he built the Church of Saint Peter.

The growing friction between his Christianized ideals and Rome's pagan population dulled the sheen of Rome for Constantine. So in 330, he changed the
name of Byzantium to Constantinople *(now known as Istanbul)*, and built a new
royal palace residence to rule - and defend - from there. Additionally, he
vastly improved the old city, and offered people instant citizenship and free
bread if they moved to Constantinople.

He did not become baptized as a Christian, however, until he was on his
deathbed. He was entombed in the Church of the Holy Apostles in Constantinople, and his tomb escaped plunder in 1204 during the 4th Crusades.

WELL, I'LL BE DAMNED!

When a Ruler was deemed to have been a 'good' ruler, he was officially deified by the Senate upon his death. He was "**Consecrated**" *~ made sacred, remembered as Gods ~ and to his memory, a temple was built so that citizens could forever go to pay homage. Julius Caesar, for example, was consecrated and had a Temple built that partially remains today in the Roman Forum.*

On the other hand, if a Ruler was deemed to have been a 'bad' ruler, the Senate would do everything possible to erase his/her memory from history. This included the destruction of paintings, sculptures, monuments, etc. This practice was called "**Damnatio Memoriae.**"

This list of Roman Rulers shows whether they were Consecrated or Damned:

SCORE CARD
Consecrated = 34   Damned = 27   Sainted = 1

Augustus 100 - *Consecrated*
Tiberius 103 - *unknown*
Caligula 104 - *Damnatio Memoriae*
Claudius - *Consecrated*
Nero 108 - *Damnatio Memoriae*
Galba - *Damnatio Memoriae*
Vitellius - *Damnatio Memoriae*
Otho - *Damnatio Memoriae*
Vespasian - *Consecrated*
Titus - *Consecrated*
Domitian - *Damnatio Memoriae*
Nerva - *Consecrated*
Trajan 110 - *Consecrated*
Hadrian 111 - *Consecrated*
Antoninus Pius - *Consecrated*
Marcus Aurelius - *Consecrated*
Lucius Verus - *Consecrated*
Avidius Cassius - *Damnatio Memoriae*
Commodus - *Damnatio Memoriae*
Pertinax - *Consecrated*
Didius Julianus - *Damnatio Memoriae*
Pescennius Niger - *Damnatio Memoriae*
Clodius Albinus - *Damnatio Memoriae*
Septimius **Severus** - *Consecrated.*
Caracalla - *unknown*
Geta - *Damnatio Memoriae*
Macrinus - *Damnatio Memoriae*
Heliogabalus - *Damnatio Memoriae*
Severus Alexander - *Consecrated*
Maximinus Thrax - *Damnatio Memoriae*
Gordian I - *Consecrated*
Gordian II - *Consecrated*
Pupienus - *Damnatio Memoriae*
Balbinus - *Damnatio Memoriae*

Gordian III - *Consecrated*
Philippus Arabs - *Consecrated*
Decius - *Consecrated*
Trebonianus Gallus - *Damnatio Memoriae*
Aemilianus - *Damnatio Memoriae*
Valerian - *Consecrated?*
Gallienus - *Consecrated*
Claudius II - *Consecrated*
Aurelian - *Consecrated*
Tacitus - *unknown*
Florianus - *unknown*
Probus - *Consecrated*
Carus - *Damnatio Memoriae*
Numerianus - *Damnatio Memoriae*
Carinus - *Damnatio Memoriae*
Diocletian 112 - *Consecrated*
Maximianus - *Damnatio Memoriae*
Constantius I Chlorus - *Consecrated*
Galerius - *Consecrated*
Maximinus Daia - *Damnatio Memoriae*
Severus II - *unknown*
Maxentius - *Damnatio Memoriae*
Licinius - *Damnatio Memoriae*
Constantine I 114 - Canonized *in the East*
Constantine II - *Damnatio Memoriae*
Constans - *Consecrated*
Constantius II - *Consecrated*
Julian the Apostate - *Consecrated*
Jovian - *Consecrated*
Valentinian I - *Consecrated*
Valens - *Consecrated*
Gratian - *Consecrated*
Valentinian II - *Consecrated*
Theodosius I - *Consecrated*

RULERS & INFLUENCERS

MUSEUMS

So much of Rome has been excavated, dug through, reburied, and built upon. Additionally, remarkable artists, wealthy collectors, and extravagant individuals have passed valuable pieces back and forth among themselves for Millennia. Fortunately, much of Rome's illustrious past has been preserved in glorious museums for your personal enjoyment. And please do. Enjoy them, that is!

...AT A GLANCE

120 Vatican Museum
After 500 years of perpetual collecting, there is so much to see! Here are a few of my very favorite pieces and places where you should spend a few extra moments to internalize their beauty.

126 Galleria/Villa Borghese
Probably the most sublime museum in Rome, the Galleria Borghese houses an extensive collection of the most cherished works of Renaissance and Baroque art in the western world. Lending to the enjoyment is the luxurious setting in a country Villa.

130 Capitoline Museum
Straddling both sides of Piazza del Campidoglio 220 are the Capitoline Museums 130. This is probably the most excellent collection of ancient sculpture, art, and historical pieces in Rome today.

134 Palazzo Barbarini
When you are a Pope (Urban VIII 214) and you are from the Barbarini family, you will enjoy only the finest that Rome can dish up for you. The Palazzo Barbarini is no exception. A remarkable collection of Renaissance and Baroque art...

MUSEUMS

MUSEUMS

148 Vittoriano

This giant wedding vake of a building hides so much. Climb to the various levels for a hug variety of views. The museum inside tells about the trials and tribulations of trying to unify Italy. Then climb to the horses on top!

141 Ara Pacis

When he returned from successful missions in Spain and Gaul, (Octavian) Augustus **100** *learned that his people had created this monument in his honor. Walk in. It's gorgeous!*

146 Trajan's Marketplace/ Imperial Forum Museum

The Museum of Trajan's Market **58** *and the Imperial Forum is the result of some of the best archaeology in the world. The museum examines the architecture and decorative...*

64 Baths of Diocletian

Diocletian ruled from the Eastern Empire, rather than from Rome. In fact, he came to Rome only once, toward the end of his reign. But he left this wonderful gift for the Romans!

79 Crypta Balbi

The 'Lasagne' of Rome, it is the excavation of a square city block and its residents. The layers of this dig site illustrate the many people and uses that occupied this piece of land for 2,000 years!

150 Villa Torlonia

Mussolini leased this villa for the equivalent of $1. Underneath the property, he dug up the ancient catacombs and turned them into WWII bomb shelters that YOU CAN ENTER!

The GLORIOUS
Vatican Museum

The **Hall of Statues** *is lined with a far-reaching collection of ancient figures from antiquity.*

The **Hall of Maps** *features a collection of hand-drawn maps depicting parts of the world as they knew them to be at that time.*

MUSEUMS

VATICAN MUSEUM
VIALE VATICANO

The conversion of the Vatican into a museum began in the 1600s under the tutelage of Pope Julius II **208** with the ancient sculpture of Laocoön and his Sons *(below)*. Found near Santa Maria Maggiore in an old vineyard, Julius sent Michelangelo and Giuliano da Sangallo, an architect/artist, to get their approval. After giving their approval, Julius II put the sublime sculpture on display for all to enjoy. This began a long-standing trend of Popes purchasing art and putting them on display in the Vatican. Today, the Vatican sees 6,000,000 visitors per year, making it one of the most visited art museums in the world.

After 500 years of perpetual collecting, there is so much to see! Here are a few of my very favorite pieces and places where you should spend a few extra moments to absorb their beauty. Among the ones pictured in this section, make sure to go through these areas:

In the **Gregorian Egyptian Gallery**, take a look at the Mummy of Amenirdis, and the distinct Shroud of the Lady of the Vatican. Incredible!

The **Gregorian Etruscan Museum** boasts an enlightening collection of pieces from the people that inhabited the area before the Romans. One of my favorites is the Sarcophagus with polychrome relief.

The **Alexander VI** section shows off its ultra lavish architectural and decorative finishes, suitable for the likes of a Borgia.

The following pages are not meant to act as a guide, but to merely point out some of the areas through which to move very slowly to enjoy. Wow!

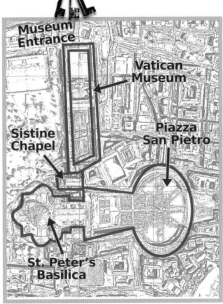

*The **Vatican Museum** is the grand rectangular area north of St. Peter's Basilica. The center is a large open-air courtyard. The galleries and halls comprise the outer perimeter of the rectangle.*

*Laocoön, a Trojan Priest, being attacked by Serpents. Approved by Michelangelo, this sculpture began what we now know as the Vatican **Museum** during the tenure of Pope Julius II in the 1600s.*

VATICAN MUSEUM

MUSEUMS

FIRST FLOOR

1-16 MUSEUM of POPE CLEMENT
1 - Arium of the 4 Gates
2 - Simonetta Scale
3 - Salon of the Greek Cross
4 - The Round Salon (Sala Rotunda)
5 - Salon of the Muses
6 - Salon of the Animals
7 - Gallery of Statues
8 - Cabinet of Masks
9 - Open Loggia
10 - Salon of Busts
11 - Octogonal Courtyard
12 - Bramante's Stairway
13 - Vestibule
14 - Cabinet of Apoxyomenos
15 - Round Vestibule
16 - Square Vestibule

17 - 25 Gregorian Egyptian Museum
21 - Terrace of the Hemicycle
26 - Chiaramonti Gallery
27 - Braccio Nuovo
28 - Pinecone Courtyard
29 - Lapidary Gallery
30 - Library Courtyard
31 - Sistine Salon
32 - Belvedere Courtyard
33 - 43 Borgia Apartments
33 - Pontiff's Hall
34 - Audience Chamber
35 - Pappagallo Room
36 - Vestments Room
37 - Flap Room
38 - Cubicle of Nicolas V

40 - Hall of Mysteries
41 - Room of Saints
42 - Room of Liberal Arts
43 - Bedroom & Treasure Room
of Pope Alexander VI (Borgia)
44 - Borgia Courtyard
45 - 46 Borgia Tower
45 - Hall of Belief
46 - Hall of the Prophet
47 - Sentinel Courtyard
48 - Sistine Chapel
49 - Control Room

50 - 63 Vatican Library
50 - Address Room of Pius IX
51 - Chapel of St. Pius V
52 - Address Room
53 - Aldobrandini Wedding Hall
54 - Room of Papers
55 - Sacred Museum
56 - Gallery of Urban VIII
57 - 58 Sistine Salon
59 - 60 Pauline's Room
61 - Alessandrina's Room
62 - Gallery of Clementina
63 - Religious Museum

121

"School of Athens" - by Raphael
fresco, 1509-1511 (Stanza della Segnatura, Palazzi Pontifici, Vatican City)

Alexander the Great   Socrates   Plato *(da Vinci?)*   Aristotle   Epicuras   Zoroaster   Raphael

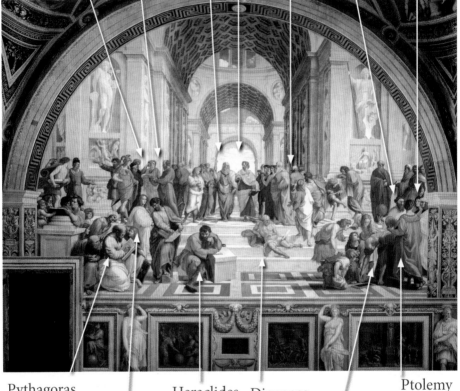

Pythagoras *(a²+b²=c²)*   Hypatia *(La Fornarina?)*   Heraclides *(played by Michelangelo)*   Diogenes   Euclid or Archimedes *(Bramante?)*   Ptolemy

The superstar of the Raphael Rooms is the "School of Athens." Created in 1511 at the behest of Pope Julius II, Raphael's "School of Athens" attempts to reconcile Philosophy, Astrology, Geometry and Poetry with Theology by depicting the most famous names from ancient Greece. Although the foreground is characteristic of Greek architecture, the main hall and the background hall seem to questioningly depict a more Romanesque architectural style. This fresco measures 25.5 feet in width.

Roman Factoids

~ Women in ancient Rome used goat fat and beechwood ash to dye their hair. Their favorite colors were blonde and red.

~ Today's Rome has 280 fountains and an excess of 900 churches.

~ The first shopping mall was built in Rome by Emperor Trajan **110**.

~ In Rome, you can find a museum devoted simply to pasta.

MUSEUMS

The **Hall of Busts** is a great example of their obsession with ancient Greek and Roman art. This obsession started the Renaissance Era in the early 1400s.

A visitor favorite is the **Room of Animals,** exhibiting a surprising array of animals from around the world.

The alabaster jaguar was mistakenly thought to be ancient. But jaguars, from S. America, hadn't yet been discovered.

The Room of Muses plays host to the enigmatic Belvedere Torso. Around the room are representatives of the nine Greek Muses of art and literature.

VATICAN MUSEUM, Cont'd.

Will the REAL Bramante please step up? Both of these staircases are named after the famed Roman artist Donato Bramante.

The original Bramante **154** *stair-case was created in 1505 by* **Donato Bramante** *himself. It was considered to be a marvel because it had no central pillar of support, a break-through concept at the time. The 'ramp' style was designed to assist Pope Julius II* **208** *to ascend while sitting within his horse-drawn carriage. This staircase can only been seen during special tours.*

Called the **Modern Bramante Staircase***, it was designed in 1932 by Giuseppe Momo. It has a clever double-helix scheme ensuring that people going up or down will not pass each other on the way.*

This sculpture is called The Strigil, named after the tool this man is using to scrape dirt and sweat from his athlete's skin.

MUSEUMS

The Papal Master of Ceremonies, Biagio da Cesena, openly and publicly criticized Michelangelo's "Last Judgement." So Michelangelo portrayed him with donkey ears, and an enormous snake grabbing his genitals.

This is the largest intact basin from antiquity. The room was modelled after the Pantheon. Study the mosaic floor. It is truly sensational!

The ceiling of the Sistine Chapel, painted by Michelangelo Buonarotti, is said to be the most popular piece of art of all time around the globe!

VILLA BORGHESE
PIAZZALE SCIPIONE BORGHESE, 5

Probably the most sublime museum in Rome, the Galleria Borghese houses an extensive collection of the most valuable, cherished works of art in the western world. Lending to the enjoyment is the luxurious setting in a country Villa. Unlike the typical encyclopedic museum setting, the lush beauty of this palatial Villa creates a warm, inviting environment, making it easy to pass an entire day here.

Designed by Flaminio Ponzio for Cardinal Scipione Borghese's art collection, the facility feels more significant on the inside than the outside. Wait until you see what is waiting for you: a vast selection of sculptures and paintings that have knocked the socks off visitors for centuries!

The Borghese Gallery is the perfect place to become familiar with the likes of Raphael, Bernini, Caravaggio, Bronzino, del Sarto, and Perugino. Of course, we can't forget our Venetian favorites, Titian and Veronese.

Set aside enough time to browse the spaces within this unmatched museum. Allow yourself to melt like warm soft butter when you first lay eyes on Bernini's **Apollo and Daphne**, and Titian's **Sacred and Profane Love**. The Borghese is home to an unmatched collection of fine art in a boutique setting that is unrivaled anywhere in the world.

Allow the images on these pages to lure you into this extraordinary treat for your eyes that you will remember for the rest of your life.

Paolina Bonaparte Borghese, by Antonio Canova, will set your heart aflutter! The exquisite detail in this life-sized masterpiece will make you want to walk around the entire piece. Do so. The mattress and pillows are an example of how important gravity is to creating realism in stone. The way her body sags at the waistline, the folds in her wrap, the bulging pillows and wrinkled mattress are all ways that you can sense gravity in this breathtaking stone. (BTW, it's ok to fall in love. I did!)

Titian's "Sacred and Profane Love" displays a 'classical grandeur ' in an 1899 world. Rothschilds once bid on this piece, offering more than the value of the Villa Borghese itself.

Sandro Botticelli's "Virgin and Child with Six Angels and John the Baptist" was a surprise to find in the Borghese. Botticelli was one of the most cherished Medici artists of the Florentine Renaissance. Although his style faded in popularity toward the end of his lifetime, his work was posthumously rediscovered in later years, thankfully for us. A consummate Botticelli fan, I would be remiss to leave this perfect piece out of this section.

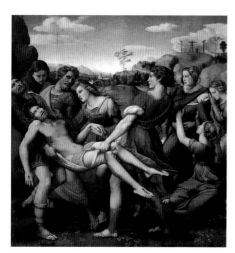

Raphaello **162** *Sanzio de Urbino was another extremely prolific Renaissance artist that is claimed by both Florence and Rome. Although he died at*

the age of 37, he managed to leave many works for our enjoyment, including these, "The Deposition" and "Lady with a Unicorn."

MUSEUMS

VILLA BORGHESE, CONT'D.

Caravaggio **166***, Rome's dark darling of the arts, casts himself as a* **Sick Bacchus** *in this self portrait. Pale lips, uninspired eyes, and sallow skin create a version of Bacchus quite unique to all others. Caravaggio's sheer talent using light and shadow are not absent from the techniques used to create an ill Bacchus.*

This is a more vivid use of darkness - to enhance the drama of the moment that young **David** *separated Goliath from his head. The story was told in an outdoor space, but Caravaggio preferred this deep darkness to mimic the darkness that David had to find in his own soul in order to decapitate Goliath.*

So much has occurred under the roof of the Borghese Gallery. Deals have been struck to acquire these inconceivable works of art. The marriage of Camillo Borghese to Paolina Bonaparte was a way to fatten the Borghese family coffers. However, Napoleon saw it differently. As an art connoisseur, this was the perfect way for him to get his hands on the very valuable Borghese art collection. And because of Napoleon, numerous pieces now appear in the Louvre.

*"**Apollo and Daphne**" Gian Lorenzo Bernini* **170** *almost single-handedly ushered in the Baroque Era with his flaming passion for motion, drama, and dynamism. In this story, Daphne is fleeing Apollo's advances. As she runs, she calls to her father to help her. Dad turns her into a tree so that Apollo can never have her. Bernini captures the exact moment that the transformation into a tree begins and she slows enough that Apollo catches up to her and takes her around her waist. But alas...*
The magic of Bernini's true gift lies in the details of wild motion. Fabric flies, winds blow, hair gets tousled. This style is diametrically opposed to the still, posed stances of sculptures of the preceding Renaissance Era. The Borghese Gallery is home to many luscious works of Bernini, all exhibiting his inimitable ability to grasp and illustrate the most agitated moment of any given story.

CAPITOLINE MUSEUM 💟
PIAZZA DEL CAMPIDOGLIO, 1

Straddling both sides of **Piazza del Campidoglio** 220 are the Capitoline Museums. Their exteriors are excellent examples of architecture from the newly-enlightened Renaissance period, as is much of the interior. The rooms themselves hold in their bosom some of the most cherished treasures from the history of magnificent Rome.

The museum began when Pope Sixtus IV do-nated a series of bronze statues in 1472. This began a long tradition of collecting supremely valuable pieces from Rome's history. With a broad selection of exhibits, there is something for everyone in these impressive collections.

"Boy with a Thorn" is a Greco-Roman crowd favorite. Buried for nearly 1,000 years, it was discovered in the 1100s, then placed in the hands of Sixtus IV.

"Cupid Kissing Psyche" After long lascivious kisses, Psyche married Cupid and became a Goddess herself.

MUSEUMS

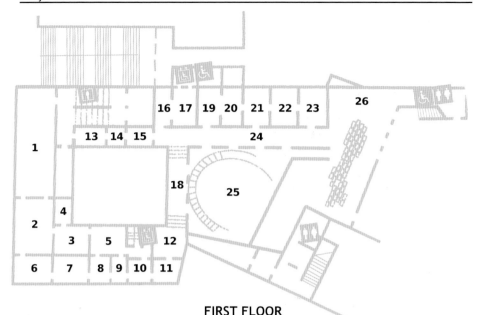

FIRST FLOOR

1. Room of the Orazi and Curiazi
2. Hall of Captains
3. Hannibal's Hall
4. Chapel
5. Tapestry Room
6. Room of Triumphs
7. Room of the She Wolf
8. Hall of Geese
9. Hall of Eagles
10. Castellani Collection
11. Castellani Collection
12. Castellani Collection
13. Salon of Modern Splendors
14. Gallery
15. Halls of the Lamian Gardens
16. Halls of the Lamian Gardens
17. Halls of the Lamian Gardens
18. Halls of the Lamian Gardens
19. Salons of the Tauriani & Vettiani Gardens
20. Salons of the Tauriani & Vettiani Gardens
21. Halls of the Mecenate Gardens
22. Halls of the Mecenate Gardens
23. Halls of the Mecenate Gardens
24. Gallery
25. Statue of Marcus Aurelius
26. Temple of Jupiter Capitoline

SECOND FLOOR

Capitoline Picture Gallery
Main Works
Palazzo Clementino-Caffarelli

THIRD FLOOR

- Tabularium
- Lapidary Gallery
- Gabularium Gallery
- Palazzo Nuovo courtyard
- Hall of Egyptian Monuments
- Earthly Rooms
- Picture Gallery
- Hall of Doves
- Cabinet of Venus
- Hall of Emperors
- Hall of Philosophers
- Hall of the Faun
- Galata Room
- Centrale Montemartini
Other Works

CAPITOLINE MUSEUM, Cont'd.

(**1**) *Twins Romulus & Remus suckle the She Wolf that adopted them, creating the legend of the beginning of Rome.* (**2**) *The Hand of Constantine* **114**. (**3**) *The Medusa looks forlorn with a head full of snakes.* (**4**) *Oceanus, the River God, reclines while soaking up the sunshine.*

MUSEUMS

(**1**) *The Lion Attacking the Horse is a well-known Roman symbol for victory and defeat.* (**2**) *A Greco-Roman theater mask.* (**3**) *"Tensa Capitolina" is a bronze chariot decorated with scenes from Achilles.* (**4**) *To get from the first building to the second building across the Piazza, you must proceed through this underground passage that appropriately exhibits headstones and stellae.* (**5**) *The "Capitoline Venus" is one of the 'Modest Venus' sculptures, of which there are several versions. She is one of the most famous sculptures in Rome. Botticelli was influenced by this ancient pose in his painting "The Birth of Venus."*

PALAZZO BARBARINI
VIA DELLE QUATTRO FONTANE, 13

When you are a Pope *(Urban VIII* **214***)* and you are from
the Barbarini family, you will enjoy only the finest that
Rome can give to you. Palazzo Barbarini is no exception.
An exquisite collection of Renaissance and Baroque art,
all housed in a sumptuously architected palace will keep
you thrilled and enthralled for hours. Inside the palace, you will find a vast collection of sculptures and
paintings that are considered to be one of the best
collections in Rome.

The Palace itself is a sumptuous affair, where
it is easy to imagine the lavish events that
have occurred under its roof.

Initially, the design of the building was
given to the great architect Carlo Maderno. He brought in **Francesco Borromini**
176 to assist. But when Maderno died,
the powers that be did not continue with
Borromini. Instead, master architect **Gian
Lorenzo Bernini** **170** was brought in to
complete the job.

Many pieces of the architecture have
since been repeated in various palaces
throughout Europe, proving the influence
of Palazzo Barbarini.

The Italian Institute of Numismatics
lives under the roof of the Palazzo.

Archaeology in the Back Yard
*In 1936, archaeologists located an ancient
Mithraeum in the back yard of Palazzo Bar-
barini.*

Borromini's **176** helicoidal staircase exhibits its unique double Doric twisted columns and oval, longitudinally flattened shape creating an easier climb than typically round staircases.

Women in Venice would wear these **Platform Shoes called "Chopines"** to keep their dresses from getting muddy and wet. The higher the shoe, the higher the wearer's social status.

"Portrait of a Young Woman" is one of the most cherished works of Raphael **162**. She was Margherita Luti, the Baker's Daughter, and Raphael's girlfriend. He wrote his name on her arm band.

"Allegory of Divine Providence and Barberini Power" 1639 by Pietro Cortona

"Judith Beheading Holofernes" is an exceptional example of Caravaggio's **166** prowess with light and dark. Light reveals only the most important parts of the scene while the background is veiled in darkness. This is the most poignant moment of the story just after Judith sneaked up on a sleeping Holofernes, and with stern determination, she grabs his hair and slices his neck in one single movement. The old crone, Judith's handmaiden, stands by to put the head in a cloth sack.

(Opposite): Antonio Corradini, the master of veiled sculpture, boasts his skills at creating feather-light, transparent fabrics from marble in this "Vestal Virgin Tuccia" who was wrongly accused of being unchaste.

VILLA FARNESINA 💠
VIA DELLA LUNGARA, 230

"Villa Farnesina, is considered one of the noblest and most harmonious creations of Italian Renaissance." So says the Villa itself, and they are absolutely correct!

Nestled against the Tiber in the picturesque Trastevere neighborhood of Rome, the Villa Farnesina is a shining jewel in the giant treasure chest that is Rome.

The Villa was originally owned by Agostino Chigi, a renaissance banker and great lover of fine art. He hung out with Popes Alexander VI **207**, Julius II **208**, and Leo X **209**. *(Chigi was the treasurer of Pope Alexander VI, Rodrigo Borgia.)* Chigi also maintained close friendships with some of the most renowned Renaissance artists in Rome, such as Raphael **162**, Baldassarre Peruzzi, Sebastiano del Piombo, and Sodoma.

The interior of the villa is decorated with frescoes by Raphael, Sebastiano del Piombo, Giovanni da Udine, Giovanni Bazzi *(known as il Sodoma)*, Giulio Romano, Giovan Francesco Penni, and Baldassarre Peruzzi, himself the architect of the home. At the end of the sixteenth century the Villa was purchased by Cardinal Alessandro Farnese from whom it takes its name "Farnesina" to distinguish it from Palazzo Farnese on the other side of the Tiber.

Raphael fans will rejoice when they view the volume of Raphael frescoes in the Villa Farnesina.

The Trompe l'oeil rooms will astound your eyes! What is real, and what is painted? These are some of the most beautifully decorated rooms in Rome!

DORIA PAMPHILJ
VIA DEL CORSO, 305

MUSEUMS

Some of Rome's most aristocratic families including the Aldobrandinis, the Dorias, the Landis, and the Papal Pamphilj family have combined over the centuries. Today, their palace, known as the Doria Pamphilj, is the sumptuous home to the works from some of Italy's most important artists. The works therein include masterpieces from the likes of Gian Lorenzo Bernini **170**, Caravaggio **166**, Raphael **162**, Lippi, Titian, Vasari, and countless other greats. The palace itself, centered around the Bramanti **154** courtyard, has gone through numerous remodels over the centuries. Today's grand and glorious Palazzo is as enjoyable to experience as is the art within these luxuriant walls. A mere 5-minute walk from the

Gian Lorenzo Bernini's "Pope Innocent X," (1644-1655), nee Giovanni Battista Pamphilj

Vittoriano **148** at the center of Rome, a visit to the Doria Pamphilj is a gift to yourself that will last your lifetime.

(**1**) *The opulent hall of mirrors is lined with a collection of sculptures.* (**2**) *The Pussino Room boasts a sublime gathering of works to ponder.* (**3**) *Caravaggio's "Penitent Magdalene" sheds a single tear.* (**4**) *Raphael's 'Double Portrait' declares the artist's sheer expertise with darkness.*

PALAZZO ALTEMPS

PIAZZA DI SANT'APOLLINARE, 46

NATIONAL ROMAN MUSEUM

Palazzo Altemps, one of the four **National Roman Museums**, contains possibly the most exquisite collection of ancient Greek and Roman statuary in the city.

The Palazzo itself makes for the perfect setting for this selection of sculptures. Designed in the 15th century for the nephew of Pope Sixtus IV, Girolamo Riario. The Riario family, with a very storied past, ultimately lost their standing when the Pope died.

The Palazzo fell to the Soderini family, who, when they lost vast sums, sold it to the Altemps. Altemps was the nephew of Pope Pius IV.

The collection consists of over one hundred sculptures, belonging to a small number of Roman Noble families that have demonstrated a distinct love for the ancient arts.

The quality of the pieces in Altemps is exceptional, and well worth a small piece of your trip to Rome to investigate.

(**1**) *2nd century bce, The Gallatian Suicide of a defeated warrior from Gall killing his wife, then himself.*

(**2**) *The Palazzo itself is a stunning exhibit of pristine architecture and frescoes.*

(**3**) *Artemis of Ephesus, taken from Hadrian's Villa in Tivoli, is represented with many bull scrota hanging from her neck as teats. The castration of bulls assures her fertility, and exemplifies her power over men.*

(**4**) *The Ancient Roman Ludovisi Battle Sarcophagus, known for its densely packed high relief that tells, in great detail, the story of the battle. c 260ce.*

PALAZZO MASSIMO

NATIONAL ROMAN MUSEUM

LARGO DI VILLA PERETTI, 2

MUSEUMS

Rome continues to astonish with yet another fantastic assemblage of ancient art housed in yet another perfect Palace. Palazzo Massimo is "truly one of the best collections of classical art in the world!"

The museum houses the ancient sculpture, painting, mosaics, and goldsmith's crafts from the Republican Age to the Late Antiquity, as well as a numismatic collection spread throughout the later centuries.

(**1**) *An array of statuary elegantly exhibited make it easy to walk among the ancients.*

(**2**) *The classic Medusa with snakes for hair created in a stunning mosaic.*

(**3**) *Some of the best-preserved frescoes from antiquity are displayed in Palazzo Massimo. These walls were removed from the ancient Villa of Livia, Emperor Augustus' wife, and placed here. Visualizing this stunning room is now so easy to do!*

JEWISH MUSEUM
VIA CATALANA

MUSEUMS

Museo Ebraico di Roma

This exemplary museum does an excellent job of presenting not just the Jewish history of Rome, but the relationship of the Jewish community with the city of Rome itself.

Established in 1960, it tells the story of the long history of Jews in Rome. It begins as far back as the 2nd century bce, moving into a focus on the period between 1550 and 1870 when all Jewish citizens were forced to live in a small area.

The art, all donated, is presented in a straight-forward, easy-to-understand fashion. The collection includes illuminated parchments, textiles, silver, and over 100 marble pieces.

The exhibit is broken down into the following areas of interest:

- The Ancient Marble Gallery
- The Textile Preservation Center
- From Judaei to Jews: features tombstones from the ancient Catacombs
- Year and Life Cycle Celebrations
- Treasures of the Cinque Scole
- Life and Synagogues of the Ghetto
- From emancipation to the present day
- Libyan Judaism

The museum also offers daily tours of Rome's Jewish Quarter.

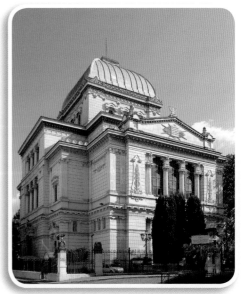

The Jewish Museum is located in the basement of the Great Synagogue of Rome.

ARA PACIS
LUNGOTEVERE IN AUGUSTA

MUSEUMS

Monument to Augustan Peace

When he returned from successful missions in Spain and Gaul, *(Octavian)* Augustus 100 learned that his people had created a monument in his honor. A man born to create peace for Rome, the people cherished him for creating a period of peace that would last for the next 200 years. This period became known as the Pax Romana. Ara Pacis *(above)* and the Obelisk of Montecitorio *(below-left)* were set up in a flat area *(below)* in the part of Rome known as Campus Martius. The Obelisk was erected of Egyptian marble *(although little of the original stone remains)*, as a symbol of Rome's newfound control over Egypt. Its shadow would point to the entryway of Ara Pacis on the Autumnal Equinox - Augustus' birthday. As a sun dial, it would efficiently keep the time, days, months, seasons, and current signs of the Zodiac.

The reliefs around the inside of the monument depict the rules of the ritual sacrifices required annually to maintain the peace in Rome. The condition of the tiny building is beautiful with carved reliefs covering nearly all of its surfaces.

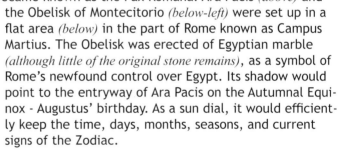

Ara Pacis was excavated and reconstructed inside a beautiful building of steel, travertine, and glass designed by architect Richard Meier, 2006.

MUSEUMS

NAT'L ETRUSCAN MUSEUM
PIAZZALE DI VILLA GIULIA 9

The design if the Villa is a hemicyclical design that surrounds three courtyards. Doric pillars, bays, and covered terraces survive intact after a scandalous Papacy and nearly 500 years of tumultuous history.

Villa Giulia

Created for the illustrious Pope Julius III *(Papacy: 1550-1555)*, the Villa Giulia is a study in Mannerist architecture. The Pope was formally educated in the arts, and hired the best artists and architects to create his new home. Even an elderly Michelangelo spent a little time perfecting details of this house.

The Villa was designed by Giacomo Barozzi da Vignola, supervised by Giorgio Vasari, with a city-facing front, and a vineyard-facing back. A stylish practice was to straddle your home between the two opposing worlds of city and country.

Behind the Villa, the Pope's personal vineyards led down toward the River. He enjoyed his walks through the Vineyard that led to the docks. There he would board a little boat, take it to work, and disembark at the Vatican gates. Then he would go back the same way in the evenings, avoiding the city both ways.

Today, the vineyards are gone, but the structure remains for your enjoyment. In the twentieth century it was given to the National Etruscan Museum as the formal exhibit space to tell the story of the ancient culture that inhabited such a large part of what is today's Italy.

WHO WERE THE ETRUSCANS?

The Etruscans were a native people that occupied the land between and including Tuscany and Lazio *(Rome)* called Etruria. The word 'Tuscany' was derived from the word 'Etruscan.' They were at the height of their culture from 800 - 500bce, although parts of their culture survived until nearly 100bce.

They were a culture rich in literature, art, mathematics, music and the sciences. Surprisingly, women actively participated in public life alongside men in the Etruscan world. They were a happy people that commonly traded with the Greeks and enjoyed the many Greek influences. Because they were skilled

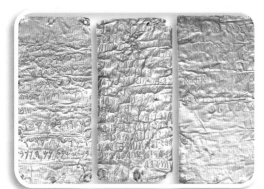

The history of the Etruscans has been shrouded in mystery, largely because we couldn't read their language. In 1964, the Pyrgi Tablets were discovered. Much like the Rosetta Stone, which brought to light the Egyptian language, the Pyrgi Tablets taught us the ancient language of the Etruscans, illuminating their story. Two of them were written in the unknown Etruscan, and the third was written in the known Phoenician language.

This whole room was taken from its archaeological site and placed in this museum intact. The walls and ceiling are emblazoned with frescoes that tell the stories of their everyday life, and important ceremonies.

MUSEUMS

National Etruscan Museum - Cont'd.

in metallurgy, Etruscan jewelry was creative as well as ornate. Much pottery has been unearthed as both a utility as well as a decoration. It is common to see Etruscan vases sporting Grecian-influenced designs on their exteriors.

The Romans, on the other hand, were brutish farmers that learned all they could from the Etruscans, then proceeded to eliminate them from history.

Fans of Etrurea
The Vatican Museum **120** contains a world class collection of Etruscan archaeological art and artifacts.

Let's Talk
What separated the Etruscans from the surrounding populations was their unique language and hence, their culture. Because their language lay uninterpreted as recently as the 1960s, the Etruscan culture has been shrouded in mystery and conundrum until very recently. Many of the mysteries have since been solved by archaeologists who have worked to translate their writings, scrolls, etchings, etc. Their burial rituals now make sense, and the remains of their dwellings and religious structures now tell a more complete story.

Thankfully. the Etruscan Museum in Rome does a wonderful job of telling that story for the educated, loving people that occupied so much of the Italian peninsula. This is an excellent museum, definitely worth visiting if you are interested in learning more about pre-Roman Italy.

The Etruscans were extremely skilled artisans and craftsmen. Their society was strong enough to support a deep artistic culture. This culture represented all aspects of their lives from their religious beliefs to their fears to their everyday loves. This creativity extended into their funeral rituals, bringing them into the afterlife.

This beautiful bronze pendant was found in an Etruscan excavation. The stone is amber, a stone commonly found in Greece. During Biblical times, a slave could be purchased with a piece of amber.

Greek styled art was popular among the Etruscans. They were adept at using art to tell their own stories on jars and vessels.

This piece was found shattered into more than four hundred broken shards of terracotta. Its reassembly revealed this exceptional sarcophagus. Etruscan men and women shared responsibilities and voice in their everyday lives. Laying down to dine was commonplace in the ancient world. This couple will be dining together forever in the afterlife. The concept of eternal love was commonplace, as is depicted in this captivating work of art. The artist is, sadly, forever unknown.

MUSEUMS

145

IMPERIAL FORUM MUSEUM
VIA QUATTRO NOVEMBRE, 94

MUSEUMS

 Trajan's Marketplace is often quiet. Although it is located directly across the street from the Roman Forum, many visitors don't realize the entrance is around the corner on Via Quattro Novembre.

The Museum of Trajan's Market **58** and the Imperial Forum is the result of some of the best archaeology in the world. The museum examines the architecture and decorative aspects of these structures. The various forms the marketplace has taken over the centuries is illustrated throughout. The point is to give the visitor an idea of how this area evolved over time. The exhibits themselves are in one of the original buildings, enabling you to stroll casually through the ancient structure.

As a visitor, you can enjoy the exhibits, then proceed outside to the open market area. From there you can go in and out of all of the porticoes. This is a truly authentic Roman experience, one that any fan of archaeology shouldn't miss.

The museum is within the ancient structure, lending a true authenticity to the exhibits. 　　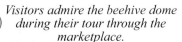 *Visitors admire the beehive dome during their tour through the marketplace.*

MUSEUMS

The Imperial Forum consists of the Forums of the Emperors Trajan, Augustus, Nerva, and Vespasian. Trajan's Forum was by far the largest of them. The Roman Forum was created before the Roman Empire.

Construction of the marketplace occurred between 100-110ce, headed up by Apollodorus of Damascus. Apollodorus, a sculptor, designer, engineer, and architect, was the favorite of Emperor Trajan. He was also responsible for the Column of Trajan, and the Trajan's baths that were built on top of Nero's coveted Domus Aurea.

Ancient Trade was a Complex Affair

Like any other market in the world, a vast amount of trading took place here. The room below exhibits the vessels that held wine and oils. Archaeologists have traced the origin of these products, some by the stamps on the vessels, and others by the shape and materials of the vessels themselves. Once identified, they created a route map to better understand relationships with other countries. Surprisingly, these vessels came from all over Europe, Russia, China, and around the African continent. Trade relationships were quite complex by the Empirical period, and Emperors enjoyed providing new and unheard-of goods to the citizens of Rome.

VITTORIANO-ALTARE della PATRIA
PIAZZA VENEZIA

MUSEUMS

UNCROWDED! TRULY STUNNING! Must-See GEM!

Near the ROMAN FORUM! PHOTO OPS ROOFTOP!

Built at the turn into the 20th Century, this massive stack of marble sits at the geographic center of the city and can be seen from nearly all of Rome. It was created as a monument to the first King of Italy (*after the unification of Italy in 1861*), Victor Emanuele II.

The Tomb of the Unknown Soldier sits under the watchful eye of the Goddess Roma, on the first level of steps, along with the Eternal Flame flanked by guards.

The building houses a museum dedicated to the Risorgimento: current events of the time, photos of famous people, and it tells the story of the state of the world at the time of Italy's Unification.

Nicknamed the 'Wedding Cake,' it has been the brunt of controversy among Romans, primarily because the offcials chopped out a large chunk of the medieval part of the city to accommodate it.

Although the horses at the very top seem inaccessible from the ground level, they are quite easy to reach. Doing so will reward you with one of the most spectacular views in Rome. *[Read the 'Getting High' section* **245** *for instructions how to reach the top.]*

The views as you climb are stunning! This unique vantage point places the Winged Victory sculptures between the pillars.

This red building was built by Cardinal Venezia as his personal Palace. It later became the seat for La Serenissima, the Republic of Venice. During WWII it was taken over by Mussolini as his office. Crowds would fill the Piazza to hear him speak from the over-looking balcony.

Called the 'Bonaparte' this building was once the home of Napoleon's mother.

Via del Corso

Emperor Hadrian's Auditorium

From the middle deck you are treated to an exquisite view straight up Via del Corso all the way to its conclusion at Piazza del Popolo.

Facing Southward is a great view looking down over the Forum as well as the magnificent Colosseum down the street.

Looking down from the East side of the building is an expansive view of Trajan's Marketplace and forum.

MUSEUMS

VILLA TORLONIA
Via Nomentana, 70

Wealthy banker Giovanni Torlonia began construction of the Villa. Over the decades, other buildings were added to the property to include the roads through the grounds, the False Ruins, the Tribuna con Fontana, and the Temple of Saturn. The landscaping was judiciously upgraded to included a wide variety of trees and gardens.

In 1925, Benito Mussolini rented the Villa for 1 Lira per year from the Torlonia family, making it into the official home of the Prime Minister and his family. While there, he made few changes to the structure itself.

However, as his political ideals created many enemies, Mussolini took control of the on-site ancient Jewish catacombs and converted them into a bomb shelter for his own protection.

Benito Mussolini
Prime Minister
1922 - 1943

As the years moved forward and WWII neared, he created a second bomb shelter that ran underneath the Villa itself. This newer shelter (3) was an air-tight, concrete-lined underground refuge that would not only protect him from bombs, but also from gaseous attacks.

Mussolini, his family, and close associates spent much time in these shelters during a variety of attacks. They suffered through at least 3 attacks per week, lasting nearly 4 years.

Today, visitors can purchase tickets to enter the bomb shelters while loud recordings of air raids and bombings scream from the vibrating walls. INTENSE!!

The Death of Mussolini

Mussolini and his mistress Claretta Petacci were captured near Lake Como in April 1945, and were shot the next day, (2 days before Hitler's suicide). Their bodies were taken to Milan and hung upside down at a gas station, where the public threw stones and beat them with sticks. His body was then hidden for 11 years, and eventually interred in his family's tomb in Predappio, Italy.

(1) *The Villa and grounds lie 1 mile east of the Borghese Gallery.* (2) *Entrance to the bomb shelter that was once an ancient Jewish Catacomb.* (3) *The newer bomb shelter with heavily-lined cement walls, a toilet and sink, a desk, and benches along the walls, kept the family safe during WWII.* (4) *The desk within the underground bomb shelter where Mussolini worked.* (5) *Gas masks with use instructions were readily available throughout the main house and the underground shelters.*

MUSEUMS

ARTISTS & ARCHITECTS

Rome is old. Its art is rich and abundant. But so many of the artists, because they lived in antiquity, are not known by name. Who was the Etruscan artist that created the profoundly sublime Sarcophagus of the Spouses? Or what about the Modest Venus in the Capitoline Museum? Even though we do not know their names, we will continue to remember them through their transcendent works of art forever.

...AT A GLANCE

154 Bramante

An architect, Bramante made a permanent mark on Rome with his creativity and foresight. This staircase, which can be found in the Vatican, was designed as a spiral ramp to make it easier to ascend than steps. It was also easier for loaded pack animals to ascend as well. Bramante's touch is in churches all over the city.

156 Michelangelo

When he was a child, Michelangelo Buonarroti was fascinated with stone. He loved to carve. His father and his uncles admonished him severely by beating him and telling him that "...sculpting was the basest of all careers" and that he should stop this sculpting business and stick to the respectable (and well-paying) job of 'lettering' or even goldsmithing.

162 Raphael

Raphael was appointed as 'Prefect' over all archaeological antiquities relating to ancient Rome that were being discovered all around the city. Wishing to create a visual survey in an attempt to organize this large variety of discoveries, he asked Pope Leo X (Giovanni de' Medici) to halt the destruction of the old Roman monuments so this could...

ARTISTS & ARCHITECTS

...AT A GLANCE

Caravaggio 166

He appeared in Rome, nude, broke, and hungry. He found a place to stay with a man that went by the name of Monsignor Insalata. The man was able to find a little work for our young Caravaggio, who was moody, temperamental, poorly dressed, and ill-mannered. He wasn't the kind of fellow one would see at Papal events. And yet, there he was.

Gian Lorenzo Bernini 170

Rome's most famous home-grown artist, Bernini was considered the king of Baroque sculpture. Having been trained as a young lad in the theater, this sculpting Maestro exhibited the unique ability to capture the single most dramatic moment in a story. His 'David,' in mid-motion, has tousled hair, flying fabric, and dynamic body positioning. You will notice these elements in all of his pieces, and lacking in other artists.

Borromini 176

There were three superstars responsible, at least architecturally, for Rome's headlong foray into the Baroque Era: Bernini, Cortona, and Francesco Borromini. Plagued with a deep melancholy that was interspersed with hot temper tantrums and flights of intensity, he made many enemies along his path. One such famous rivalry is depicted in the tales about Borromini and his 'nemesis' Bernini 170 .

BRAMANTE
1444 - 1514

Donato Bramante was born in Urbino where he learned mathematics and painting. And it was in Urbino that he began his career and received his first commissions for architectural design.

He later moved to Milan where he started over, and became the favored architect for Ludovico Svorza, the Duke of Milan. His designs earned him lavish praise until the Svorzas were chased out of Milan by the French army.

Knowing he had to begin his career for yet a third time, Bramante moved to Rome. Here, he quickly caught the attention of Cardinal della Rovere, who eventually became Pope Julius II **208**.

BRAMANTE DA VRBINO ARCHITETTO

He received commissions for many projects around Rome, including the Cloister of Santa Maria della Pace, and what is considered to be a valued gem of Rome, the Tempietto *(below-left)* of San Pietro in Montorio on Janiculum Hill. The Tempietto is thought to be the perfect building, architecturally speaking.

After that, he received the order to design the largest, most incredible church in Christendom, Saint Peter's Basilica. Although his plan was near complete, he died before his designs were executed.

 Bramante's Staircase in the Vatican was made as a winding ramp so that pack animals could ascend/descend easily. This staircase is kept closed to the general public, but special tours are available to see it. Ask your guide in advance.

Bramante's 'perfect' Tempietto was created atop the spot where St. Peter was martyred on the cross, upside down.

ARTISTS & ARCHITECTS

MICHELANGELO
1475 - 1564

ARTISTS & ARCHITECTS

When he was a child, Michelangelo Buonar-roti was fascinated with stone. He loved to carve. His father and his uncles admonished him severely by beating him and telling him that "...sculpting was the basest of all careers" and that he should stop this sculpting business and stick to the respectable (and well-paying) job of 'lettering' or even gold-smithing. But thankfully, these incidents only solidified the boy's steadfast drive toward drawing and sculpting. Michelangelo grew to become the most famous (and highest paid) artist in the world.

In Florence, Lorenzo de' Medici, a wealthy banker and art lover, had an art school near the Church of Santa Croce where he paid the artistic Master Masaccio to teach young artists to paint and to sculpt. Masaccio found two young boys who showed exquisite talent, and so brought them into his

Michelangelo Buonarroti
by Jacopino del Conte

garden. One of them was Michelangelo. One day, Lorenzo visited the garden and picked up a crumpled scrap of paper from the floor. Seeing that it had incredible potential, he asked who was responsible for the drawing. He was told that a teen-aged boy by the name of Michelangelo drew it. Medici went to the boy and saw that he was working on a sculpture of a fully-toothed gargoyle. Lorenzo chuckled and said that gargoyles had fewer and more ugly teeth. After he left, Michelangelo, wanting nothing more than to please his Master, hit the statue with a hammer knocking out its teeth. Inspired by the boy's raw genius at such a young age, Lorenzo de' Medici contacted the father of the boy and agreed to pay him if he allowed the boy to stay and to be raised by the Medici family and schooled professionally. And so it was that Michelangelo spent his teen years in the House of Medici.

Leaving his Mark

Michelangelo was known to have spent weeks selecting the perfect piece of stone. Once found, he would sketch the piece, complete with its natural lines and striations. This way he would know that the correct stone was delivered when it arrived to him several months later.

Making of a Maestro

Michelangelo spent the next several years in the Medici household, where he was treated as though he were another Medici child. He was allowed to freely explore his imagination and to test his

Punching Michelangelo

Michelangelo's unfailing reputation for having an ill temper is legendary. Even in his youth, he was known to often provoke anger. So it goes that one day while in art school in the beautiful garden of Lorenzo de' Medici, he said something to anger a fellow young artist. This artist, Pietro Torrigiano, was so incensed by Michelangelo's insult that he hauled off and punched him square in the nose so hard that Cellini quoted Torrigiano as saying "I felt bone and cartilage go down like a biscuit beneath my knuckles." For this, Torrigiano was banished from Florence by Lorenzo de' Medici. But the question that hung in the air since that time was whether or not Michelangelo had learned from this incident to keep his insults inside.

(Not a chance! But then again, we wouldn't want to change a single thing about this rare genius.)

abilities by experimenting with a variety of media. Although he demonstrated great promise in several of them - especially drawing and painting - he felt the strongest pull toward the toughest of them all: sculpting from stone.

During some evenings, young Michelangelo was allowed to sit quietly and unobtrusively in the parlor as the elite, educated gentlemen of the city would visit to drink a sweet liqueur and discuss the issues of the city and the world. One of the more popular topics was the one that intrigued Michelangelo so much that it had a colossal effect on his art for the rest of his life. Those were the legends of the ancient Greeks and the Roman empire.

Through those stories, he came to understand that over 1,000 years before, there existed giant cultures that lived a life so vastly different than the one he had always known. He learned that back in those days, music and the performing arts were boundless. But more important than anything else to our young Michelangelo: there was a vast array of visual art everywhere! Not just paintings and sculptures that tell the stories of the bible, or those that were created to live inside the walls of the churches, or those stories of just one God. He was, for the first time, seeing art that told wild stories of a whole hoard of gods! There was Bacchus, the god of wine. And a god named Apollo who was the god of truth and prophecy. And Diana the goddess of the hunt. There was the god of love that the Greeks called Eros and that the Romans called Cupid. And the list went on and on. There was a god or goddess that controlled pretty much everything.

The stories that went along with these gods were mystifying and altogether fantastic to the ears of our young Michelangelo. He sat in awed silence, listening as these ancient stories unfolded before him.

MICHELANGELO Cont'd.

The images created in his mind were strange, and foreign and provocative. "So," he began asking himself, "What if I carved something from one of those ancient stories instead of the standard biblical stories that all of the other guys have been carving for the past centuries?" His mind flooded with images and scenes and people and stories that began to permeate all of his thoughts, his dreams at night, his very soul. And all he wanted was for the world to get out of his way so that he could release these images from inside his head.

Greatness Set Loose Upon the World

In 1492, Michelangelo was 17 when his beloved Master Lorenzo de' Medici passed away leaving Michelangelo both distraught, and unemployed. At that time, the city of Florence was in turmoil as rival factions vied to fill the empty seat of supremacy left vacant by the death of Lorenzo.

Confused and grieving, Michelangelo left Florence and went to Rome where he found work as a sculptor and a painter.

In 1499, Michelangelo was hired by a French Cardinal to carve the Pietà: Mary cradling her dead son. He personally went to the quarry in the town of Carrara to supervise the cutting and transportation of the marble. Upon its completion, the Pietà was hailed as a masterpiece. But this was not enough for the temperamental artist. He needed to find a project that would not just make him famous in his lifetime; he wanted eternal fame.
Periodically, he would return to Florence to visit his father and to complete a variety of projects, one of which was the tomb for his beloved patron Lorenzo de' Medici and his brother Giovanni de' Medici. Today these tombs can be found in the Cappella Medici in the Basilica di San Lorenzo in Florence.

He accepted commissions for projects all over Tuscany and down into Rome. They were all nice, but still he searched for the one single project that would once and for all, separate himself from the hoards of hacks who dared to call themselves artists. And he found one. When he learned that the Church elders wanted a statue from the biblical story of "David and Goliath" to be sculpted for the top of the Church of Santa Maria del Fiore...!

And if that great sculpture weren't enough, as surely it was, he later returned to Rome where he created what was to become one of the most

Eww, Those Feet!

After Michelangelo died, the mortician had to carefully peel the boots from Michelangelo's legs and feet. This was due to the fact that Michelangelo had not removed the boots for an unknown number of years, and the skin had grown to the leather in various places.

Sitting alone behind triple-layered bullet-proof glass in Saint Peter's Basilica is Michelangelo's only signature sculpture, the Pietà. Created when he was a mere 23 years of age, it demonstrates gravity in the most profound ways: the draping of Mary's robes, the sagging heaviness of the body of Jesus, and the way Mary's fingers push into his skin under his arm. Additionally, the body of Jesus reflects Michelangelo's deep study of the human body, as the veins nearly pulse, and the stomach almost breathes. Although he had created several pieces before this, the Pietà was clearly the breakout piece that brought him global, lasting fame. Sadly, because it rests so far behind the glass, the viewing intimacy has been removed.

reproduced paintings in all of history: the ceiling of the Vatican's Sistine Chapel. And the rest, as they say, is history.

Michelangelo died in Rome at the age of 88. He had previously made it clear that he wished to be entombed in the Florentine Church of Santa Croce, which is where you will find his tomb today.

Marriage? Me? Never!

When asked why he never married, Michelangelo replied, "I have too much of a wife in this art that has always afflicted me, and the works I shall leave behind will be my children, and even if they are nothing, they will live for a long while." ~ Smithsonian.com

Body Snatching

After his death, Michelangelo was buried in Rome. However, the Florentines knew of his wishes to be buried in his beloved Florence. Funded by Florentines, a pair of thieves went to Rome to steal Michelangelo's body and bring it to Florence for a proper burial. They located the body, and hid it under the hay in their oxcart for transport back to Florence. After this successful effort, Michelangelo's body was carefully interred in the Church of Santa Croce in Florence where you will find his tomb today.

MICHELANGELO, Cont'd.

Tomb of Pope Julius II
(Located in San Pietro in Vincoli) **196**

Michelangelo was called to Rome in 1505 when Pope Julius II came upon the idea of having a memorial made for himself. He wished for Michelangelo to create for him the largest and most grandiose tomb ever seen. Michelangelo sketched out a rendering of the perfect tomb that consisted of forty separate statues with Moses as the central character. It also included six slaves: two of which currently reside in the Louvre, and four in the *Accademia* in Florence -near Michelangelo's beloved statue of *"David."*

However, a number of conflicts arose during its creation that forced Michelangelo to stop work in the middle of its progress. Some of these conflicts are said to originate in jealousy from the architect **Bramante 154** *(Michelangelo was quite vocal about the flaws in Bramante's work)* who convinced the Pope that it was bad luck to create a tomb before you are dead. And from a younger **Raphael Sanzio 162** who convinced the Pope to recast Michelangelo into the role of a painter. Feeling that Michelangelo, who had never worked with color before, would prove that Raphael was a better painter than he, Raphael went so far as to suggest that for a project, Michelangelo could paint the ceiling of the Sistine Chapel **124**. The Pope loved the idea. Michelangelo, a sculptor to the bone, felt that painting was beneath his talents. Nevertheless, he showed everyone who the grand master really was when he created on the chapel ceiling *"The Creation"* and later *"The Resurrection"* behind the altar within the same chapel.

The tomb, however remained unfinished until Michelangelo had completed the **Sistine Chapel** (1512), at which point he resumed and sculpted two of the Slaves and Moses. Upon the death of **Julius II 208** in 1513, the Papal administration drew up a new contract to change the original free-standing tomb to a wall-mounted structure. As the 'powers that be' changed over the next couple of decades, new contracts continued to change the structure. The final Tomb, much smaller and less ambitious than Michelangelo had planned, was finally completed in 1545 ~ after 40 years. Some of the statues that exist on the tomb today were not created by Michelangelo himself.

"Gesu" or "Risen Christ" sculpture in Santa Maria sopra Minerva **200**

Porta Pia, the city gate in the north side of the Aurelian Wall.

Finding Michelangelo in Rome

Campidoglio **220**
  Piazza Campidoglio - overall-
  Palazzo Senatorio
  Palazzo dei Conservatori
  Palazzo Nuovo

Palazzo Farnesi **161**
  Courtyard
  Façade

Tomb of Pope Julius II **208**
  Overall Design
  Moses
  Rachel & Lea

Santa Maria degli Angeli **198**
  Overall design
  Interior
  Cloister

St. Peter's Basilica **161**
  Dome

City Gate
  Porta Pia

Sta Maria sopra Minerva **200**
  "Risen Christ"

Michelangelo designed the whole of Piazza Campidoglio, including the Palazzo Senatorio that today houses the Mayor's office. He decorated the Piazza with statuary from antiquity, ie, the twins Castor & Pollux, and Marcus Aurelius on horseback.

ARTISTS & ARCHITECTS

RAPHAEL
1483 - 1520

ARTISTS & ARCHITECTS

He was known by many names: Raffaello Santi, Raffaello de Urbino, Rafael Sanzio di Urbino, and just plain Raphael. Little was known about his early life, because written evidence such as personal letters or journals have never been produced. This has led many a historian to speculate about his life. Born in Urbino, Italy he was schooled in the well-established and famous school of the arts in Florence. In addition, he was also known as a draftsman and an architect. Inheriting his talents and sensitivities from his father, who was an artist and a poet, and his mother who was schooled in both visual arts as well as music, Raphael learned his famously good graces and manners from being brought up in the world of the court where his parents often worked.

Raphael ~
a Self Portrait

His rare and cherished talents as a painter covered a wide gamut of media, such as canvas, frescoes and tapestries. He was commonly commissioned to paint portraits of the rich and famous, from Lorenzo de' Medici to a variety of popes.

While in Rome, Raphael was appointed as 'Prefect' over all archaeological antiquities relating to ancient Rome that were being discovered all around the city. Wishing to create a visual survey in an attempt to organize this large variety of discoveries, he asked Pope Leo X (Giovanni di Lorenzo de' Medici) to halt the destruction of the old Roman monuments so this could be done. But the Pope wanted to see the new construction of St. Peter's Basilica, because its completion would help satisfy a few financial 'issues.'

Raphael's works in Rome are still well-known today, as are the mysteries that surrounded his life. No jottings, not even doodles on scraps, have ever been found that were written in his hand. This lack of documentation has created many legends and even cults that were all created around the mysterious life - and abruptly premature death - of this most prolific artist. His tragic death represented the end of the 'High Renaissance' period.

Raphael's position in the Renaissance

Thirsting to learn from the Florentine greats such as da Vinci and Michelangelo **156**, Raphael moved to Florence shortly after his 21st birthday in 1504. At that point, da Vinci was at the height of his career as was Michelangelo. Raphael proceeded to copy *(as was - and is - a common learning practice in art schools)* the most important works by both da Vinci and Michelangelo as well. By this time, Michelangelo point had already amassed a healthy hatred for

*(Left) The Sistine Madonna, (Center) La Crocefissione, (right) La Fornarina all demonstrate
Raphael's recognizable style of 'clarity,' which was initially gleaned from Perugino who apprenticed
Raphael as a child.*

elder da Vinci. And when the clearly gifted talents of Raphael began to appear around town, Michelangelo found room in his heart to hate him too.

Raphael's generally-known style of painting clearly acknowledges his early apprenticeship under the master Perugino. Perugino was known for the 'clarity' in his work, and Raphael took that concept of 'clarity' to new heights, in addition to adding his own interpretations of what he had learned from the Florentine masters Leonardo da Vinci and Michelangelo.

A common definition of the 'High Renaissance period' was punctuated by the trilogy of da Vinci, Michelangelo and Raphael. Some feel that the High Renaissance ended upon the death of Raphael in 1520. Even though he was not born in nor did he die in Florence, he is never-the-less considered to be the endpoint of the Florentine High Renaissance because of the deep influences of the masters and how Raphael in turn combined those influences into his own masterful, and never-to-be-forgotten works.

Raphael the Architect

As a personal friend of the esteemed architect Donato Bramante **154**, Raphael studied architecture with a fervor to match his study of the painting of the masters. The results of these studies are evident in many of his paintings and frescoes, most notably his "School of Athens" which can be seen today in the Vatican **119**. Upon Bramante's death, the commission to build the new St. Peter's Basilica in Rome was given to Raphael. Unfortunately, much of his contribution there - as well as his other architectural accomplishments - have been lost, altered or destroyed. Pope Julius II **208** was in the midst of

Raphael, Cont'd.

a restructuring of some of the streets and alleys in the city, on which he envisioned a number of beautiful new buildings and structures. Raphael is known to have designed the Palazzo Branconio dell'Aquila, the Chigi Chapel in the Villa Farnesina **136**, Palazzo di Jacobo da Brescia, and the Villa Madama for Giulio de' Medici which is said to be the most sophisticated villa to date and had a great influence over architectural design from that point forward.

You can visit the tomb of Rome's beloved Raphael inside the Pantheon **186**.

Finding RAPHAEL IN ROME

Vatican Museums
  "School of Athens"
  Raphael Rooms

Villa Madama
  Overall design
  Loggia di Raffaello

Villa Farnesina
  Cupid and the Three Graces
  Council of Gods
  The Loggia of Psyche
  The Voyage of Galatea
  Venus and Cupid
  Venus and Jupiter
  Wedding Banquet

Sta Maria del Popolo
  Chigi Chapel Dome

Galleria Doria Pamphilj
  Double Portrait

Palazzo Branconio dell'Aquila

Palazzo Barbarini
  La Fornarina
  Portrait of a Young Woman

Borghese Gallery
  Lady with a Unicorn
  Portrait of a Man
  The Entombment

Sta Maria della Pace
  Siblys and Prophets - Fresco

Sant'Agostino
  The Prophet Isaiah

ARTISTS & ARCHITECTS

THE TWO FACES OF RAPHAEL

His gentle handsomeness is well documented from his own hand. In existence today are several self-portraits where some admirers have been quoted as saying that Raphael's beautifully defined facial features are so perfect that they resemble those perfect features known of Jesus Christ.

> "Time is a vindictive bandit to steal the beauty of our former selves." ~ **Raphael**

To match his perfect appearance was his reputation as a patient and even-handed boss. His workshop produced a highly unusual quantity of art pieces, as he utilized the talents of many artists to accommodate the wide variety of eager patrons who wanted to maintain their 'chic-ness' by possessing some of his artwork. The 'delicate' temperaments of many of his artists often clashed with the fustian dispositions of many a patron, which caused a commonly seen number of rifts between them. Raphael's good manners and ability to sooth both sides produced a working environment that many knew to be of a calmer atmosphere than some of the other studios.

But it appeared that there was also another side to this well-heeled gentle man. His reputation as a 'womanizer' was truly legend. His friend the Cardinal Bernardo Bibbiena talked Raphael into proposing to the Cardinal's niece Maria Bibbiena. However, once done, Raphael had second thoughts and was less than enthusiastic about this engagement and proceeded down a path of continuous affairs. His 'romps' became well known, as was his favorite relationship with the daughter of a 'fornaro' (baker) by the name of Margherita Luti, who became known simply as his 'fornarina'. And it was after one rumbustious night with his fornarina that Raphael fell ill. Being too embarrassed to tell his doctors that this happened as a result of that raucous night, it is said that he was misdiagnosed, given the wrong treatments, and tragically passed away within three weeks. He was only 37 years old. Upon his death, the Pope wept grievously and publicly, making it known that his sadness was deepened because he had not acted on his personal wish to make Raphael a cardinal.

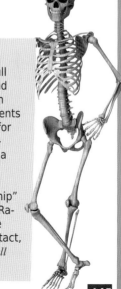

Skull Worship

In the early 1700's, Raphael's skull was removed from its skeleton and displayed in the Accademia di San Luca in Rome where new art students would place their pencils upon it for inspiration. Even Goethe, who admired its "perfect brain-pan" had a cast of the skull made so that he could take it home and admire it daily. This practice of "Skull Worship" was maintained until 1833 when Raphael's tomb was opened and the skeleton was found completely intact, complete with skull. *(So, whose skull was actually being worshipped?)*

ARTISTS & ARCHITECTS

CARAVAGGIO
1571 - 1610 The 'Bad Boy.' Rome's Dark Darling of the Arts.

Born and raised near Milan as Michelangelo Merisi, his family moved to the nearby town of Caravaggio when he was a child. He eventually became known as Michelangelo Merisi da Caravaggio, or simply Caravaggio.

His teen years saw the budding of a creative genius with ill manners and a temper to match. In Milan, he was known to be involved in several brawls. When he was in his early twenties, he injured a cop, provoking him to flee to Rome.

He appeared in Rome, nude, broke, and hungry. He found a place to stay with a man that went by the name of Monsignor Insalata. The man was able to find a little work for our young Caravaggio.

Chalk drawing by Ottavio Leoni, c. 1621.

As his work began to get noticed by Rome's art aficionados, Caravaggio struck out on his own, accepting more prestigious commissions.

When he worked, he stopped pre-sketching his paintings. He took to painting directly onto the canvas with a clarity few possess. His ultra-realistic figures were a significant departure from the Renaissance style, as he single-handedly ushered in the Baroque era of painting. His dramatic use of darkness and light transcended the known chiaroscuro techniques and dove deeper into a style known as tenebrism. This created a hallmark that eventually influenced the likes of Rembrandt.

The Light and Dark Sides of Caravaggio

Interestingly, his own life seemed to reflect a dramatic contrast of light and dark as well. On the light side, his work was coveted by artists and patrons alike. He was invited to all standout events, and everyone wanted to be seen with him.

However, on the dark side, he was moody, temperamental, poorly dressed, and ill-mannered. He wasn't the kind of fellow one would see at a Papal event, and yet there he was.

By the time he was thirty years old, he was the most famous artist in Rome. However, between commissions, he would transform into a staggering drunkard searching for a fight.

ARTISTS & ARCHITECTS

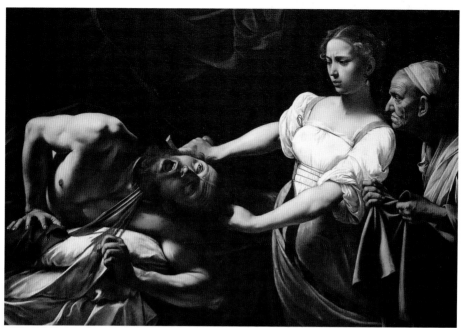

"Judith Beheading Holofernes" is an exceptional example of Caravaggio's prowess with light and dark. Light reveals only the most important parts of the scene while the background is veiled in darkness. Palazzo Barbarini **134**.

With sallow skin and lips, Caravaggio used his own image in his "Sick Bacchus." Galleria Borghese **126**

Caravaggio portrays St. Peter being crucified upside down, because Peter didn't feel he wasn't good enough to die as Jesus did. Santa Maria del Popolo.

CARAVAGGIO

Caravaggio's "The Calling of Michael" depicts Christ, on the right partially blocked by Peter, points at Michael, saying "You. Come with me." A red-bearded Michael looks up as if to say, "Who me?" Once again, Caravaggio's use of darkness penetrated by the perfect spots of light to tell his story. And, like the artist, the darkness seems to rule the story. You can find this painting in Rome's Church of San Luigi dei Francesi.

Over the years, Caravaggio found himself in court repeatedly for throwing artichokes at a waiter, illegally carrying a sword and knife, insulting a woman, and penning illicit poetry about a competitor that ended in a libel suit.

One day, a back-alley brawl resulted in Caravaggio severely cutting a man's leg during an argument. The man bled out and died. Caravaggio or not, the Pope sentenced him to death, so he fled Rome to stay alive.

Caravaggio found himself in Sicily, and Naples, all the while searching for commissions for new paintings. Characteristically, he continued to argue with patrons, and brawl with anyone who was willing or able. His temperament worsened as he moved through his thirties.

While in exile, he painted his "David Holding the Head of Goliath" **126** *(using his own face as Goliath)* as a gift to the Pope ~ as a plea for forgiveness. But the Pope did not give in.

Ultimately, Caravaggio found himself in Tuscany, where he died of a fever in the coastal town of Porto Ercole. He was 38 years old.

In "The Fortune Teller," Caravaggio depicts a young man being stolen from. Capitoline Museum.

Death of Caravaggio

The cause of his death has been narrowed to either an infected knife wound from yet another brawl, or from extensive lead poisoning from his paints. Or both. Perhaps the lead poisoning caused his worsened temperament? In any case, this is one more example of how the intense drama of Caravaggio's life was reflected in his art.

FINDING CARAVAGGIO IN ROME

Galleria Borghese
"Boy with a Basket of Fruit"
"Madonna dei Palafrenieri"
"Sick Bacchus"
"David with the Head of Goliath"
"St. Jerome"
"St. John the Baptist"
"Still-life with Flowers and Fruit"

Sant'Agostino
Capella Cavaletti
"Madonna di Loreto"

San Luigi dei Francesi
Contarelli Chapel
"Calling of St. Matthew"
"Inspiration of St Matthew"
"Martyrdom of St Matthew"

Santa Maria del Popolo
Cerasi Chapel
"Conversion / Way to Damascus"
"Crucifixion of St. Peter"

Villa Boncompagni
Jupiter, Neptune, Pluto ceiling

Nat'l Gallery of Art Antica
"Judith Beheading Holofernes"
"Narcissus"
"St Francis in Meditation"
"St John the Baptist"

Galleria Doria Pamphilj
"Mary Magdalene"
"Rest on Flight to Egypt"

Pinocoteca Capitolina
"St. John the Baptist"
"The Fortune Teller"

Odescalchi Balbi Collection
"Conversion of St. Paul"

San Silvestro al Quirinale
"Noli me Tangere"

BERNINI
1598 - 1680

Gian Lorenzo Bernini, was one of the key artists to usher in the Baroque era. Following a century of the predictable symmetry and static poses of the Renaissance period, artists like Bernini enjoyed 'coloring outside the lines.' The Baroque era brought us wildly ornate textures and colors; blendings of patterns, and to some, overly-decorated styles. These styles influenced everything from art to architecture, from fashion to music. Beginning in the very last years of the 16th century, the Baroque era lasted about 150 years until 1750.

Gian Lorenzo Bernini
~ a Self Portrait

Bernini was considered the king of Baroque sculpture. His early years were spent in the environs of the theater as an actor, a director, and a stage designer. He brought these well-honed skills to his work as a sculptor in a way that was unique to artists in his day.

"The Blessed Soul"

Unlike the Renaissance period where sculptures were likened to 'photographs in stone,' Bernini envisioned wild movement in every single piece he created. In busts, hair and beards were not simple lumps on heads. They were unruly. Fabric didn't simply lay flat. He was quite liberal with wrinkles, folds and layers. The best example of his style is exhibited in the breathtaking *"Apollo and Daphne"* at the Villa Borghese Gallery 126.

"The Damned Soul"

In addition to a sculptor, Bernini was also a highly accomplished architect as well. He was hired by Pope Urban VIII 214 as head architect of St. Peter's Basilica 180. Part of this project included twin bell towers. But while working on the second tower, the first developed cracks. Bernini's rival Borromini instilled fear and loathing into the Papacy, saying that it would all come tumbling down and it was all Bernini's fault. This besmirched Bernini's reputation around the city for a couple of years, creating a dark, lonely period in his life.

However, he won the job of creating the Fountain of Four Rivers in the Piazza Navona, which was so popular that everyone forgot about the Tower 'fiasco,' and Bernini went back to being Rome's darling of sculpture.

The Rivalry

Bernini and Borromini were born 1 year apart, and spent a good deal of their lives competing for architectural projects.

Borromini had a noxious personality, adding to his already ill temperament.

Although the two architects had worked together on a couple of projects, they really didn't like each other much.

In Piazza Navona, for example, Borromini designed the dazzling Church Sant'Agnese in Agone, while Bernini created the Fountain of the Four Rivers just outside.

After Pope Urban VIII died, Bernini lost the commission to remodel the Palace of the Propagation of the Faith. The job went to Borromini instead. The building was next door to Bernini's own house, so Borromini chiselled donkey ears on that side of the building. Bernini retaliated by sculpting a phallus on his balcony, pointing to Borromini's building. The city eventually had them removed for the sake of decency.

These tales continue, but the fact that both were exceptional architects should not go ignored.

Memorial for Santa Maria Riggi, 1651
Found in Sta Maria Sopra Minerva

The Elephant and the Obelisk, 1667
Found in Piazza Minerva

Saint Peter's Colonnade

ARTISTS & ARCHITECTS

ARTISTS & ARCHITECTS

"Ecstasy of Santa Teresa"
Gian Lorenzo Bernini
in the Church of Santa Maria della Vittoria 192

Bernini, when given this assignment to create a Santa Teresa sculpture, set about to read her story. A passage describing her vision of 'Bridal Mysticism' contained a most poignant moment.

> *"In this vision it pleased the Lord that I should see it thus. He was not tall, but short, marvellously beautiful, with a face which shone as though he were one of the highest of the angels, who seem to be all of fire: they must be those whom we call Seraphim.... I saw in his hands a long golden spear, and at the point of the iron there seemed to be a little fire. This I thought that he thrust several times into my heart, and that it penetrated to my entrails. When he drew out the spear he seemed to be drawing them with it, leaving me all on fire with a wondrous love for God. The pain was so great that it caused me to utter several moans; and yet so exceedingly sweet is this greatest of pains that it is impossible to desire to be rid of it, or for the soul to be content with less than God." (Peers, 197)*

Bernini perfectly visualized this moment and brought forth her sensual, erotic statement in stone. Called a 'transverberation,' this is the moment of contact between Earth and Heaven. Teresa pose, in this piece, bears a striking resemblance to that of an orgasm. There is a hidden skylight above the sculpture: when the sun shines down, the brilliant rays fall upon the scene, creating an ethereal and highly emotional aura.

Bernini was trained in the theater early in his life. He loved the theater! Here Bernini utilizes the whole space to include stucco, fresco, plaster, stone, and metal. Notice the theater boxes with four men in each, watching this event as though it were a stage production. Those eight gentlemen include the primary donor of this piece, Cardinal Cornaro & family (all of whom happened to be Bishops at the time).

In the base of the Ecstasy, Bernini included a bronze sculpture of the Last Supper. Unfortunately, it rarely gets its due notice because of the fabulous Santa Teresa above it.

BERNINI, CONT'D.

Bernini's "David" ~ 1624   *Michelangelo's "David" ~ 1504*

It is difficult to compare art, especially when looking at the work of some of the greatest artists in the world. The tools that each artist had to work with in this case are vastly different, lending to the completely different natures of the finished pieces. For example, on the left, Bernini excels in capturing the height of agitation in the scene where David prepares to cast the stone that slew Goliath. His 'David' is in full motion, with tousled hair and flying fabric. While Michelangelo's 'David' on the right, stands to his full vertical height. Michelangelo's genius was in capturing that pensive moment of indecision just before David decided to cast the stone. Bernini's 'David' had already made the decision, and is now dealing with that moment. Additionally, the stone that Michealangelo was given to sculpt was 17 feet tall, thin and narrow. In fact, he utilized so much of the rock that in certain places, the rough spots of the outer stone can still be seen. Like the top of his head, and the edge of his elbow. Clearly, Bernini had the pleasure of working with a chunkier piece of stone, enabling him to produce his 'David' with the depth required for the motion being depicted. Michelangelo's 'posed' style was the height of artistic fashion during his Renaissance period, while Bernini made conscious decisions to cast off the staidness of the Renaissance, and create with all the gusto he could muster. When Michelangelo's 'David' was produced 100 years earlier, people had never seen such an incredible statue ever created in their time.

Our hero Aeneas bravely saves his crippled father and his young son from the burning city of Troy. "Aeneas, Anchises and Ascanius." ~ Villa Borghese

FINDING BERNINI in ROME

• • • • • • • • • • • • • • • • • • • •

Sculptures

Aeneas, Anchises and Ascanius *Borghese*
Angel with Crown of Thorns *S. Andrea delle Fratte*
Apollo and Daphne, Aeneas *Borghese*
Blessed Ludovica Albertoni *San Francesco a Ripa*
Bust of Antonio Cepparelli *Museum of Sacred Art*
Coppola & Gabriele *Basilica di S. Lorenzo in Lucina*
Bust of Innocent X *(2 versions) Galleria Doria Pamphilj*
Bust of Paul V *Borghese*
Bust of Scipione Borghese *(2 versions) Borghese*
Bust of The Saviour *Bslca di S. Sebastiano*
The Blessed Soul & the Damned Soul *Spanish embassy*
David *Borghese*
Ecstasy of St Teresa *Santa Maria della Vittoria*
Equestrian statue of Constantine *St Peter's Basilica*
Memorial to Maria Raggi *Santa Maria sopra Minerva*
St Bibiana *Chiesa di S. Bibiana*
St Longinus *St Peter's Basilica*
The Goat Amalthea *Borghese*
The Rape of Proserpine *Borghese*
Truth Unveiled by Time *Borghese*

Architecture

St Peter's Square
Façade of Church of S. Bibiana
Palazzo Montecitorio
Palazzo Chigi-Odescalchi
Palazzo Barberini
Scala Regia *St Peter's Square*

Monuments

Baldachin *St Peter's Basilica*
Tomb of Urban VIII *St Peter's Basilica*
Tomb of Alessandro VII *St Peter's Basilica*
Elephant & Obelisk *Piazza della Minerva*
Cornaro Chapel *S. Maria della Vittoria*
Tabernacle *St Peter's Basilica*
Raimondi Chapel *St Pietro in Montorio*
Altieri Chapel *San Francesco a Ripa*

Fountains

Fountain of the Four Rivers *Piazza Navona*
Fountain of the Moor *Piazza Navona*
Fontana del Tritone *Piazza Barberini*
Fontana of the Bees *Piazza Barberini*
Fontana della Barcaccia *(Bernini & Dad?) Piazza di Spagna*

Paintings

Portrait of a Boy *Galleria Borghese*
Self portrait *Galleria Borghese*
Self portrait *Galleria Borghese*
Portrait of Urbano VIII *Palazzo Barberini*

BORROMINI   Archichitect
1599 - 1667

ARTISTS & ARCHITECTS

There were three stand-out superstars responsible, at least architecturally, for Rome's headlong foray into the Baroque Era: Bernini, Cortona, and Francesco Borromini.

Born in Bissone, which is now known as the Piedmont/Lombardy area, Borromini was the son of a stone mason, and grew up as a stone mason himself. When he was old enough, he left to go to school in Milan where he could deepen his knowledge of his craft.

He dove deeply into the architectural concepts and principles of the ancient Romans and Greeks, appreciating the Vetruvian concepts of architecture: A building must achieve a balance between beauty, strength, and utility.

Francesco Borromini

Plagued with a deep melancholy that was interspersed with hot temper tantrums and flights of intensity, he made many enemies along his path. One such famous rivalry are the tales that are perpetuated about Borromini and his 'nemesis' Bernini **171** .

Because of his early formal training, Borromini's design style seemed to have a command over engineering structure, where Bernini and Cortona were clearly trained first in the visual arts.

After his completion of the Capella di Falconieri, Borromini committed suicide, wanting no name on his grave. He was 67 years old.

* *

◀ *The double-doric-pillared oval staircase in Palazzo Barbarini.*
The other famous staircase in Palazzo Barbarini was designed by Bernini.

 Borromini's interior redesign of the Basilica of St. John in Lateran.

The stunning Baroque style of the exterior of San Carlo of the 4 Fountains.

Borromini in Rome

1. The Oratory and Palazzo dei Filippini
2. Palazzo Falconieri
3. Palazzo Spada
4. St. Angnes in Agone
5. Sant'Ivo Sapienza
6. Collegio de Propaganda Fide
7. Sant'Andrea delle Fratte
8. Palazzo Barbarini
9. San Carlo of the 4 Fountains
10. St. John in Lateran

NOTABLE CHURCHES

Inside the Aurelian walls, Rome boasts 19 Basilicas (3 Major and 16 Minor) and over 200 churches. The greatest artists in Rome have contributed to many of the interior works, especially in the Patriarchal Basilicas. For 1,000 years, the Church was, by and large, the most prominent patron of the arts. This is why there is SO MUCH of the very best art inside the Churches of Italy. Eventually, beginning with the Medici in Renaissance Florence, wealthy private citizens upped the art ante by paying the best artists to create pieces for their own private collections. But Rome's churches can be considered some of the greatest art museums in the world!

...AT A GLANCE

180 ### Saint Peter's Basilica
Simon Peter (who knew that St. Peter's first name was Simon?) was executed for his faith. He asked to be crucified upside down because he did not feel worthy enough to be crucified as Jesus was.

186 ### Pantheon
Designed by Marcus Agrippa in the early first century as a Roman Temple, it was rebuilt over 100 years later by Emperor Hadrian, and commemorated around 126ce. Don't forget to visit Raphael's tomb inside.

188 ### Santa Maria Maggiore
I overheard someone nearby whisper that "If you aren't already Catholic, this Church might make you join." Santa Maria Maggiore is considered by some to be the most beautiful Church in Rome. Check out the gold!

192 ### Santa Maria della Vittoria
***"Santa Teresa in Ecstasy"** is the reason to get here. See the relics while you're here. Then sneak around to the surprise room that awaits your visit. What a gem of a Church this is!*

192 ### Santa Maria del Popolo
This Minor Basilica was the solution that solved the problem of a walnut tree that was haunted by Nero's evil spirit. Today it is home to some of the most cherished works by Caravaggio, Raphael, and others. Definitely worth a visit!

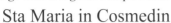

...AT A GLANCE

Sant'Ignazio 194

This little church really wanted a real dome, but they couldn't afford one. So they paid an artist to paint one. And Wow! It truly is convincing! This is a great trompe l'oeil.

Sta Maria in Cosmedin 195

So you got here because of the Mouth of Truth outside. But inside, you'll find the Skull of St. Valentine, and you'll get to visit the underground tomb of Adriano.

St. Pietro in Vincoli 196

When Michelangelo finished sculpting his sublime 'Moses', he hit it with a hammer, and commanded "Speak!" An 8-minute walk from the Colosseum. See the relic: the Chains that bound St. Peter.

Santa Maria degli Angeli 198

Michelangelo originally designed the church. But here's the cool part: when the sun shines through a hole in the wall on certain days, it shines onto the floor tracking important dates of the year, the Zodiac, and...

Sta Maria Sopra Minerva 200

Just behind the Pantheon lies little-known secret: a church that houses Michelangelo's Gesu. Additionally, it boasts a gorgeous marble Bernini scroll that, at nearly 2,000lbs, it appears to float.

St. John in Laterano 202

This is the oldest public church in the city of Rome, and the highest-ranking of the 4 Papal Basilicas. This gives it the unique and prestigious title of Archbasilica.

Basilica di San Clemente 82

A church like no other. Street level: you've gone back 1,000 years. Down a level: you've gone back 1,700 years. Down another level: you are now back 2,000 years, into the Secret Mithraic Cult rooms.

NOTABLE CHURCHES

ST. PETER'S BASILICA
VATICAN CITY

NOTABLE CHURCHES

Simon Peter *(who knew that St. Peter's first name was Simon?)* was executed for his faith. He asked to be crucified upside down because he did not feel worthy enough to be crucified the same way as Jesus. He was entombed in Rome, in a quiet area north of the River Tiber, on what was known as the Vatican Hill. His martyrdom created a growing pilgrimage to his grave. Eventually, the Church of St. Peter was built in his honor on the spot of his burial. Over the centuries, the Church grew, morphed, and was remodeled.

The Basilica you see today is the physical and spiritual center of the Catholic world. Visitors come from around the globe to pay homage to St. Peter, and to visit what is considered to be the most beautiful church in the world. And for good reason.

St. Peter's Basilica was designed by Western history's greatest artists and architects. The overall design of the Basilica endured many versions, because the architects kept dying. Each new architect wished the Church to bear his own design.

Beginning with Pope Nicholas V *(mid-1400's)* who hired Rosellino who wanted to raze the original church and build a new one. But Nicholas died, and so the following seven Popes opted for working with the old church. Around 50 years later, **Pope Julius II 208** hired **Bramante 154** who had the brilliant idea of creating the overall shape of a Greek Cross *(rather than the traditional*

The columned hemicycle around the Piazza San Pietro was the masterful touch of Gian Lorenzo Bernini.

NOTABLE CHURCHES

Latin Cross), with a huge dome to tower over it. Then Julius died, and so did Bramante. Next came **Pope Leo X** 209 *(a Medici Pope)* who brought his favorite Renaissance guy into play: **Raphael** 162. But Raphael died at the unfortunate early age of 37, leaving his touches unseen. Sangallo was later hired to oversee the project to its conclusion.

It is interesting to realize that the ground broke in 1506 and finished in 1626. 120 years and a long lineup of Popes, architects, designers, artists, and workers comprised the thousands of people that contributed to the creation of this, arguably, most exquisite structure in the world.

*The bronze Baldacchino, beautifully designed by **Bernini**, stands over 94' tall under the dome. At the time, it was known to be the largest bronze sculpture in the world! The Tomb of Saint Peter lies directly beneath the Baldacchino.*

All over the Baldacchino, in fact, all over St. Peter's, you will see bees. These were from the Barbarini family crest, from which Pope Urban VIII 214 *hailed.*

If you climb the 496 steps to the top of the dome, the view inside is as great as the view outside!

Inspired in part by the Pantheon and by Brunelleschi's dome in Florence, Michelangelo created the most photographed dome in the world.

The mosaic-encrusted interior of the Cupola was designed by Cavalier d'Arpino.

See the row of windows? Just below it is a railing with tiny little visitors on their way up the top of the Dome. Their views are magnificent!

When you look around this massive Basilica, you will see art everywere. Bear in mind that the paintings you see on the walls and floors are not paintings: they are mosaics. The original paintings throughout were removed and re-placed by mosaics to increase the longevity of the art within the church.

4 Major Basilicas in Rome

- Saint John Lateran (San Giovanni) **202**
- Saint Peter's (San Pietro) **180**

Saint Paul's (San Paolo) (outside the wall)

- Saint Mary Major (Santa Maria Maggiore) **188**

Left: *Michelangelo's* **156** *cov-eted "Pieta" sits annoyingly behind bullet-proof glass. Very protected yes, but intimate no.* ***Below:*** *The pillared colonnade around St. Peter's Piazza is the stunning crea-tion of Gian Lorenzo Bernini.* **170** *Opposite page: (1) The Relic of St. Peter's chair is surrounded by Bernini's "Throne of St. Peter." (2) "St. Longinus" displays Bernini's sense of free-flowing motion in stone. (3) Bernini created this Tomb for his beloved Patron Pope Urban VII* **214**. *(4) The "Tomb of Alexander VII" showcases Bernini's ability to mold stone as if it were clay. (5) The gold-gilded Altar Cross was created by Gian Lorenzo Bernini.*

Gian Lorenzo Bernini **174** was the head of the architectural committee during its rebuilding in the 1600's. Everywhere you look, you will see Bernini's touch. The regal flooring, the decorative niches, the ceilings and domes, the minor spaces that fill between the great spaces: all Bernini. Pope Urban VIII (Mafeo Barbarini) viewed Bernini as his own private Michelangelo, an artist that would influence art in the hearts and souls of the world. And he was right. Bernini's works dominate the spaces throughout St. Peter's Basilica.

NOTABLE CHURCHES

Halfway to the top, you will find yourself on a rooftop, with still a bit more to climb. But from here, you get a splendid look at Michelangelo's design genius and workmanship on the dome. Clearly influenced by Brunelleschi's incredible dome of Santa Maria della Fiore in Florence, and Agrippa's/Hadrian's superb dome on the Pantheon in Rome, Michelangelo has embraced the classical heart of Renaissance style: the lines, the symmetry, the understated grace.

 If at this point you are seeking a break, this is the place. While you are on this level, you will find a little rooftop cafe where you can stop for a sandwich and vino to cool down and re-energize for the rest of the climb to the top of the dome.

The reconstruction of St. Peter's Basilica took 21 Popes 120 years to complete. It began with Pope Julius II in 1506 and finished with Pope Innocent X in 1626.

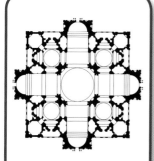

Bramante's original plan was a High Renaissance design, taking directly from Vitruvius' concept of the perfect design. Bramante was infatuated with the rediscovered Archaic approach to architecture from the ancient Romans & Greeks. His plan takes the shape of a Greek Cross. Alas, Bramante died before his plans broke ground.

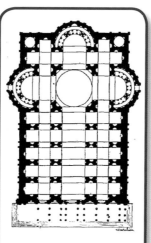

Raphael's plan was to move away from Bramante's Greek Cross. By expanding to make room to hold a large audience, he created more of a Latin Cross shape. Alas, he too died before his plan was used.

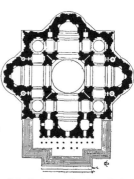

Michelangelo decided to create a plan that was closer to Bramante's plan of a Greek Cross. Additionally, he moved the main pillars outward making room for the huge dome that you see today. His dome was inspired by the Pantheon, and Brunelleschi's design of the Duomo in Florence.

PANTHEON
PIAZZA DELLA ROTONDA

Latin Inscription
"Here lies Raphael, by whom nature herself feared to be outdone while he lived, and when he died, feared that she herself would die."

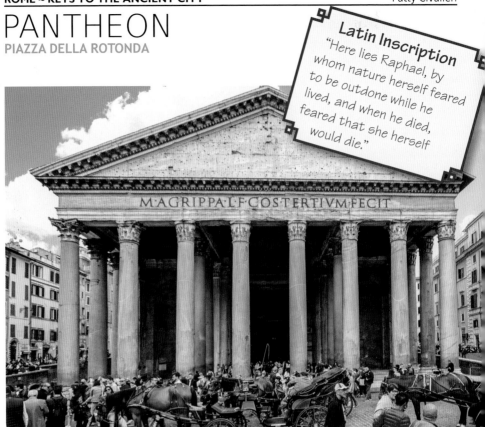

MAGRIPPA·L·F·COS·TERTIVM·FECIT

Designed by Marcus Agrippa **102**, then rebuilt in the early first century as a Roman Temple, it was completed over 100 years later by Emperor Hadrian, and commemorated around 126ce. The Pantheon is the most unharmed religious structure left from ancient Rome. The magic was in their knowledge of how to construct this magnificent dome without supporting beams or posts. 2,000 years later, this is still the largest support-free dome in the world!

Esteemed artist Raphael, who maintained quite a cult following during his short life, is entombed inside the Pantheon *(right)*. This is a privilege offered to only a select few. Raphael was truly loved.

Across the room, Vittorio Emanuele II who, after his reign as the King of Sardinia, became the first King of Italy after the Unification of the country in 1861.

Pantheonic Fun Facts

- "PANTHEON" came from the Greek word meaning "All Gods." It was meant to welcome all people of all religions.
- [Legend] The first time the Catholic Prelates entered the building, 7 Devils fled the building. These were the 'other' Gods.
- [Legend] One of the Devils flew threw the oculus knocking down a giant Pine Cone, which blocked the hole in the dome, down to the ground below. The Piazza below became known as Piazza della Pina.
- Bernini built 2 towers outside the Pantheon. The locals did not like them, and so named them the "Asses Ears." They were eventually demolished.
- It was once believed that it never rained in the Pantheon. Because thousands of candles used to light the interior, rain would evaporate before hitting the floor. The floor is concave, and the drain holes capture the water.
- [Legend] During construction, the Dome area was filled with dirt containing gold coins. When finished creating the Dome, the locals were told to remove the dirt and keep any coins they found.
- [Reality] The 16 granite columns in the Portico were quarried in Egypt and transported to Rome.

NOTABLE CHURCHES

SANTA MARIA MAGGIORE
PIAZZA DI SANTA MARIA MAGGIORE

Dedicated to the memory of Saint Mary are 26 Basilicas in Rome. Of those, Santa Maria Maggiore is the largest. Originally constructed in 435ce, the luxuriant Baroque-era decor will make you stand agape when first you enter its doors. I overheard someone nearby whisper that "...if you aren't already Catholic, this Church would make you join." Santa Maria Maggiore is considered by some to be the most beautiful church in Rome, surpassing even St. Peter's Basilica.

Queen Isabella of Spain donated gold to the Vatican which was used to decorate the church *(far right)*, thus strengthening the bond between the Church and Spain.

The lush decor continues through a wealth of gorgeous story-telling mosaics on the walls, floors, and apse. The paintings throughout are numerous and stunning, as expected. A floor mosaic depicts the Borghese **126** coat-of-arms, touting an eagle and a dragon.

The main apse focuses around the crypt *(right inset)* which holds the relic of the Holy Crib. To see it, descend the steps to gaze upon the crystal crib that contains the relic. A larger-than-life-sized sculpture of Pope Pius IX kneels before the Crib. He held the Holy Crib to such esteem that he commissioned the creation of this area.

The Sistine Chapel on the right side of the church *(the chapel is called 'Sistine' because it was dedicated to Pope Sixtus V)* is richly decorated with gold, frescoes, and mosaics. The centerpiece of the chapel is the reliquary that holds a piece of the Holy Crib.

A look at the upstairs balcony tells of the remodeling of the original architecture over the centuries. Notice how the design and artwork have evolved. Going further, you will enter the changing room of the Archbishop as well as see a variety of wardrobes *(above)* worn by past Archbishops. Peek through the far door to get a glimpse of the secret spiral staircase *(left)* in the back that was designed by Bernini.

Speaking of Bernini: Outside the Sistine Chapel, you will see a simple tomb slab on the floor covering the Bernini family tomb entrance. Sad that one of his magnificent sculptures isn't here to watch over him for all of eternity.

Secret residential staircase inside Santa Maria Maggiore was designed by Bernini.

SANTA MARIA del POPOLO
PIAZZA DEL POPOLO, 12

The minor Basilica of Santa Maria del Popolo has a somewhat untraditional origin. At least, as the legends tell it.

The time was the very early 1100s. It seems that, according to legend, a beautiful walnut tree grew in the spot where the church resides now. This area was at the Flaminian Port, the spot where visitors from the north would first enter the city. Back in the day, the first thing travelers would see was this fabulous walnut tree.

In the tree, lived demons *(according to one legend)*, black crows *(according to another)*, ghouls, and spirits *(according to yet another)*. For many years, an excessive amount of strange reports passed through the city. Some people said they were attacked, some robbed. Some were beaten, some strangled, and some were haunted in their dreams. But all of these stories were centered around the evil walnut tree.

Pope Paschal II, tired of these reports, decided to fix the problem. So he performed an exorcism on the tree, while his men beat the roots of the tree with sticks. Afterward, they dug up the tree from its roots.

What they found buried in the roots gave them a rather sobering shock!

For, entangled in the roots of the tree were the remains of Emperor Nero who had been buried in that place nearly 1,000 years earlier! Well, that answered everything! The evil spirit of their former tormented Emperor was at the root of all this evil. *(Is this where that saying came from?)*

The solution was now clear. Pope Paschal II laid a stone on the ground where the tree used to be. That stone was made into the first original altar in the new church. Dedicated to Saint Mary, it was built to cleanse the area of those evils, forever. And it worked. The stories ceased at once.

In reality, archaeologists report that Nero's remains were located in that area, but further up the hill, not in the precise place where Santa Maria del Popolo lies. However, that wouldn't stop our superstitious Romans from conjuring these great tales, now would it?

During the 1200s, the church was given over to

*This flambouyant sculpture, **Daniel and the Lion,** graces the corner of the Chigi Chapel, created for Pope Alexander VII. ~ Gian Lorenzo Bernini, 1657*

The Dome was de- ①
signed by Raphael as
a cartoon. The painting
was completed by Venetian
Luigi da Pace. Raphael's
hands touched every cor-
ner of the Chigi Chapel.

This mosaic floor, ②
created by Bernini, is
often misinterpreted as a
secret code, when MDCL
was simply the Jubilee year,
1650. Mors aD CaeLos =
Through Death to Heaven.

Caravaggio's **Cruci-** ③
fixion of Saint Peter
depicts Peter being execut-
ed upside down because he
did not feel he rated high
enough to be executed as
Jesus was. Truly exquisite!!

the Augustinian Order, who took charge of its care and feeding. In the 1400s, the church was knocked down during the great renovation of Rome, on the order of Pope Sixtus IV, to create the exquisite Renaissance Basilica that you see today.

The architectural design has been graced to us by the likes of Raphael **162**, Donato Bramante **154**, and Gianlorenzo Bernini **170**.

Santa Maria del Popolo is a veritable treasure trove of supremely important art and architecture. The star of the show is the Chigi Chapel *(1 & 2 above)*. Chigi, Pope Alexander VII, commissioned Raphael to design and decorate the Chigi family Chapel.

What's the Difference?

A **Church** is a local congregation and is run by a Priest who is in charge of the area called the Parish.

A **Cathedral** is a church run by the Bishop, who is in charge of a large area called a Diocese. He may oversee many Churches.

A **Basilica** There are 2 kinds of Basilicas, Major and Minor. There are 4 major Basilicas, the personal churches of the Pope. All are in Rome. The Minor Basilicas are globally located, and were granted this status because of significant history, spirituality or architecture.

NOTABLE CHURCHES

SANTA MARIA della VITTORIA
VIA VENTI SETTEMBRE, 17,

GREAT FIND!   Must-See ART!   Must-See GEM!

NOTABLE CHURCHES

If you come to this church for no other reason than to see Bernini's "Ecstacy of Santa Teresa," you've done yourself a great honor!

A GEM OF A CHURCH! This little church is jam-packed with Baroque era treasures for your spirit. A truly remarkable experience, Vittoria promises to leave you agape.

Built during the early 1600s for the Discalced *(barefoot)* Carmelites, Santa Maria della Vittoria boasts a host of Baroque decor from floor to ceiling.

Huge ornate capitals support the broad nave and single-vaulted ceiling. Angels & Putti are abundant throughout. Of the three chapels, the Cornaro Chapel commands the largest audience.

Designed and executed by Rome's most beloved Baroque sculptor, Gian Lorenzo Bernini **170** created for us his interpretation of "The Ecstacy of Santa Teresa." After reading the account of one of Teresa's dreams **172**, this masterpiece illustrates in vivid detail, her account of being touched by the arrow of an angel. And wow!

Bernini shares with us his love for the theater as he creates the environs for this sculpture. Using the natural light from a hidden skylight above the chapel, Bernini adds golden bars that pick up the intense sunlight. It shines down upon the event as though it was an observant approval from heaven itself.
The sheer drama created by this

scene seems to have attracted an audience. Notice the two theater boxes filled with people watching the event on each wall next to the sculpture. They are Cardinal Federico Cornaro, and the Doge Giovanni I Cornaro, while the others are Bishops of the Cornaro family. *(Coincidently, they all happen to be related to the Cardinal.)* This entire setting seems to draw us into the scene, completing Bernini's atmosphere of a grand theater.

> For Robert Langdon fans, Santa Maria della Vittoria is a must-visit, as it was featured prominently in Dan Brown's blockbuster book and movie "Angels and Demons." ©Pocket Books.

The splendid Cantoria inside Santa Maria della Vittoria was lavishly created by Mattia de Rossi.

Go behind the Altar to find a little shop filled with items created personally by the Carmelites, which they sell to raise funds. Items like Grappa, Honey, Jams, and Remedies can be found here. The Monk at the desk will gladly take your order.

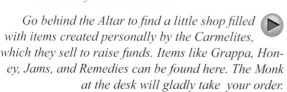

NOTABLE CHURCHES

SANT'IGNAZIO (Fake Dome)
VIA DEL CARAVITA, 8A

GREAT FIND!

Near TREVI Fountain

PHOTO OPS

The ceiling vault was created with a 'feeling of infinite space' by Andrea Pozzo, depicting the glory of Saint Ignatius of Loyola.

Sant'Ignazio is a beautiful little Baroque-era church located between Trevi Fountain and the Pantheon. The church leaders wanted a large impressive dome during its design in the 1620s. But alas, they did not have the funds to buy an expensive dome. So they hired Andrea Pozzo, a renowned Baroque artist, to paint a dome using his exquisite 3D techniques to achieve a perception of depth *(below-right)*. This dome was among his most famous works. He moved the vanishing point toward the vault to enhance its realism for people as they entered the church. The dome looks real, even as you approach directly under it.

Near the entrance is a surprise. A local artisan, Vincenzo Pandolfi (1907-2005), began this wooden model (below) when he was 70 years old. He finished 28 years later at 98, then died in 2005. This wood model represents globally-important churches of every religion. Pandolfi's message is clear: all religions are one, all faiths are welcome.

NOTABLE CHURCHES

SANTA MARIA in COSMEDIN

PIAZZA DELLA BOCCA DELLA VERITÀ, 18

Situated in an ancient cattle market known historically as the Forum Boarium, lies the minor Basilica of Santa Maria in Cosmedin built in the Byzantine era. *('Cosmedin' comes from the Greek word 'kosmidion' meaning 'ornate.')* After having passed the test of the Bocca della Verita **152** in the outer Portico, you will be granted entrance to the Church. The simple Romanesque-styled interior will provide you with several points of interest.

The Skull of St. Valentine lies in wait. (Or DOES he?)

> Santa Maria in Cosmedin's bell tower is the tallest Medieval bell tower in the city of Rome.

First, note the gorgeous wood-beamed ceiling, a rarity in today's Roman churches. This is reminiscent of the many wooden-ceilinged churches throughout the city of Venice.

Bocca della Verita, the Mouth of Truth.

On the left, you will find a glass reliquary *(above right)* which holds the Skull of Saint Valentine.

Several factors point to the question of the true identity of the skull. One reason is that during the Victorian Era, bones and relics were lavishly distributed throughout Europe, seven of them claiming to be the skull of St. Valentine. Enough said.

Legend has it that the Altar was originally built to honor Hercules **152**.

Walk toward the front of the church to find an attendant at a table who, if you donate a couple Euro, will let you pass through a gate and down into the Tomb of Pope Adriano I, the man who created the beautiful diaconate.

The Tomb of Pope Adrian.

195

SAN PIETR VINCOLI
PIAZZA DI SAN PIETRO IN VINCOLI, 4

GREAT FIND!   **FAMOUS ART!**   **Near the COLOSSEUM!**   **Must-See GEM!**   **TRULY STUNNING!**

Located on the Oppian Hill near the Cavour Metro Station, and a mere 8-minute-walk from the Colosseum **42**, is a rather plain-looking building. Approaching it is a little deceiving because it looks more like a regular building than a church. But enter ahead.

Directly up front and center is the pride and joy of the Church: their Relic of the Chains that bound Peter. Peter was the fellow who asked to be crucified upside-down because he did not feel deserving enough to die as Jesus did. To the right is another pride of not just the Church, but of all of Italy: Michelangelo's Tomb of Pope Julius II **208**.

The Pope wanted a colossal tomb to be created in his memory, so he asked Michelangelo **156** to come up with a 2-story, 4-sided design. After several iterations, they settled on a very lavish, 4-sided, free-standing version. This was never to be finished because Michelangelo was reassigned to paint the ceiling of the Sistine Chapel, and the Pope died. His family later paid Michelangelo to create a less ornate tomb which is the one you see here today, a 2-story, 1-sided design.

This is the 2nd iteration of Michelangelo's design for the tomb. Note his 'Slaves' that are placed all around the tomb. 4 of them can be found on display in the Florence Accademia near the 'David,' while the other 2 are displayed in the Louvre.

Nonetheless, his Moses is considered to be one of his most sublime sculptures of all time.

This sculpture is not promoted well to mass tourists, and so goes unseen by most. This assures you the probability of a clear and uncrowded viewing. Enjoy!

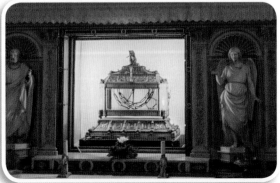

The Relic of St. Peter's Chains are exhibited in San Pietro in Vincoli.

Talk to Me!

When Michelangelo finished his Moses, he felt the spirit of the sculpture so clearly that he struck it with a hammer and shouted "SPEAK!"

Pride

Michelangelo felt this was the greatest sculpture he ever created! --->

Not Horns

It is said that Moses appeared to have two rays of light reflecting from his forehead. Michelangelo's interpretation seems to look like horns. But, Nay.

SANTA MARIA degli ANGELI
PIAZZA DELLA REPUBLICA

Don't let the modest entrance fool you. **Michelangelo Buonarroti** formulated the design of this Basilica to nestle comfortably into the 1,500-year-old wrinkled ruins of the Baths of Diocletian *(Terme di Diocleziano)* `64.` But the inside is jaw-dropping!

Michelangelo's original design has been re-modeled since the 1600s. Instead of entering in the rear of the Church, the entrance is now on the side. This alters your perception considerably, as the expanses fill your sight from left to the right, instead of deeply in front of you.

The use of sumptuous marbles is a visual feast! **Michelangelo** `156` created the general layout of the Church based on a Greek cross: a massive, airy transept with spacious chapels to each side.

The most exciting feature is the Meridian Line that shoots nearly 150 feet diagonally across the floor of the Basilica. Created to pinpoint the exact date of Easter, it also points directly to the Solstices and the Equinoxes. Additionally, it marks each of the Zodiac signs and determines the precise length of the year.

In the early 1700s, Pope Clement XI commissioned Francesco Bianchini, an astronomer, mathematician, archaeologist, historian, and philosopher, to create the Meridian Line in the Church. It seems that a famous Meridian Line had already existed in a church in Bologna, and the Pope, frankly, wanted a better one.

And better it is. Its accuracy is substantially better than the one in Bologna. Since the ground underneath the ruins of Diocletian has long ago settled, they can count on this Meridian Line to remain accurate for centuries to come.

(1) *The modest entrance conforms with the exterior of the ruins of the Baths of Diocletian.*
(2) *A 16-foot sculpture of Galileo Galilee acknowledges the appreciation of the sciences.*

(**3** & **5**) *The nearly 150-foot-long Meridian Line juts across the floor of the Basilica accurately measuring the true date of Easter, the Solstices & Equinoxes, the precise length of the year, the arrival of the Seasons, even the placement of certain constellations. A tiny hole placed high on a wall (4) on the sun-side of the building, casts a beam of light down to various spots on the Meridian Line to illuminate differing pieces of information throughout the year.*

Santa Maria Sopra MINERVA

If you are hanging around near the Pantheon, the Church of Minerva is a mere 45-second walk around the back. **This will become your new favorite church in Rome!**

GREAT FIND!

Must-See GEM!

TRULY STUNNING!

Must-See ART!

Near the PANTHEON!

Michelangelo's **156** exalted "Cristo della Minerva" *(below)* is a marvelous reason to visit this little-known church. But continue to explore its interior because there is an abundance of treats that await you here in every corner.

When you first enter, look up to see a most unusual shade of blue that you won't soon forget. When this church was built, the color of blue came from pigments of ground-up lapis lazuli, which always came from Afghanistan. But this blue came from an unknown mineral with Egyptian origins. Let this blue stay in your dreams, because it will.

The interior of the church is a mash-up of Medieval, Renaissance, and Baroque architecture, tastes, and decor. And in every part lies a treasure.

Any Medici fans out there? The Altar is a beautiful tribute to the two Medici Popes, **Leo X 209** and Clemente VII. In front of the altar lies the body *(but not the head)* of Saint Catherine in a state of Serenity *(bottom right)*.

The Convent of Minerva was where the Congregation of the Holy Office met secretly to hand out the punishments of the Roman Inquisitions.

It is not widely known that this church houses a Michelangelo. This is apparent by the lack of crowds. Know the privilege when you visit this incomparable work by the ultimate Master of Sculpture.

The Carafa Chapel was designed by the Florentine artist Filippino Lippi. And hanging airily from a front-facing pillar is the "Memorial to Maria Raggi." How an 2-ton, 8-foot-tall marble sculpture can hang 'airily' is a miracle that only Gian Lorenzo Bernini could pull off! *(opposite)*

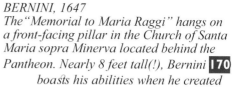

BERNINI, 1647
The "Memorial to Maria Raggi" hangs on a front-facing pillar in the Church of Santa Maria sopra Minerva located behind the Pantheon. Nearly 8 feet tall(!), Bernini **170** *boasts his abilities when he created this luscious piece. The black and beige marbles dance together in perfect lock-step, in and out of every single wrinkle in the 'cloth.' It is as if they were formed together by Mother Nature herself. The golden bronze medallion is framed by two Putis holding an image of a penitent Maria Raggi. Most pass this by when visiting the Church of Minerva, but when you find it, you won't soon forget it.*

I spotted this lonely little fellow (artist unknown) near the door as I departed Minerva. I simply couldn't leave him out of this book, as he looks like he could use our company.

The body of Saint Catherine of Siena lays in state, except of course, her head, which is kept in the city of Siena.

ST. JOHN OF LATERAN

PIAZZA DI S. GIOVANNI IN LATERANO, 4

This is the oldest public church in the city of Rome, and the highest-ranking of the 4 Papal Basilicas. Not only is it the oldest public Basilica in Rome, but of the entire Western World. It carries the unique and prestigious title of Archbasilica. It houses the cathedral of the Roman bishop, and has the title of Ecumenical Mother Church of the Catholic faithful.

The church sits atop the ruins of the New Fort of the Roman Imperial Cavalry Body-guards. The Cavalry was dissolved after Constantine I 114 won the Battle of the Milvian Bridge

Inside, visit the stunning Altar of St. Mary that has been rebuilt several times in history. The collection of Relics is impressive, including the Arm of St. Helen, the Chin of St. John, the Column of Flagellation, and a piece of the True Cross.

Because it has been updated over the centuries, you will see a combination of ancient, Byzantine, Renaissance, and Baroque decor and style.

This is the Ceremonial Key to the Basilica.

The Byzantine dome features this sumptuous scene illuminated in gold.

San Giovanni il Batiste, St. John the Baptist watches over the tombs.

A stunning Egyptian Obelisk stands watch outside the Basilica.

Take a walk around all sides of the Baldechino. Marble and gold resound!

NOTABLE CHURCHES

NOTABLE POPES

The transformation from the little-known leaders of a small cult in Rome, to the all-powerful leaders of the Western Empire was a long difficult road for the Papacy. Like any other legacy of powerful leaders, the lineage includes men of greed, men of lust, men of valor, and men of courage. Our lineup has included a bit of everyone. These are the ruling Popes that you will see and hear about most often during your visit to Rome, as their influences, reputations, and legends still echo through the streets of Rome these many centuries later.

...AT A GLANCE

206 John XXIII *(AntiPope)*
Baldesarre Cossa 1410 - 1415
The Pirate Pope: Once upon an afternoon during the dismally Dark Ages, two guys sat in a tavern slugging down their tankards of ale. One was a Pirate, and the other was a Medici.

207 Alexander VI
Rodrigo Borgia, 1492 - 1503
The infamous Borgia family has created quite a reputation for themselves over the centuries, especially in Hollywood movies!

208 Julius II
Giuliano della Rovere 1503 - 1513
This was the man that contributed so much to the art and architecture of the Rome that you see today. He named himself not after the original Julius, but after Julius Caesar!

209 Leo X:
Giovanni de' Medici 1513 - 1521
The eldest son of Lorenzo (il Magnifico) de' Medici, he was raised in a household of free-thinking, well-educated, rich Medici family. But did he break the Papal bank?

210 Paul III:
Alessandro Farnese, 1534 - 49
Born into the wealthy Farnese family, he enacted the Inquisitions to ferret out the Protestants and either bring them into the fold, or...!

...AT A GLANCE

Gregory XIII 211

Ugo Boncompagni, 1572 - 1585

Born Ugo Boncompagni in Bologna in 1470, Gregory XIII was responsible for re-calculating the highly inaccurate calendar, and creating the calendar we use today: the Gregorian Calendar.

Paul V 213

Camillo Borghese, 1605 - 21

Camillo Borghese was born into the wealthy Borghese family from Siena. As a moderate, he was easily elected as Pope in an environment where polarized controversy had made weary the patience of the College of Cardinals.

Urban VIII 214

Maffeo Barberini, 1623 - 44

A zealous nepotist, he placed many of his relatives in positions of power inside the church, the military, and the government. It is said that the Barbarini family amassed 105 million scudi, the equivalent of $1.2B today!

Innocent X 215

Giovanni Battista Pamphilj, 1644 - 55

His first task at hand was to create a law suit against the Barbarini family for misappropriation of Papal funds, and lavishly overspending. He was also the guy that after 120 years, finished St. Peter's Basilica.

Pope Joan 216

A Woman Pope? 855 - 857

A young, intelligent ninth-century woman followed her boyfriend to Greece. While there, she would dress as a man and use the name Johannes Anglicus so that she could get an education. How did she become Pope?

NOTABLE POPES

NOTABLE POPES

POPE JOHN XXIII (Anti)Pope: 1410-1415
Baldessare Cossa

The Pirate Pope

Once upon an afternoon during the dismally Dark Ages, in the tiny walled-in town of Florence, two guys sat in a tavern slugging down their tankards of ale. Their names were Giovanni de' Medici and Baldassarre Cossa. Cossa was an honest-to-goodness pirate who had recently found himself in Florence, where he befriended Medici, the wealthy owner of the fast-growing Medici bank.

On this particular afternoon, Medici asked of Cossa "What would you like to be when you grow up?" Gnawing thoughtfully on his half-eaten drumstick, Cossa, full-mouthed, spewed "I would like to work at the Vatican." "Oh really?" chuckled the affable Medici. "Yeah," continued Cossa, "but not just in ANY position. I want to be Pope, and I want YOU to give me the money I will need to make that happen!"

> ### The Medici Popes
> The Medici family created four popes of their own:
> Giovanni de' Medici became Pope Leo X: 1513
> Giulio di Giuliano de' Medici became Pope Clement VII: 1523
> Giovanni Angelo Medici became Pope Pius IV: 1559
> Alessandro Ottaviano de' Medici became Pope Leo XI: 1605
> ...and the Vatican has never been the same since.

After a hardy round of thigh-smacking laughter, Medici straightened up and said, "OK, my friend. I'll put up the money. But when you become Pope, you had better remember who got you there." So they banged their tankards together and shook on it.

The years passed, and Cossa advanced quickly through the ranks to the exalted position of Cardinal. One night, Cossa invited the current pope *(Alexander V)* over for dinner. The funny thing, however, was that the pope returned the next day, dead. Cossa quickly took advantage of the sudden space at the top of the papal heap and claimed the papacy for himself as Pope John XXIII.

Remembering his old Medici friend, our new pope granted all of the Vatican's loans to the Medici bank. This resulted in catapulting the Medici bank - and its family - to the top of the Florentine social heap, where Giovanni de' Medici became known as "God's Banker."

P.S. After several years and a tumultuous career, Pope John XXIII was defrocked, publicly humiliated, and imprisoned for corruption and fornication *(over 40 counts!)*. At that point, it became necessary once again for Cosimo to pull out his checkbook to bail Cossa out of jail.

A few short months later, after Cossa's death, Medici doled out yet another pouch of gold florins to pay Donatello and Michelozzo to sculpt a more-than-adequately ornate tomb for our 'Pirate Pope.' Today, the tomb of the 'Pirate Pope' can be found in the city of Florence in the octagonal Baptistery of San Giovanni.

Adapted from the book "FLORENCE Gems & Giants" by Patty Civalleri

POPE ALEXANDER VI

Papacy: 1492-1503

Rodrigo Borgia

Born and raised in Xativa, Spain (near Valencia), Rodrigo traveled to Bologna to earn a degree in Law. He then entered the Priesthood, and very quickly, he advanced to the position of Bishop, later Cardinal. More naturally adept at the skills required of lawyering than of Spiritual work, Borgia proved to be an adept Politician, making him quite valuable to each Pontiff.

When Pope Innocent VIII held the Papal Throne, Borgia began distributing wealth to other Cardinals to buy votes. Upon the death of Innocent, three Cardinals became official candidates to the Papacy: Ascanio Sforza from Milan, Giuliano Della Rovere for the French, and Rodrigo Borgia. Borgia outright purchased the votes he needed to become Pope. Knowing that Sforza was in deep debt, Borgia 'gifted' him with four mules full of silver to back off from the election. At 61 years of age, Rodrigo Borgia became Pope Alexander VI. Bear in mind that bribery for Papal votes was not unusual in those days. Both of the other candidates were happy to bribe for votes, but they couldn't match Borgia's wealth.

Pope Alexander VI was known as a man that deeply loved his family. Having fathered twelve illegitimate children by a variety of mistresses, he loved them all, especially the four he bore with Vannozza (Giovanna) dei Cattanei: Cesare, Giovanni (Juan), Lucrezia, and Gioffre.

Alexander VI enjoyed living in the Vatican's Papal Suites **120**, safe from public scrutiny. He built magnificent apartments inside, that you can visit today.

He was known for his lavish lifestyle, lavish enough to threaten the Papal coffers. To raise money, he would sell Cardinalships for vast sums. Additionally, he would sell Indulgences: a written paper that would promise passage into heaven to a person and/or their descendants in the afterlife.

When people would speak out against him, i.e., the Dominican Monk Savonarola from Florence, Alexander VI would have them arrested, found guilty, then disappeared them. *(Burned at the stake, in Savonarola's case.)*

A young German monk, Martin Luther, was so appalled at the Pope's behavior that he started a movement called the Protestant Reformation.

After 11 years as Pope, Borgia fell ill and died. His body was unusually purple, black, and bloated after only 24 hours. Was it Malaria? Was it poison? Or was he cursed? Nobody knows.

POPE JULIUS II
Giuliano della Rovere

Papacy: 1503-1513

NOTABLE POPES

Portrait of Pope Julius II by Raphael

After the death of **Pope Alexander VI** *(Borgia)*, a very ill Pope Pius III held the Papal Throne for 26 days. Knowing his reign would be brief, the Church was prepared to elect the next Pope unanimously during the shortest Conclave in history. But it took four times in the Papal Conclave before he was finally chosen to be Pope.

Della Rovere chose the name of Julius II to honor his own personal hero, **Julius Caesar 96**, rather than to dignify the previous Pope Julius I. And, like Julius Caesar, Julius II was a military might that changed the overall makeup of Italy during the Italian wars.

At the time he came into control, Italy was being torn into pieces by the European powers. France had control of Milan and Florence. Spain was a political power under the Borgias that ruled Naples, and the Austrians and the French were vying for Venice. Julius II brought Milan under the Italian control of the Sforzas, and Florence back under the Italian control of the Medicis. He booted out the Spanish from Naples, and created an alliance with Venice against France.

In Rome, Julius II was making his mark locally as well. He hired **Bramante 154** to create a plan to rebuild a crumbling Saint Peter's Basilica. When Bramante unexpectedly died, Julius II brought in Raphael to head the project. But when **Raphael 162** died unexpectedly at age 37, Julius II assigned the project to **Michelangelo 92** to continue and hopefully complete the job.

He so loved the work of Michelangelo, that he asked Michelangelo to create a giant 4-sided tomb for him. But he died before Michelangelo could finish it. Decades after Julius' death, his family reached out to Michelangelo, convincing him to take the time to complete the deceased Pope's tomb. Michelangelo complied. However, the tomb he completed was much smaller than the originally planned tomb. This tomb *(right)* can be visited at a small church called **San Pietro in Vincoli** (*St. Peter in Chains* **196**) near the Colosseum.

Tomb of Pope Julius II by Michelangelo Buonarotti

Papacy: 1513-1521 # POPE LEO X
Giovanni de' Medici

As the eldest son of Lorenzo *(il Magnifico)* de' Medici, Giovanni was raised in a household of the free-thinking, well-educated, wealthy Medici family of Florence. In Medici style, he was educated in the arts, sciences, and philosophies of the ancient Romans and Greeks. His father Lorenzo adopted a teen-aged **Michelangelo** , and raised him like a brother to young Giovanni. Other artists, like Sandro Botticelli, hung out at the Medici household, becoming best buddies with Giovanni.

Once he became Pope Leo X, Giovanni continued his fervent love for the arts by spending lavishly on art and artists to beautify Rome. Additionally, he continued Papal support of the rebuilding of the **"St. Peter's Basilica" on page 180** 180. Once again we had a Pope that couldn't control spending on his favorite issues, and once again, the Papal coffers suffered. In order to raise money, he would give Indulgences *(the granting of after-life guarantees to a person and their family)* to people that donated heavily to the Church.

Golden Trumpet

After his election as Pope, Leo X wanted to trumpet the return of the Golden Age by hosting a lavish party in Florence. A gold-painted little boy was featured to dance on the tabletops. Alas, the boy died a few days later from the gold paint.

Martin Luther, was vehemently vocal about the wrongness of 'Indulgences,' thus creating the straw that caused his excommunication from the Church. This, in turn, caused him to start the Protestant Reformation movement.

Pope Leo X extended the horrendous Spanish Inquisitions into Portugal, creating a fear of speaking or thinking without the dread of mortal punishment to that country.

But when all was said and done, Pope Leo X's memorial legacy is about the lavish way in which he doled out Indulgences instead of money to get what he wanted.

The Tomb of Pope Leo X is in the Basilica of Santa Maria sopra Minerva 200, *a 45-second walk behind the Pantheon* 178, *along with the tomb of Pope Clemente VII, his cousin Giuliano de' Medici. Note the familiar Medici Crest over each tomb.*

NOTABLE POPES

209

POPE PAUL III   Papacy: 1534 - 1549
Alessandro Farnese

NOTABLE POPES

Born into the wealthy Farnese family, Alessandro was the favored Cardinal under Pope Clement VII *(Giulio de' Medici)*. He became Pope Paul III upon the death of Clement.

He took the Papal Throne during the rough period after the Sack of Rome *(1527)* and the Protestant Reformation. The latter created upheaval and distrust among the Catholic world.

Paul III had enough of all this nonsense, so he formed a Counter Reformation beginning with the Council of Trent. His intent was to 'clean up' the practices of Catholics, to convince stray followers to return to the Church, and to take the strength out of the Protestant Reformation's complaints in Rome. Another

Pope Paul III by Titian

effort was to enact the Inquisitions to find out who the Protestants were, and to either bring them into the fold, or...!

Villa Farnesina **136** *was the palatial Farnese family home. Today, it is a museum decorated in large part by the delightful art of Raphael. Rooms like this, filled with Trompe L'oeil, will amaze and bewilder your eyes!*

During this mess, he managed to heap a large dollop of nepotism into his political and religious world. He made his son Pier Luigi Farnese into the Duke of Parma; his grandson Alessandro into a Cardinal at the age of 14; his grandson Ranuccio Farnese into a Cardinal at the age of 15, and so on. Additionally, his sister Giulia was the preferred mistress of Pope Alexander VI, Rodrigo Borgia.

A tremendous patron of the arts, he reinstated Clemente VII's commission for **Michelangelo** **156** to paint the "Last Judgement" in the Sistine Chapel. Additionally, he appointed Michelangelo, 80 years old at this time, to take over the completion of the rebuilding of St. Peter's Basilica, which he did, masterfully.

After a tumultuous 15-year term as Pope, a single word seems to resonate commonly with his memory: nepotism.

Pope Paul III's tomb can be found in Saint Peter's Basilica.

POPE GREGORY XIII
Papacy: 1572 - 1585

Ugo Boncompagni

Pope Gregory XIII

Born Ugo Boncompagni in Bologna in 1502, our future Pope studied and excelled at law, becoming a professor of law for several years. He moved up to become a judge of the capital, an abbreviator, and vice-chancellor of the Campagna e Marittima.

He bore an illegitimate son, but it did not count against him because he had not yet accepted his Holy Orders until he was 40.

Although Pope Gregory XIII is best remembered for the recalculation and recreation of the Gregorian Calendar, a rather unfortunate incident of timing left a dark stain on his reputation. It seems that in 1572, four thousand Huguenots *(French Protestants)* were brutally murdered under the orders of Catherine de' Medici. This event was to become known at the St. Bartholomew's Day Massacre. Pope Gregory wept irascibly through the night at the appalling incident. However, because he

Making significant changes to the previous Julian calendar, this Gregorian calendar is the one used most in the world today.

had scheduled a party to celebrate the fact that Charles IX's life was not lost, it was announced that the Pope was taking hysterical joy at this horrible incident. The public got it into their heads that he was celebrating the massacre, earning him great disdain.

On a positive note: to make up for lost ground during the Protestant Reformation, there needed to be a better way to spread the Catholic word further. Punishment, via the Inqui-

sitions, had not worked, and fear served only to shrink the following. He felt that education was a better route, and well-educated priests should be sent around the globe on Missions to spread the faith. This turned out to prove much more successful over the next centuries.

The Dragon on his family's Coat of Arms represents power, wisdom, and astuteness. The missing tail represents the absence of evil.

NOTABLE POPES

JULIAN VS. GREGORIAN CALENDARS

When Julius Caesar **96** came into power, the 10-month Roman calendar was the standard chart for tracking time. But it quickly fell out of sync with the seasons, so Caesar changed the 'algorithm' and added his own month of July to bring it closer in sync with astronomical events. He called it the Julian Calendar. But this too quickly fell out of sync. So Octavian **100** (Augustus) came along a few decades later and added HIS OWN month of August to the calendar. But alas, this too fell away from the seasons. After that, nobody could agree upon a better solution, so this latest version of the Julian calendar stayed in play for the next 1,500 years! Eventually, Pope Gregory XIII *(previous page)* came along and recalculated the whole inaccurate mess, and came up with the calendar that we use today: the Gregorian Calendar.

The BIG LEAP

It took 170 years for North America to conform to the new Gregorian Calendar. When they finally made the switch, they were so far out of sync that Wednesday September 2 was immediately followed by Thursday September 14, 1752. It took 300 years for the rest of the world to convert to the Gregorian Calendar.

September 1752						
Sunday	Monday	Tuesday	Wednesday	Thursday	Friday	Saturday
		1	2	14	15	16
17	18	19	20	21	22	23
24	25	26	27	28	29	30

◑ 15th   ○ 23rd   ◑ 30th

Calculating the Leap Years

The big challenge to an accurate calendar is fine-tuning the calculation for the Leap Years. This is how our Calendar (the Gregorian) is calculated:

> Every year that is exactly divisible by four is a leap year, except for years that are exactly divisible by 100. The centurial years are leap years if (and only if) they are exactly divisible by 400. For example, the years 1700, 1800, and 1900 are not leap years, but the year 2000 is.

(Whew!! I think we need to throw a computer at this issue. It still has a few rough spots, eh?)

Papacy: 1605-21 # POPE PAUL V
Camillo Borghese

Camillo Borghese was born into the wealthy Borghese family from Siena. As a moderate, he was easily elected as Pope in an environment where polarized controversy had made weary the patience of the College of Cardinals.

Although he was considered to be a moderate, his personality shared more in common with a defense lawyer than a Saintly Pontiff. This caused many a riff with the non-Catholics of the world.

An on-going battle between Venice and the Pope continued to polarize both populations. It seems that the Venetian government preferred a clear separation between the Church and the State. One issue was that they felt the Church shouldn't be able to blindly come to Venice,

Portrait of Pope Paul V by Caravaggio

clear real estate from under its residents, and build church after church wherever they wanted. One Venetian Catholic Priest, Paolo Sarpi, was empowered by Venice to speak in their behalf to the Pope. This had the unfortunate result of Sarpi being mysteriously stabbed 15 times, but he survived. Relations between Venice and Rome ultimately relaxed, however, grumblings still occur between the two entities, even today.

Another hot spot was the Gun Powder Plot against King James I in England. James outlawed anyone that didn't vow a loyal allegiance to his Throne, angering the Pope who wanted allegiance only to God and the Pope.

Nepotism was still practiced in the Papacy. He installed his nephew Scipione Borghese as Cardinal, giving him enormous power to facilitate the growth of the Borghese fortune.

A visit to the Borghese Museum, will treat you to one of the most exquisite art collections in the world. The Borghese gardens are world famous for performances, picnics, and romantic strolls alike.

POPE URBAN VIII
Maffeo Barberini

Papacy: 1623-44

Born into the noble Florentine Barberini family, young Maffeo was educated by the Jesuits, then earned a Doctorate of Law as a young adult.

As Pope, Urban VIII, he showed little interest in foreign affairs; he was more interested in how to grow the power of the Church in Rome and in Italy.

With impeccable taste in art, he commissioned only the very best artists and architects to upgrade Rome. This included a remodel of **Castel Sant'Angelo 66**, a stronger defense at the **Port of Ostia 280**, and a wide variety of repairs around the city.

*Pope Urban VIII
by Caravaggio*

A zealous nepotist, he placed many of his relatives in positions of power inside the church, the military, and the government. It is said that the Barbarini family amassed 105 million scudi *(approx $1.2 billion today)* in family wealth.

He purchased a palace in Rome, and proceeded to fill it by commissioning Bernini to improve the building, create new pieces for it, and by purchasing great works from the likes of **Raphael 162**. At the significant cost of Rome's own cultural heritage, he fervently ripped apart ancient buildings to reuse materials in his new buildings. A common joke was *"What the Barbarians didn't do [to destroy Rome], the Barbarinis did."*

He so successfully drained the Papal coffers that his successors never fully recovered the traditional financial strength of the Catholic Church.

 Piazza Barbarini

Raphael's "La Fornarina" re-  *sides inside Palazzo Barbarini 134, now a fabulous museum of Renaissance and Classical art.*

POPE INNOCENT X
Papacy: 1644-1655

Giovanni Battista Pamphilj

*Pope Innocent X
by Diego Velasquez*

The Pamphilj family is renowned for their exquisite taste and influence in the art community. Born and raised in Rome, Giovanni graduated from the Collegio Romana with a degree in Law.

He was elected in 1644 after a bitter Conclave between its French and Spanish members.

After taking the Papal Throne, his first task at hand was to create a law suit against the Barbarini family for misappropriation of Papal funds, and lavishly overspending. Determined not to face these charges, the Barbarinis fled to France to gain the protection of Cardinal Mazarin. The Pope applied continuous pressure on the Cardinal to return the Barbarinis, so the Cardinal responded by threatening war by sending his own army into Italy. This worked, making the Pope back off his pressures.

The widow of the Pope's deceased brother, Olimpia Maidalchini, became the chief advisor to the Pope. She so dominated his decisions that Emperors, Cardinals and Kings realized that they must go through Olimpia to get the Pope's ear. Rumors of illicit behavior circulated, but were never proven.

When Portugal broke away from Spain, the Pope refused to recognize them, and consequently did not recognize Portugal's nominations of Bishops, nor their stance as an independent country.

His reputation as a bitter old Pope gave ample material for artistic satire. Artist Guido Reni painted such a piece that today hangs in the Capuchin church of Santa Maria della Concezione **85**. It is the image of Michael the Archangel stomping on the head of Satan, which bears the face of our Pope Innocent X.

The Pamphilj family were influential in the worlds of art and architecture. Their family Palazzo **137***, a quick walk from the Forum, is today a fantastic museum that includes pieces from Raphael, Titian, and Caravaggio.*

PALAZZO
DORIA PAMPHILJ

NOTABLE POPES

POPE JOHN VIII (Pope Joan)
Legend of the Only Female Pope   Papacy: 855 - 857

This story is a highly contested legend, with many who believe, matched by many who do not. As legends are told by word of mouth and tend to vary in each telling, it is difficult, over 1,000 years later, to prove or disprove with any sense of validity. Oft-times, legends have some basis in truth. So, as the story goes...

A young, intelligent ninth-century woman followed her boyfriend to Greece. While there, she would dress as a man and use the name Johannes Anglicus so that she could get an education. She learned mathematics, philosophy, finance, music, poetry, and politics. She was such a learned woman that she gleaned much respect everywhere she went. Eventually, her boyfriend traveled to Rome. Our smart young woman, posing as a Priest, followed. Again,

Artist's concept of the female Pope wearing the Papal Tiara. Artist unknown, c. 1560

gaining such respect that she garnered many job offers. One such proposal was as the Curial Secretary, which was a position she held (as a man) for several years.

Continuing to gain a growing number of admiring followers, she continued to advance as a person of worldly intelligence. Eventually, she became Cardinal; then ultimately, she was elected as Pope John VIII, in 855.

One day, as Pope John VIII led a procession down the Via Sacra near the Basilica di San Clemente, she went into labor!

The result of this story has several endings, depending upon the teller.

1. She died during childbirth
2. She died during a public stoning.
3. She died because she was roped around her feet, and dragged behind a horse, all-the-while being stoned by the public.
4. She was fired from the Papacy. Her baby grew up to be the eventual Bishop of Ostia.

But no matter how the story was told, it is certainly a provocative topic that continues to create more legend, even today!

Funky
HISTORY

Is He Dead Yet?

When a Pope died during Medieval times, the Camerlengo *(Chamberlain)* would tap-tap-tap the forehead of the deceased Pope with a silver hammer. If there was no response, death was formally declared.

One Flew Over the Cardinal's Head

Pope Fabian, whose Papacy lasted from 236-250ce, is famous because of the unusual way in which he was chosen to be Pope. In those days, there was no College of Cardinals to manage the election process. In Fabian's case, a Dove landed on his head right after the previous Pope died. That was enough to declare it a miracle. After his death, he was given Sainthood and is now known as Saint Fabian.

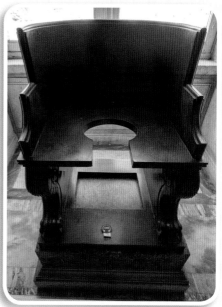

It was once said that when a Pope was elected, he must go through a few days of testing before he can officially take the Papal Throne. One such test involves the Sedia Stercoraria, this keyholed chair.

This chair sat on a fairly high pedestal. The newly-elected Pope would climb up (unclad) and sit. A trusted person would look under the chair and reach up to give our newly elected a Pontifical Tug (Pope Grope?), declaring "Duos habet et bene pendentes" meaning "He has two, and they hang nicely." This would ensure the new Pope was not a woman. (See previous page.)

It is important to know that the use of this chair is, in itself, another legend. Some claim that it was called the 'Dung Chair' and the new Pope would sit in it, and throw out 3 pouches of silver as a symbol of distributing his wealth to the masses. Another stated use was as a birthing chair.

In any case, there are three chairs: one in St. John Lateran, one in the Louvre, and this chair can be found in the Vatican Museum.

NOTABLE POPES

PIAZZAS

WHAT'S A PIAZZA?

Good question! And a common question. Simply put, a Piazza is an open gathering space outside of a church. The area is used for every sort of social gathering you can think of. But the most common activity is *(drum roll, please)* people watching. Most Piazzas have eateries so you can sit and enjoy this favored pasttime. But you may be treated to music, vendors, acrobats, parades, or who knows what can happen in a Piazza! Here are 10 popular Piazzas to keep you watching!

...AT A GLANCE

220 Campidoglio
Poised majestically atop the Capitoline Hill lies the ineffable Campidoglio. It boasts an elegance of Renaissance design that is exclusive in Rome, because it was designed by Michelangelo himself.

222 Piazza del Popolo
Piazza del Popolo (Piazza of the People) is a hemicycle-shaped Piazza that stands immediately inside Rome's northern Aurelian Gate. In the center stands an Obelisk from Egypt's Ramses the Great.

223 Campo dei Fiori
Campo dei Fiori, Field of Flowers, was open area between the Theatre of Pompey and the Tiber. Today, you'll find a local market featuring fresh produce from the fields of Italy.

224 Piazza Navona
Most visitors eventually find themselves in Piazza Navona. But only a few know that you can actually go underneath it to see the ancient Sports Arena that lies underground!

225 Piazza delle Minerva
Located just behind the Pantheon's southeast side, you'll find the Piazza della Minerva. You'll instantly recognize Bernini's delightful Obelisk and Elephant.

PIAZZAS

...AT A GLANCE

Piazza Barbarini  `226`

When you're a Pope (Urban VIII `214`*) and Barbarini as your last name, you get a Piazza named after you. And not one, but two fountains. And what's with all of those Bees?*

Spanish Steps `227`

It may be a bit difficult to understand why these steps are so popular. After all, they are merely a flight of steps. But the picturesque way in which all of the surrounding pieces comes together...

Piazza della Rotonda `228`

A favorite site in Rome is the Pantheon. The Piazza just outside is the Piazza della Rotonda, lined with restaurants and people watchers. This could be you!

Piazza della Madonna dei Monti `229`

If you want to go where the locals are, this is the place. During the day, it is quite quiet. But from 4:00pm until midnight, this place jumps with college students and young couples.

Piazza della Repubblica `230`

Piazza della Republica is one of the most striking Piazzas in Rome. It was created when Rome became the Capital of Italy in 1870. Straddling the top of the Viminal Hill...

Piazza Mincio `232`

And the Fountain of the Frogs. Piazza Mincio is where Dr. Seuss might live in Rome. Architecturally speaking, its kind of whimsical and fun. But also clever and creative. Gotta see it!

Piazza di Santa Maria in Trastevere `234`

Trastevere is possibly the most romantic neighborhood in Rome. Small streets and alleyways are lively with scattered umbrella-embellished tables, and strolling minstrels.

PIAZZAS

CAMPIDOGLIO
PIAZZA DEL CAMPIDOGLIO
(Entrance to the Capitoline Museum **130***)*

TRULY STUNNING!

PHOTO OPS

Poised majestically atop the Capitoline Hill lies the ineffable Campidoglio. Definitely my favorite Piazza in all of Rome, it boasts a Renaissance elegance that is not only unique to Michelangelo, but is exclusive within Rome.

Hired during the Papal reign of **Pope Paul III 210**, **Michelangelo 156** was responsible for much of the artistic renewal of the city, a movement spearheaded by the Papacy in general.

Michelangelo's architectural prowess is not as well-known as his expertise at sculpting or painting, but he was quite skilled at designing architectural settings, as is made clear in Campidoglio. *[Campidoglio translates to Capital.]*

Your first glimpse of the tall staircase that leads up from Via di Teatro di Marcello to Piazza del Campidoglio will be daunting at first. But our friend Michelangelo created a series of shallow steps that make for an easy climb. The top of the staircase is flanked by a pair of horses and men; the men are Castor and Pollux, the twin sons of Zeus and Leda. The horses were created in antiquity and were placed here in the sixteenth century.

As you step between the twins and into the Piazza, you will immediately be taken by the clean lines and picturesque symmetry of Michelangelo's Renaissance style.

The statue of Marcus Aurelius on horseback is a copy *(the original is inside the Capitoline Museum)* and was moved here by the Pope. The 2 buildings on

The entrance to the Piazza is flanked by two horses and the Gemini Twins, Castor and Pollux. All of these were created in antiquity, and placed here by Michelangelo.

either side comprise the Capitoline Museum, as does the space underneath the Piazza.

Note the extended star design in the ground *(above)*. This was part of Michelangelo's original design, but it wasn't placed here until after his death.

The building on the far end of the Piazza is Palazzo Senatorio, which contains the administrative offices of the city, including the Mayor's office.

Campidoglio lacks bars and eateries but is nevertheless a stunning setting for a brief respite.

PIAZZA del POPOLO

PIAZZAS

Piazza del Popolo *(Piazza of the People)* is a hemicycle-shaped Piazza that stands immediately inside Rome's northern City Gate *(below-left)*. In the center of the Piazza stands the Egyptian Obelisk of Ramses II *(Ramses the Great)* from Heliopolis, Egypt.

The near twin domes *(right)* of Santa Maria in Monsanto and Santa Maria dei Miracoli create a stately entrance from the south. These churches each contain famous works of art, featuring paintings by Rome's darling of the dark, Caravaggio.

Scattered around the perimeter of the Piazza are four neo-classical statues that represent each of the seasons of the year. Can you identify them?

Dea Roma *(below-right)* sits to the east, accompanied by the legendary She-Wolf suckling the infants Romulus and Remus. Behind is the Terrazza del Pincio, Napoleon's Piazzale. Pincio Hill is decorated with a series of private gardens, and it provides access to the Borghese Gardens on one side, and a stunning view over Piazza del Popolo on the other.

The best gift in Piazza del Popolo is the Minor Basilica of Santa Maria del Popolo **190**.

Featured in Dan Brown's ground-breaking novel "Angels & Demons™" and designed by history's most favored architects, like Bramante, Bernini, and Raphael, it serves as a model of Renaissance architecture.

Inside, however, are the greatest treasures of all! The best paintings from Caravaggio, sculptures from Bernini, and a Chapel by Raphael.

CAMPO dei FIORI

Campo dei Fiori, Field of Flowers, was the open area between the Theatre of Pompey and the Tiber River. For centuries, this area remained open fields because of the regular flooding from the River. Today, you will enjoy the local market that features fresh produce from the fields of Italy.

Historically, it evolved into the hub of local commerce, with streets named Via dei Balestrari *(crossbow-makers)*, Via dei Baullari *(coffer-makers)*, Via dei Cappellari *(hat-makers)*, Via dei Chiavari *(key-makers)* and Via dei Giubbonari *(tailors)*.

Eventually, the horse market became popular, ushering in hotels, inns and taverns. One that still remains today and once belonged to Rodrigo Borgia's mistress Vannozza dei Cattanei, is the Taverna della Vacca *(Cow's Inn)*.

Famed Martyr of Free Thinking, Philosopher Giordano Bruno *(1548-1600)*, was burned alive in Campo dei Fiori. A sculpture acknowledging his life and works stands today in the Campo in the exact spot where he was executed by the Catholic Church for heresy. His books were placed in the index of Forbidden Books in the Holy Office.

PIAZZAS

PIAZZA NAVONA

Piazza Navona is one of the most popular Piazzas in Rome, above ground and below. Two thousand years ago, the Stadium of Domitian, several blocks long, was created as a Circus, or horse race track. In fact, many visitors don't know that you can actually go UNDER Piazza Navona to see the remains of the original Circus and the museum they created for it down below.

The fountain *(inset)* was created by Gian Lorenzo Bernini **170**. Called the Fontana dei Quattro Fiumi *(Fountain of the Four Rivers)*, it is an exquisite piece of work from the master of Roman Baroque sculpture, topped by the Obelisk of Domitian.

The church in the center of the Piazza *(below)* was designed by the Rainald-is, then was taken over by Bernini's rival, Francesco Borromini **176**. Called Sant'Agnese in Agone *(St. Agnes of the Games)*, Borromini couldn't finish it because its patron, Pope Innocent X, died. It was later completed by others.

The Piazza, lined with restaurants and ca-fes, remains a crowded and popular hang-out, nearly 24/7. Musicians and entertain-ers of every sort hang out here regularly. On special religious occasions, parades and processions will pass through as well.

PIAZZA della MINERVA

1.) Located just behind the Pantheon's southeast side, you'll find the Piazza della Minerva. You'll instantly recognize Bernini's **170** delightful Obelisk and Elephant. The Obelisk was carved from Egyptian granite and shipped here centuries ago. The elephant is cute enough to be hired to star in a Disney movie! This sculpture lends a unique family air to this Piazza.

2.) Take a look at the outside wall of the church, to the right of it's entrance. Notice the squares with Roman writing. The fingers mark the height of the water during various floods that filled this Piazza, once upon a year. Can you read them and recognize the months and the years that the floods occurred? Brush off your knowledge of Roman numerals for this one!

3.) If you wait long enough, a local entertainer may come out and keep you humming to your favorite Italian tunes!

PIAZZA BARBARINI

When you're a Pope *(Urban VIII* `214`*)* and Barbarini as your last name, you get a Piazza named after you. It's going to have in it not one, but two fountains sculpted by the world-famous Roman sculptor, **Gian Lorenzo Bernini** `170`.

This fountain *(right)* is the Fontana delle Api, or the Fountain of the Bees. Why you ask? The Barbarini family crest has 3 bees on it. Everywhere you see 3 bees carved on a statue, a building, in a fresco, or in a church *(they are ALL OVER the city),* you will know that a Barbarini family member had something to do with it. Most likely, they paid for that building or piece of art, or whatever it is. I have even seen 3 bees on a building way up in Venice. Who knew?

The bodies of unknown corpses would be displayed in this Piazza with the hopes that someone could identify them. This practice stopped in the 1700s.

The fountain of the Triton, or Fontana delle Tritone. On it you will see the Sea God Triton who sits on a seashell that is supported by four dolphins. This was one of Bernini's own favorite sculptures.

PIAZZA DI SPAGNA
SPANISH STEPS

It may be a bit difficult to understand why these steps are so popular. After all, they are merely a flight of steps.

But the picturesque way in which all of the surrounding pieces come together is stunning nevertheless.

During the early 20th century, photographers would bring their models to the Spanish Steps to shoot for a variety of magazines. It became known around the wealthy neighborhood that beautiful young women were often found, making it a regular hangout for wealthy young men. This grew to become a 'thing,' bringing crowds of all types to the steps. This was the beginning of its crowded popularity, and it hasn't stopped since.

The twin-towered church on top, Santissima Trinità dei Monti, and its Egyptian granite obelisk sit prettily atop the steps. Looking down from the church level is a pleasant, very Roman experience.

The beautiful balustrades in the center, designed by Francesco de Sanctis, who won the design contest in 1717, creates an unusual midpoint stop and softens the appearance as a whole.

The fountain *(bottom-right)*, Fontana della Barcaccia, was sculpted by Pietro Bernini, who, it seems, was assisted by his ultimately famous son, Gian Lorenzo Bernini.

If you are headed down the steps, the orange house down on the left was the home of the English Poets **Shelly & Keats 260**, now a museum dedicated to their lives and work.

PIAZZA della ROTONDA
WHERE THE PANTHEON LIVES

PIAZZAS

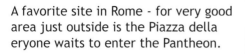

A favorite site in Rome - for very good reason - is the Pantheon. The area just outside is the Piazza della Rotonda, the place where everyone waits to enter the Pantheon.

Standing erect and proud in the center of the Piazza is the Fontana del Pantheon. The fountain was commissioned by Pope Gregory XIII **211** in 1575, who hired Leonardo Sormani to sculpt it. 150 years later, Pope Clemente XI had it redesigned. This was when they added the distinctive Egyptian Obelisk, made from Egyptian granite and carved during the time of Ramses II *(Ramses the Great, 1304bce)*.

Plenty goes on around the fountain. This is where the horse carriages line up to find passengers. Vendors like to set up their carts to sell their goodies. Musicians and acrobats alike enjoy entertaining the captive audience patiently waiting for their turn to enter the Pantheon.

But every day is an excellent day to people-watch. If this is your thing, then hanging out at the fountain and just watching will keep you amused and amazed for hours.

PIAZZA della MADONNA dei MONTI

If you are new in town, or you simply want to go where the locals are, this is the place. During the day, it is quite quiet. But from 4:00pm until midnight, this place jumps with college students and young couples alike!

This is the Monti district, a few blocks East of the Colosseum and the Forum. This is arguably the last local neighborhood in Rome. There are many tiny streets packed with local shops; dozens of restaurants almost all within eye-sight of this popular Piazza; bars, pubs, and eateries with inside and outside seating. And people everywhere!

Many of the local apartments have very small kitchens, so eating out is the norm here. At 4:00pm, people come out post-siesta to enjoy a mid-day aperitif with a glass of wine. *(Remember, Romans eat after 8:00pm, so this is their midday snack time.)*

After sunset, this fountain teems with people. It is a central meeting place for locals that want to end their day together. Music bellows from the bars, and the restaurants fill up.

This is a great place to escape the tourist set, and plunge into the Roman landscape. Best of all, the food is the real Roman cuisine, prepared by the neighborhood locals. Buon Appetito!!

PIAZZA della REPUBBLICA

PIAZZAS

Piazza della Republica is one of the most beautiful Piazzas in Rome. It was created when Rome became the Capital of Italy in 1870. Straddling the top of the Viminal Hill, it is flanked on one side by the Baths of Diocletian **64**. On the other side, by the sumptuous curves of the twin buildings. One of Rome's main Boulevards, Via Nationale, begins between the two and runs across the city.

The Fountain of the Naiads *(water nymphs)*, was initially created with four lions. Later the lions were replaced with the four nude nymphs, which created quite an uproar when they first appeared here in 1901.

The naiads are the Nymph of the Lakes *(holding a swan)*, the Nymph of the Rivers *(with a monster of the rivers)*, the Nymph

of the Oceans *(riding a horse symbolizing the sea)*, and the Nymph of the Underground Waters *(over a dragon)*. Rutelli's Glauco group stands in the center of the fountain, symbolizing the dominion of man over natural forces.

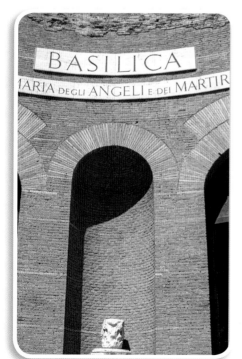

On the northeast side of the Piazza lay the gigantic **Baths of Diocletian** 64. Facing the Piazza is the Basilica of **Santa Maria of the Angels and Martyrs**. Don't be fooled by the ancient stone exterior, because you will be blown away by what waits for you inside. 198

The Basilica was carved into the Baths, with the Tepidarium of the Baths used as one of the wings of the Greek Cross plan. This plan was created by Michelangelo 156, the same exceptional artist that painted the ceiling of the Sistine Chapel 124, and sculpted the globally-famous statue of David in Florence, and the Moses (in Rome) 196 for the Tomb of Pope Julius.

PIAZZA MINCIO
Dr. Seuss' Neighborhood?

GREAT FIND! — TRULY STUNNING! — PHOTO OPS — UNCROWD

Piazza Mincio is a fun out-of-the-way neighborhood in Rome. Appealing to fantasy-lovers, this area is quite a significant departure from the typical architecture of ancient Rome.

Fiery, colorful, imaginative, kooky, whimsical, and outlandish: these are the words that come to mind when walking through the area. But all with a smile and the subliminal "Cool!" will run through your mind as you round another corner.

Famed Florentine architect, Quartière Coppedé, designed these buildings between 1916 and 1926 to amaze and amuse. And this he did, quite successfully.

Using brick, marble, and stucco, he created a fun collection of oddities for your camera. Watch for Seahorses in Chandeliers, a Flying Baby *(right)*, towers, turrets, arches, angels, and of course, the Golden spider of Palazzo della Rana.

A short taxi ride will get you here from the center of Rome, and with no entry fee, you can roam through the neighborhood freely admiring this wondrously quirky neighborhood of Rome.

PIAZZAS

PIAZZAS

PIAZZA di SANTA MARIA

Trastevere: tras-TEH-veh-reh (tras=other side, Tevere=Tiber. Trastevere= other side of the Tiber.)

Trastevere is possibly the most romantic neighborhood in Rome. Small streets and alleyways are lively with scattered umbrella-clad tables outside of the numerous cafés.

Outside of the church of Santa Maria in Trastevere *(Our Lady in Trastevere)*, the large piazza is accentuated with a Baroque fountain that was restored by both **Bernini 170** and Fontana in 1659 and 1692 accordingly.

Lined with little shops and cafés, the Piazza is a favorite hangout for young Romans, students, and tourists alike.

Trastevere is where many artists would hang out, including the likes of **Raphael 162**. Some of the local bars even boast their own 'Raphael' stories. Once the favored neighborhood of artists, writers, poets, and musicians alike, Trastevere today has settled into a warm, quaint, but not entirely quiet area of Rome.

The fountain in Piazza Trastevere is so overwhelmed with Rome's student population that many visitors have begun to seek quieter places to relax at the end of a vacation day.

IN TRASTEVERE

An evening stroll through the darling, winding streets of Trastevere will yield music to your ears, fresh simmering sauces for your nose, and plenty of romance for your heart.

GETTING HIGH

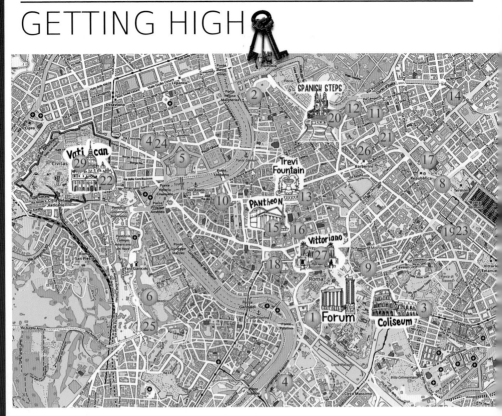

①	47 Circus Roof Garden		⑮	Minerva Roof Garden
②	Aquaroof Terrazza Molinari		⑯	Otium Hotel
③	Aroma Lounge Bar *(Palazzo Manfredi)*		⑰	Palazzo Naiadi
④	Piazza Fiorenzo Fiorentini		⑱	Palatine Hill
⑤	Castel Sant Angelo		⑲	Santa Maria Maggiore
⑥	Gianicolo, Janiculum Terrace		⑳	Spanish Steps
⑦	Hotel Albergo del Senato		㉑	Sky Blu Pool Terrace
⑧	Hotel Diana Roof Garden		㉒	Residenza Paolo VI Hotel
⑨	Hotel Forum Roof Garden		㉓	Terrazza di Papi Roof Garden Rest.
⑩	Hotel Raphaël		㉔	Terrazza Les Étoiles
⑪	Hotel Savoy		㉕	Terrazza Parrasio
⑫	La Terrasse Cuisine		㉖	The Flair at Sina Bernini Bristol
⑬	La Terrazza del Cesari		㉗	Vittoriano
⑭	Marcella Royal Hotel		㉘	Zest Bar in the Radisson Blu
	㉙ Dome of Saint Peter's Basilica			

When it's time to take a Selfie break, you can treat yourself to some cool and
quiet time - wherever you are in the city.
Enjoy, fellow travelers!

Get High in Rome? Seriously?

Most visitors to Rome have a few 'wants & wishes' in common, such as

- How to escape the stifling crowds?
- Where to find the best views/take the best photos in the city?
- Where to cool down, refresh, and enjoy a great meal after a long hot day of sightseeing in Rome?

I have skimmed the rooftops of Rome to scope out places all over the city where you can climb up, take an elevator or an escalator, and grant all three of these wishes.

There is no need to feel crowded, over-heated, or claustrophobic in Rome, as long as you know how to glide over the top of the city to get away from it all. I know that you'll love every single one of these places!

47 Circus Roof Garden ①
Via Luigi Petroselli, 47 ◄
Cool down and re-energize while you look down over the Forum Boarium **70** *and the Mouth of Truth* **262**. *Hercules will smile as you enjoy traditional Roman foods and an extensive cocktail menu.*

Aquaroof Terrazza Molinari ②
Via del Vantaggio, 14 ◄
A mere 4-minute stroll from the venerated Piazza del Popolo **222**. *Aquaroof has comfortable rooftop seating, wonderful food, and a great menu of Molinari cocktails. And, it is wheelchair accessible.*

Aroma Bar ③
Via Labicana, 125 ◄
A sublime view of the Colosseum **42**. *you won't get enough selfies at the Aroma Bar. On top of the Hotel Manfredi, it also looks down upon the Ludus Magnus* **75**, *the archaeological ruins of the ancient Gladiatorial school and practice arena.*

GETTING HIGH

GETTING HIGH - Views & Roof Tops

(4) Piazza Fiorentino Fiorentini
▶ **Via di Santa Sabina**

A walk up the gentle Aventine Hill will reward you with plenty of treats along the way, including the beautiful view from the Gardens of St. Alessio in the tree-laden Piazza Fiorentino Fiorentini. The views that surround this little park are surprising. This is a great picnic spot!

(5) Castel Sant Angelo
▶ **Lungotevere Castello, 50**

An often over-looked treat for great views is Castel Sant'Angelo **66***. It looks incredible from the outside, but inside is a genuine castle. When you near the top, stop for a cool Spritz and snack, and snap some selfies over the Tiber River* **253***.*

(6) Gianicolo, Janiculum Terrace
▶ **Piazzale Giuseppe Garibaldi**

Whoosh! What a view! This is one of the most sweeping vistas of Rome in the whole city. A beautiful park environment, a lovely walk, and perhaps if you plan ahead, a fantastic picnic. Snap away - you'll love the results!

(7) Hotel Albergo del Senato
▶ **Piazza della Rotonda, 73**

A choice location next to the Pantheon **186***. The Terrace rooftop bar offers a cocktail hour, refreshments, and a stunning view looking down over the fabulous Pantheon.One of the best people-watching views in the City!*

(8) Hotel Diana Roof Garden
▶ **Via Principe Amedeo, 4**

Near to the Roma Termini train station, Hotel Diana's rooftop has an excellent view in a southern direction at the magnificent Santa Maria Maggiore **188***. When you get to the rooftop, climb up one more level to get this flowered look at the city.*

Hotel Forum Roof Garden ⑨
Via Tor de' Conti, 25-30 ◄

A little gem of a bar, this is a fantastic place to refresh after visiting the Forum or the Colosseum **42** *. It sits over a restaurant, and both enjoy a view of the Forum as well as Vittoriano's* **148** *rooftop horses across the way. Now THIS is Roma!*

Hotel Raphaël ⑩
Largo Febo, 2 ◄

A prime location right next to Piazza Navona **224** *will ensure that you have plenty to look at. And you won't have to walk far to get to it from anywhere in the city. Capture this stunning view of Sant'Agnese in Agone, the beautiful church of Piazza Navona.*

Hotel Savoy ⑪
Via Ludovisi, 15 ◄

A twisty curvy slightly winding rooftop, it is clear that the Hotel Savoy has gone through many changes over the years. Maintaining its elegant charm, the rooftop bar sits atop a restaurant overseen by a terrific chef! Buon Appetito!

La Terrasse Cuisine ⑫
Via Lombardia 47 ◄

Located atop the Sofitel Rome Villa Borghese, this newly-remodeled hotel is clustered with some of the finest hotels in Rome, all in the Borghese **126** *neighborhood. Relax and enjoy an ice cold Spritz or one of the many specialties made by their in-house mixologist.*

La Terrazza del Cesàri ⑬
Via di Pietra, 89/a ◄

This boutique property boasts being the oldest hotel in Rome. La Terrazza rests on top with a smashing view of the Saint Ignatius of Loyola Church. Truly a hidden gem, it is a bit hard to find, but well worth the effort.

GETTING HIGH

GETTING HIGH - Views & Roof Tops

GETTING HIGH

⑭ Marcella Royal Hotel
▶ **Via Flavia 106**

The Marcella Royal Hotel was originally opened in 1967during the period of Fellini's Dolce Vita, when in the nearby Via Veneto, one of the most famous and elegant streets in the world, the stars of world cinema could be seen.

⑮ Minerva Roof Garden
▶ **Piazza della Minerva, 69**

That's the Pantheon's dome **186** *in the background. This lovely spot is a personal favorite when in Rome. Piazza Minerva* **225***is below, and you may get treated to one of the musicians that play down there regularly. And Michelangelo's* **156** *Gesu is in the church just below you.*

⑯ Otium Hotel
▶ **Via d'Aracoeli, 11**

A fantastic find is the lounge on top of the Otium Hotel! To sit and imagine being on top of that cool building with the horses, Vittoriano. **148** *Then to discover you can! This is what dreams are made of, and the Otium is where they will come true! Otium means Cultural Leisure.*

⑰ Palazzo Naiadi
▶ **Piazza della Repubblica, 47**

Posh! This is a Dedica Anthology® brand hotel, the 5-star beauty that dominates Piazza della Republica **230***. The rooftop features a lavish pool, and an enviable environment that you will want to write home about. And did I say Posh?*

⑱ Palatine Hill
▶ **Access through the Roman Forum**

One of the 7 Hills of Rome, Palatine stands in the shadow of the Colosseum **42***, and so often goes overlooked. But this was where the most affluent rulers of ancient Rome built their palaces. Both the views and the archaeological sites are splendido!* **56**

Santa Maria Maggiore ⑲
Piazza di S. Maria Maggiore ◄

Not a rooftop bar. But we would be remiss if we left out the balcony with an excellent view of its own Piazza. When you get up there, you will also be treated to a tour of the upstairs of this most incredible Basilica. (Look for the secret staircase!) **188**

Spanish Steps ⑳
Piazza di Spagna ◄

A climb up this architecture bellisima will reward you with plenty of lavish views. Bars & restaurants surround, and the Shelly/Keats **260** *house is off to the side. The luxurious balconies crown the steps while the fountain at the bottom will amuse you.*

Sky Blu Pool Terrace ㉑
Via di S. Basilio, 15 ◄

Pool beds, lounge areas, and a great blu pool. Escape the bustle of the city on top of the Aleph Rome Hotel. A Shisha corner will even give you the flavors of the Middle East. Their evening parties are a great way to end your day of sightseeing.

Residenza Paolo VI Hotel ㉒
Via Paolo VI, 29 ◄

This is the only hotel located in St. Peter's Square in Vatican City! If being close to the heart of Christendom is what you're looking for, look no further. With close-up views of the venerable St. Peter's Dome **180** *and the Apostolic Palace, you'll enjoy your wine with the most Holy scenery!*

Sky Bar ㉓
Via Carlo Alberto, 3 ◄

Sitting atop the Mecenate palace Hotel is the Sky Bar. Enjoy a delicious cocktail or an aperitif while watching the sunset over the historic skyline of Rome. The Sky Bar offers guests the perfect place to enjoy a drink on an unforgettable summer evening while you get lost in good conversation.

GETTING HIGH

GETTING HIGH - Views & Roof Tops

GETTING HIGH

(24) Terrazza Les Étoiles
VIA GIOVANNI VITELLESCHI, 34

Settled proudly on top of the Atlante Star Hotel, the Terrazza boasts Panorama and Taste. With the ideal view of the Dome of Saint Peter's Basilica **180** *on one side, and the impenetrable Castel Sant'Angelo on the other.*

(25) Terrazza Parrasio
VIA DI PORTA S. PANCRAZIO, 32

Nestled quietly in the jovial Trastevere **234** *neighborhood, Botanika Terrazza Parrasio is a place of happy music and happy people. Serving everything from Scampi to Sushi, Terrazza Parrasio is an excellent evening away in Roma.*

(26) The Flair
PIAZZA BARBERINI, 23

"Entering the The Flair means accessing an open space capable of giving a full sense of freedom and granting the privilege of looking at the chaos from above, letting yourself be surrounded only by beautiful and, of course, good things."
~ the Flair

(27) Vittoriano
PIAZZA VENEZIA

The 'Wedding Cake' of the Roman skyline, Vittoriano offers many layers of outdoor views away from the crowds. The higher you go, the fewer the people and the better the views. All around! See page **148** *to learn how to get to the top of Vittoriano! A MUST DO!*

(28) Zest Bar
VIA FILIPPO TURATI, 171

Located in the Radisson Blu Hotel, the Zest Bar offers Italian and International dishes. Buffet Brunch is available in the mornings, and the pool is the perfect cool-down after a hot afternoon of sight-seeing.

Getting high means escaping the crowds, by finding the coolest building rooftops and the highest points in the city. The oddest thing: people don't automatically think of 'going up' when it comes to visiting a city. That's why so many of these places are a welcome treat away from the pushy, exhausting crowds. Additionally, you'll enjoy sumptuous views, cool breezes, and in some places, you'll get to revel in cool refreshments or even marvelous meals. After all, isn't this what Italy is really all about?

29
Dome of Saint Peter's Basilica
Piazza San Pietro ◄

An experience unto itself is a visit to Saint Peter's Basilica. To top that experience, take yourself to the top of the Dome to get some of the best views of the city. There is a terrace on the way up that features lunch and wine to cool you down if you're needing a little break.
DO THIS ~ an absolute MUST! 180

GETTING HIGH

A couple of small blocks from Vittoriano **148** is the "Otium Hotel" Rooftop Terrace. When I first found this spot, I wished there was some way to get up to those fabulous flying horses. Little did I know...

This is a popular view over the Forum. To find it, go to Piazza del Campidoglio **220** by climbing the Michelangelo **156** staircase. Go all the way through the Piazza, and go around the either side of the building with the beautiful water fountain. You'll find yourself looking down on the luscious Roman Forum! **46**

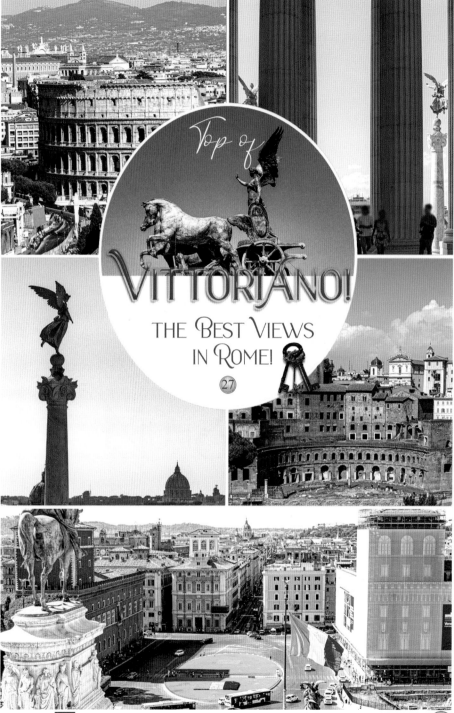

Top of

VITTORIANO!

THE BEST VIEWS IN ROME!

㉗

Vittoriano **148** *has the best 360° views in all of Rome. At every level you climb, the views get better and better. Then you get up to the elevator that whisks you up the last 10 stories to the top. This is our top recommended spot for the overall best views in the city.*

GETTING HIGH

Going to the top of the Colosseum **42** is rewarding if you're looking for great views. This stunning angle of the Arch of Constantine will give you plenty of perspective!

Top of the COLOSSEUM!

From another side on top of the Colosseum **42**, you get a striking look at the Temple of Venus and Rome in the Forum. A once grand structure, indeed.

Top of
CASTEL SANT'ANGELO

Castel Sant'Angelo **66** *is a terrific site for so many reasons. It's an amazing castle. It has a an unbelievable history. And it has some of the best views in Rome. Don't forget to stop at the little café on your way to the top to take a cool refreshing wine break while enjoying these views. Outstanding selfie spot!*

FUN FINDS

FUN FINDS

Rome has no end to oddities, peculiarities, and curiosities. All around the city you will run into things that make you laugh, feel all warm inside, or simply scratch your head in pure befuddlement. Here is a list of some of my quirky favorites that give the marvelous city of Rome even more charm and depth of personality.

...AT A GLANCE

252 Summer River Walk

The month of July brings the Summer Festival to Rome. The normally empty banks of the River Tiber become lined with tents that offer a whole variety of goodies to while away the heat. Clothing, food, bars, trinkets, arts and...

253 Boat Ride

A boat ride is a fun way to get across the city. Most folks don't think of it, so it's not usually crowded. It runs only during the high season, from April 1 to October 31. Although it is a hop-on/hop-off ride, you can opt to stay on...

254 Borghese Gardens

Once a sizeable vineyard, the land was converted into one of the largest parks in the city of Rome by Cardinal Scipione Borghese in 1605. (The other two largest parks are the Villa Doria Pamphilj **137** *and the Villa Ada.)*

255 Ponte Sant'Angelo

The picturesque Ponte Sant'Angelo is yet another enduring structure left from the second century ce by Emperor Hadrian **III**. *The bridge was created in 135ce to connect the Castel Sant'Angelo on the left bank of the River Tiber...*

256 Secret Keyhole of Malta

When you climb the Aventine Hill to this non-descript green door, you will see something that you can't see from anywhere else in Rome: 3 countries, all at once! The Templars, the mysterious Knights of Malta: all here.

FUN FINDS

...AT A GLANCE

Pyramid of Cestius   257

The year is 18bce. There is a fervent fever for all things Egyptian. Everyone wanted something in their home that looked Egyptian. If you could afford it, a Pyramid would be the cat's meow!

Fake Colosseum   259

*This building has mischievously fooled visitors for 2,000 years. Called the **Theatre of Marcellus**, it is only a couple of blocks from the Forum, and just down the street from the real Colosseum.*

Monte Testaccio   258

Broken Pot Mountain is aptly nicknamed. An entire neighborhood has been created on and around a mountainous heap of ancient pottery shards.

Keats & Shelley House   260

This house was the creative haven for the likes of John Keats, PB Shelley, Mary Shelley, Lord Byron, and many more. John Keats, an English poet, had been published for a mere four years...

Water Organ of Quirinale   261

*A rare experience, as it is not often open to the public, is the **Water Organ** commissioned by Pope Clement VIII. The instrument uses water to turn the paddle that drives the drum that...*

Mouth of Truth   262

A woman's fidelity can be tested here. Yours can be too! You must put your hand inside the mouth. If indeed you have told a lie, you will remove only a handless stump.

FUN FINDS

262 Fountain of the Turtles

This wonderful surprise, just around the corner from Largo Argentina, is not only delightful, but it is a great representation of the lengths the city pursued to make it utilities beautiful.

263 Monster House

An unusual site while walking through the lovely neighborhood at the top of the Spanish Steps, is the Bibliotheca Hertziana, or the 500-year-old Monster house. This is a fun photo op!

264 Obelisks of Rome

Obelisks are yet another remnant of the fad that swept Rome called Egyptomania. Most of the obelisks around Rome were carved in and moved from Egypt. We found 19 obelisks. How many can you find?

265 Quattro Fontana

As you wander the streets of Rome, you'll come to the **intersection of Via delle Quattro Fontane and Via Venti Settembre** *(20th of September). The uniqueness is the placement of these four fountains, one on each corner...*

il Passetto di Borgo

When Popes needed to escape safely from the Vatican, they needed a secret passageway. And guess what? Here's one now! It leads from the Pontifical Palace to Castel Sant'Angelo.

Porto Pia

Has Michelangelo touched every corner of Rome? It appears so! The Porta Pia is divinely designed by our hero of stone, Michelangelo, leaving his Renaissance touch on your gate of entry into the city.

Art on the Streets 268

Street Art comes in many forms and varieties in Rome. Creativity has no bounds, and Romans love to show off their work. Some are there to delight and amuse you, and some are there for you to purchase.

Museum of Purgatory 270

Inside the Church of the Sacred Heart, is a very small but interesting little exhibit. A visit to this little church will have you believing in Spirits and Ghosts before you leave. Mwah-ah-ah!

Magic Door 271

Porta Alchemica, or the Magic Door, stands quietly in a pretty little park in Rome. A pilgrim stayed overnight at this villa as he was passing through Rome. He was in search of the final ingredient that would enable him to create gold. And he found it here!

Skull of St. Valentine 195

When you enter the church, a reliquary on the left holds the Skull of St. Valentine. But is it the real skull? During the Victorian age, bones were liberally doled out. As it turns out, seven others claim to have his skull. Then whose head is this, anyway?

Fountain of the Frogs 232

in Piazza Mincio. This is a fun out-of-the-way neighborhood in Rome. Appealing to fantasy-lovers, this area is quite a whimsical departure from the typical architecture of ancient Rome.

Flood Tiles of Minerva 225

Take a look at the outside wall of the church of Minerva, to the right of it's entrance. Notice the squares with Roman writing. The fingers mark the height of the water during various floods that filled this Piazza!

SUMMER RIVER WALK

FUN FINDS

The month of July brings the Summer Festival to Rome. The normally empty banks of the River Tiber become lined tents that offer a whole variety of goodies to while away the heat.

Clothing, food, bars, trinkets, arts and crafts await slow-strolling visitors to stop in and browse.

Music fills the air as the sun sets over the city. The day turns to night as the aromas from fresh-cooked foods fill your nostrils.

Tents filled with games to challenge your ability to throw darts at a balloon will keep your competitive spirit alive.

Tables are abundant with plenty of folks willing to strike up a casual conversation.

If your trip to Rome is during the hot month of July, perhaps a stroll down by the river with a cold drink will ease the heat!

Images courtesy of RomeCabs.com

BOAT RIDE ON THE TIBER
ROMEBOATEXPERIENCE.COM

UNCROWDED!   PHOTO OPS   GREAT FIND!

A boat ride is a fun way to get across the city. Most folks don't think of it, so it's not usually crowded. It runs only during the high season, from April 1 to October 31. Although it is a hop-on/hop-off ride, you can opt to stay on the boat for the whole 1.5-hour tour. There are 5 places where you can get on/off:

- **ISOLA TIBERINA - on the Lungotevere Degli Anguillara side**
- **SANT ANGELO BRIDGE - on the Lungotevere Tor Di Nona side**
- **JUSTICE PALACE - Lungotevere Marzio**
- **POPOLO SQUARE - Lungotevere In Augusta**
- **VATICAN CITY - Lungotevere Castello**

(Consult a map for each of these locations.)

Also available are a **Dinner Cruise, a Sunset Cruise,** and a **Wine Bar Cruise.** Please check their website *(top-right)* for details and to purchase tickets.

FUN FINDS

BORGHESE GARDENS

Once a sizeable vineyard, the land was converted into one of the largest parks in the city of Rome (*The other two are the **Villa Doria Pamphilj** 137 and the Villa Ada.*) by Cardinal Scipione Borghese in 1605.

The property houses several villas and many points of interest. The Villa Medici contains the French Academy in Rome. The Piazza di Siena accommodated a horse training area, and played host to the equestrian events during the 1960 Olympics.

Orchards, mazes, and sculpture gardens abound. The Borghese gardens are one of the most scenic, relaxing walks in the city of Rome, and shouldn't be missed.

Clever and intricate mazes will amaze you during your stroll

The hydro-chronometer, or water clock operates 24/7.

PONTE SANT'ANGELO

The picturesque Ponte Sant'Angelo is yet another enduring structure left from the second century by **Emperor Hadrian** ▮▮▮.

The bridge was created in 135ce to connect the **Castel Sant'Angelo** 🖅 on the left bank of the River Tiber to the Campus Martius area on the right.

The robustness derives from its wide bearing on top of five stone arches. The iron balustrade was created in the 1500s by Pope Clement IV.

In the 1600s, Pope Clement VII *(de'Medici)* added the statues of Peter and Paul. Later that century, **Gian Lorenzo Bernini** 170 designed ten Angels for the bridge, each holding an Instrument of the Passions. Although he completed only two of them *(now in the church of Sant'Andrea delle Fratte)*, the rest were sculpted by other artists.

The Haunting of Beatrice Cenci

Young Beatrice (1577 - 1599) was the daughter of wealthy aristocrat Count Francesco Cenci. Francesco was a mean and angry man that violently abused his children. Beatrice, in an effort to be removed from the custody of her father, wrote a plea to the authorities, to no avail. One night after a meticulous plan, she and her siblings planned to murder the Count. They drugged him and stabbed him in the head and throat. But this did not kill him, so they bludgeoned him to death and threw him out a window. Investigators realized his injuries did not match with a 'falling accident,' so they interrogated the family. The trial created an uproar in Rome: some people were sad for the murder of the Count, while others stood up against the abuse of children. Found guilty, they were all executed in horrible ways, Beatrice by beheading with a small dull axe. To this day on September 11th at midnight, the anniversary of her execution, it is said that her ghost appears on the Ponte Sant'Angelo carrying her own head.

Note: This story has inspired many to write versions of her life. This included Stendahl, Dickens, Hawthorne, and Shelley.

KEYHOLE of the KNIGHTS of MALTA

PIAZZA DEI CAVALIERI DI MALTA, 3

GREAT FIND!   PHOTO OPS   UNCROWDED!

FUN FINDS

Behind the Green Door. *(Hmmm, sounds like an old movie.)* When you climb the Aventine Hill to this non-descript green door, little will you know what is waiting for you on the other side. Through this magical little keyhole, one of Rome's secret little gems, you will see three countries: Italy, Vatican City, and Malta - all at once!

The property where you are standing belongs to the Knights of Malta, and is not officially considered to be a part of Italy. It is, in reality, the property of the country of Malta. And of course, **Saint Peter's** Dome `180` is in Vatican City, again, its own country. Everything in between is Italy.

During the 10th century, this facility was a Benedictine monastery before it was passed to the Templars, then to the Knights Hospitallers, then to the modern order of the Knights of Malta. It later underwent a series of remodels during the 1400s-1600s.

Today, a stroll up the Aventine will afford you a variety of panoramic views of the city. And while you're here, notice the Masonic symbols on the building, along with symbols of the sea, left over from when the Aventine Hill was compared to a ship.

Was this view of 3 countries created on purpose? Or by accident?

A line of visitors wait to snap a rare photo through the keyhole.

This facility sometimes hosts events, as seen in the foreground here.

PYRAMID OF CESTIUS
VIA RAFFAELE PERSICHETTI

Back in the Republican days of Rome, they had something called the Corporation of Religion, a religious order that had nothing to do with Catholicism or religion as we think of it today. Founded in 196bce, this particular order,

the Epulones, was created because the city needed someone professional to manage the myriad of city-wide games, feasts, parties, events in general. One of the Priests from the Epulones was a guy named Gaius Cestius, an event planner par excellence.

The year is now 18bce, **Caesar 96**, Cleopatra, and the Republic are all dead. One thing remaining is a fervent fever for all things Egyptian. Everyone wanted to have something in their home that looked Egyptian.

Recycling Egyptomania

The Pyramid of Cestius was one of two pyramids in ancient Rome. The other one was built near the Mausoleum of Augustus, its origins unknown. During the Renaissance (1500s), Pope Alexander VII had it knocked down so that he could use its stone to build the new steps at St. Peter's Basilica.

Our guy Gaius Cestius was no different. He wanted the coolest Egyptian symbol ever: a tomb for himself in the shape of a Pyramid.

Created of concrete over a slab of travertine, its brick face created the smooth exterior. This construction has kept it intact for 2,000 years, making it the best-preserved structure left over from antiquity. The barrel-vaulted interior chamber was discovered with frescoes, which do not remain today.

The inner chamber can be visited, but reservations are required.

MONTE TESTACCIO
VIA NICOLA ZABAGLIA, 24

FREE!   **Quick & EASY!**

Broken Pot Mountain is aptly nick-named. An entire neighborhood has been created on and around a mountainous heap of ancient pottery shards. Where did it all come from, you ask?

Not by random accident, this monstrous mound was created intentionally, and began possibly around 150bce, before the reign of Julius Caesar. Later, the importation of oils grew to a feverish level during the height of the Roman Empire, around 100ce.

Oils were used for candles, cooking, heating, and general lubrication. Olive oils were in high demand for cooking and polishing. They were imported in 18-gallon amphorae from countries such as Greece, Africa, and more.

The amphorae were made from clays, like terra cotta, and were neatly broken and deposited here for efficient disposal.

The largest storage warehouse existed here, where in the back yard, they built a large wall, and stacked broken pottery in an orderly fashion. Paths existed for the passage of the people that were adding new broken amphorae to the stacks. Because the oldest shards are at the bottom of the piles, it is difficult to know just how old the oldest pots are.

FUN FINDS

FAKE COLOSSEUM & FORUM
VIA DEL TEATRO DI MARCELLO

Quick & EASY!   **FREE!**   **Near the ROMAN FORUM!**   **PHOTO OPS**

As large as this structure looks, it is dwarfed by the real Colosseum only a few short blocks away.

This building has mischievously fooled visitors for 2,000 years. Called the **Theatre of Marcellus (the Fake Colosseum,)** it is only a couple of blocks from the Forum, and just down the street from the real **Colosseum 42**. It was originally commissioned by **Julius Caesar 96**, but he died before construction began. **Augustus 100** decided to follow through with its construction in 12bce. The arched porticoes and the remains of the three standing ruined pillars only deepens the illusion.

Back in its heyday, the theater held as many of 20,000 spectators. Much like other theatrical structures, the Theater of Marcellus contains passageways and tunnels giving access to its performers. The arched porticos act as entry and exit points, making it easy to fill and empty the entire space.

It fell into disuse after the 400s ce, lending to its fast decay. For awhile it was used as a trash dump site. When the big Roman renewal took place during the Renaissance period, much of it was dismantled and its stone was used for other new buildings and churches around the city.

Later the top level was removed and replaced with apartments. The easiest way to tell the difference between this building and the Colosseo? The top level of the Colosseum has no apartments, Teatro di Marcellus *(above)* does.

KEATS & SHELLEY House
PIAZZA DI SPAGNA, 26

This house was the creative haven for the likes of John Keats, PB Shelley, Mary Shelley, Lord Byron, and many more.

John Keats, an English poet, had been published for a mere four years before his tragic death from tuberculosis. *"Turn the key deftly in the oiled wards, And seal the hushed Casket of my soul." ~ John Keats*

Percy Bysshe Shelley and his wife Mary lived here also, until he drowned during a 50-mile sail along Italy's west coast. He was considered to be the finest philosophical poet that England ever produced.

His wife Mary Shelley, famous for her creation of "Frankenstein," spent time at this address as well.

Today, the museum of Keats & Shelley consists of the greatest library of Romantic Literature in the world, book store, and shrine to John Keats.

The Twizy

These humorous little cartoon-like cars are quite hilarious to the eye of a large-vehicled American. But in a super-crowded city like Rome that was not built with parking garages in mind, there are many more cars than there are places to park them. Enter Twizy[tm], by Renault®. This little electric gem can easily traverse Rome's roughest streets. When finished it can fit between two cars that are already parallel-parked along the side of a street. It is as long as a typical car is wide. Talk about a BUG!

WATER ORGAN
IN THE GARDENS OF PALAZZO QUIRINALE

Nicknamed Monte Cavallo *(Horse Mountain)* because of the horses with Castor & Pollux in its Piazza, the Palace has been the personal home of 4 Kings, 30 Popes, and 12 Presidents. The most famous resident was Napoleon, who had many homes in many countries. He called this one his "residence par excellence."

Pope Gregory VIII 211 pined for a summer home somewhere near Rome. He wished to escape the stench of the River Tiber, and the unhealthful conditions of the Lateran Palace. He loved the idea of being closer to heaven on the top of the of treasured Quirinale Hill.

The gardens have enjoyed every flavor of Papally-indulgent landscaping. It was thought of as a garden island due to its cherished position at the top of the ancient Quirinale Hill. A rare experience, as it is not often open to the public, is the **Water Organ** *(inset)* commissioned by Pope Clement VIII. The instrument uses water to turn the paddle that drives the drum that creates the pressure that plays the music. Water is also used to create the wind in its chest that creates the sound in the pipes.

The top of Quirinal hill dates back to the beginnings of Rome. In 2013, archaeologists discovered a 6th century bce 2-room house, with clay-covered wooden walls. It is located next to a 5th century bce temple.

FUN FINDS

MOUTH OF TRUTH
PIAZZA DELLA BOCCA DELLA VERITÀ, 18

Bocca della Verita

POPULAR   GREAT FIND!   PHOTO OPS

This man's veracity is being tested as he places his hand into The Mouth of Truth, with the hopes that he does not pull out a bloody stump. Are you brave enough to try?

Weighing 2,866 pounds, this ancient rock might definitely apply enough pressure to take your hand! Situated next to the front entrance to the church of **Santa Maria in Cosmedin** `195`, this funny, yet stony face has been responsible for the circulation of rumors, tales, and flights of fancy for many centuries.

According to the legend, someone can ask you a question. For example, to a woman: 'Have you been unfaithful to your husband?' After the answer, you must put your hand inside the mouth. If indeed you have told a lie, you will remove only a handless stump.

For some odd reason, the Bocca della Verita is a popular site. There remains in the back of every tester's mind the slight possibility of danger that may come from Rome's very own truthometer.

FOUNTAIN OF THE TURTLES
PIAZZA MATTEI

Turtle fans unite! This Renaissance fountain is here to delight! Designed in the 1580s by famed architect Giacomo della Porta and sculpted by Taddeo Landini, this was one of the many fountains around the city created to bring water to its residents. Instead of a mere pump on a sidewalk, Rome had the forethought to find wealthy donors *(in this case, Muzio Mattei)* to pay sculptors to make them not just functional, but also delightful. The turtles were added 100 years later during its restoration.

MONSTER HOUSE
VIA GREGORIANA, 28

FUN FINDS

MAX PLANCK INSTITUTE for ART HISTORY - BIBLIOTHECA HERTZIANA

An unusual site while walking through the lovely neighborhood at the top of the Spanish Steps, is the Bibliotheca Hertziana, or the Monster house.

The gaping mouth was once the entrance gate to the garden that inhabited this space centuries ago. Its style is reminiscent of "Bomarzo Park **284**," the fantasy park that is located one hour north of Rome. The "Bomarzo" rock sculptures were created by Simone Moschino, a mannerist sculptor from the 1500s. It is possible that he was the sculptor of this Monster House.

Today, the Library "promotes scientific research in the field of Italian and global history of art and architecture. Established as a private foundation by Henriette Hertz (1846–1913), it was inaugurated in 1913 as a research center of the Kaiser-Wilhelm-Gesellschaft. Today, the Bibliotheca Hertziana is part of the Human Sciences Section of the Max Planck Society and is considered one of the world's most renowned research institutes for art history."

Although it is a private (member-only) organization, it holds regular tours to the public (in Italian only). Please do not disturb the occupants, as this is a place of deep study and research.

FUN FINDS

SERPENS ULTOR
VIA DI TOR SANGUIGNA, 3

SERPENS ULTOR

BALLISTRARIUM VERITATIS
FIDEM NON PRODERE
PERICULUM HOSTIS FACERE

Funky HISTORY

Serpens Ultor, the Avenger Serpent, is the ultimate test to see if a man has been cheating on his wife. If accused, he must pretend to urinate in the hole. If he is guilty, he will be immediately emasculated.

This serves to balance the **Bocca della Verita** *(Mouth of Truth* 262*)* across town, which was created to 'eat' the hand of a woman who has been unfaithful to her husband, or anyone else who has been telling lies.

The Serpens Ultor can be found inside the Stadium of Domitian (Circus Argonalis) 74 underneath **Piazza Navona** 224. It stands, appropriately, waist high.

OBELISKS
How Many Can You Find?

Lateran Obelisk - piazza San Giovanni in Laterano ~ 105.5'
Piazza del Popolo 222, aka the Flaminian obelisk ~ 78.5'
Vatican 120 Obelisk ~ 83'
Solar Obelisk, obelisk of Montecitorio 141
Liberian Obelisk ~ 48.5'
Quirinale Obelisk ~ 48.1'
The Mattei Obelisk- Villa Celimontana ~ 40'
Minerva Obelisk - Piazza Minerva 225 ~ 18'
Pantheon 186 Obelisk, The Macuteo Obelisk - 21'
The Dogali Obelisk at the Baths of Diocletian ~ 29'
Medici Obelisk - at the Villa Medici (Twin of the Dogali Obelisk)
Navona Obelisk - Piazza Navona 224 ~ 54'
Sallustian Obelisk, Lunar Obelisk - Spanish Steps 227 ~ 100'
Pincian Obelisk, aka Hadrian's Obelisk ~ 30.5'
Villa Borghese 126 - tiny ~ 9'
Torlonia 150 Twin Obelisks - each 33.7'
Egyptian Gate Obelisks- twin obelisks
Foro Italico Obelisk- Musollini ~ 57'
Marconi Obelisk ~ 147.5'

He Gave us a Hand with The Mattei Obelisk

In 1820, the owners decided that the obelisk needed to be moved. The operation occurred with great pomp in front of a large crowd. Unfortunately, during the procedure, the rope broke, amputating both hands of one of the workers. To this day, his hands are trapped underneath the monument.

QUATTRO FONTANE
Four Fountains

As you wander the streets of Rome, you'll come to the **intersection of Via delle Quattro Fontane and Via Venti Settembre** *(20th of September)*. The uniqueness is the placement of these four fountains, one on each corner of the intersection. Commissioned by Pope Sixtus V *(Papacy 1585-1590)*, they are a good representation of Late Renaissance sculpture. Nearby is the San Carlo alle Quattro Fontane, designed by the Baroque architect master **Francesco Borromini 176**. The symbology is debatable, a common interpretation is that they each represent a river. But perhaps not, as you can see by the descriptions below. The existence of these fountains is one more thing that gives Romes her unique depth.

Huntress Goddess Diana

The River Tiber with an oak tree.

Juno, Goddess of Marriage & Childbirth

The River Aniene provided much of Rome with water

This panorama captures the scale 3 of the 4 fountains at this intersection.

FUN FINDS

PASSETTO DI BORGO
The Popes' Secret Passageway

Passetto is a 'secret' passageway that connects the Vatican to Castel Sant'Angelo. Created in the early 1200s, it was used most notably by two Popes to facilitate their secret escape. When King Charles of France invaded Rome in 1494, Pope Alexander VI *(Borgia)* crossed it to safety. Then later in 1527 when Rome was sacked by Charles V, Pope Clement VII *(de'Medici)* fled the Vatican and successfully barricaded himself in Castel Sant'Angelo.

In Dan Brown's best selling novel "Angels & Demons" *(©Pocket Books)*, the bad guys kidnap four Cardinals and take them across the Passetto to hide them.

Occasionally, tours are available that will take visitors across Passetto.

PORTA PIA
The Port of Michelangelo

Has Michelangelo touched every corner of Rome? It appears so! Named after Pope Pious IV, Porta Pia was divinely designed by our hero of stone, Michelangelo, leaving his Renaissance touch on this busy gate of entry into the city.

A 4-sided masterpiece, Michelangelo wanted to represent the dramatic importance of entering into the greatest city in the world.

The niches in the exterior side hold sculptures of Saint Agnes and Saint Alexander between four columns.

This was Michelangelo's last work in Rome, as he died in 1564, 5 years before its completion.

Unification of Italy

In 1870, a breach in the wall at Porta Pia was created so the Berglieri troops *(members of the Royal Italian Army)* could enter and capture the city of Rome. This successful attempt was the final step in pulling power from the Papacy and uniting Rome under its King, Vittorio Emanuele II.

• • • • • • • • • • • • • • •

One day, when Mussolini was coming through the wall, an antifascist demonstrator threw a bomb at his car. No serious damage was incurred.

INTERIOR

EXTERIOR

ART ON THE STREETS

FUN FINDS

Street Art comes in many forms and varieties in Rome. Creativity has no bounds, and Romans love to show off their work. Rome is famous for its art schools, and students love to come out to practice their skills. Some are there to delight and amuse you, and some are there for you to purchase. Here a few examples of the types of creative artistry that you will find as you walk the streets of Rome. Enjoy the visions!

MUSEUM of PURGATORY
LUNGOTEVERE PRATI, 12

FUN FINDS

Away From the HEAT!   *EERIE!*   *Funky HISTORY*

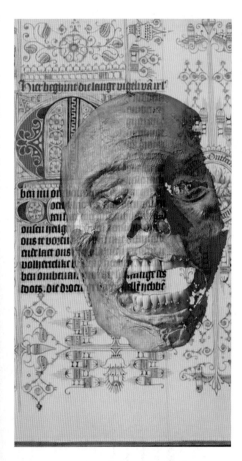

Inside the Sacro Cuore di Gesù in Prati, Church of the Sacred Heart, is a very small but interesting little exhibit.

The story took place in an old church where Father Jouet, a French Missionary, oversaw the little church. According to his story, a candle caused a nearby painting to catch fire. Witnesses to the fire reported seeing the image of a burning man in a wall near the altar. Father Jouet, deciding that there must be a man buried within the wall, chose to build a larger church around it.

Among the oddities exhibited here is a man's nightcap with the hand print of his dead wife that appeared after her death, asking him for forgiveness. Additionally, you'll find the hand prints on a book that appeared after another person died.

The bookstore carries books that explains these unusual items in further detail.

MAGIC DOOR
PIAZZA VITTORIO EMANUELE II

Funky HISTORY   GREAT FIND!   Quick & EASY!

FUN FINDS

Porta Alchemica, or the Magic Door, stands quietly in a pretty little park in Rome.

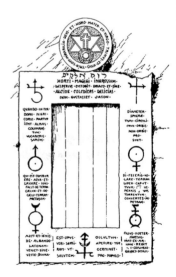

As the legend goes, a pilgrim that went by the name of Giustiniano Bono, stayed overnight at a villa as he was passing through Rome. Giustiniano, as it happened, was an Alchemist who had heard that a rare herb, a key ingredient to concocting gold, grew outside of this villa. He had searched far and wide for it, and was so happy when he discovered it here. In the middle of the night, he harvested the herb, and was seen disappearing through a door, never to be seen again. But he left behind 2 things: a piece of paper with strange symbols on it, and a few gold flakes near the door. The owner of the villa, a Marquis, had the symbols carved into the door with the hopes that a passerby might be able to translate it, enabling him to create gold from an herb.

The 2 statues that stand guard on either side of the door are of the Egyptian Deity Bes. To the Egyptians, Bes is the god of childbirth, fertility, sexuality, humor, and war, but served primarily as a protector god of pregnant women and children. He is regularly depicted as a dwarf with large ears, long-hair and beard, with prominent genitals, and bowed legs.

DAY TRIPS

...AT A GLANCE

Pompeii 286

In a single 24-hour period, a cata-strophic volcano buried this luxuri-ous city deep under ash and lava, as much as 30 feet deep in some places. Today, it can be visited on foot thanks to over a century of archaeological excavations.

Herculaneum 290

Herculaneum is thought of as the little sister to Pompeii. Eventually, when archaeologists have uncovered more of the city, it may match Pom-peii in size. Currently, only 25% of it has been properly excavated. But what a spectacular 25% it is!

Nemi 290

Nemi, the easily-accessible lake-front village with rural-cool breezes, was the country home for many Roman influencers. This included the most infamous Emperor, Caligula 104 who made a home here, and this is where he kept his party barges.

The romance of Cupid and Psyche is legendary. This beguiling sculpture (reproduc-tion) can be found amid the ruins of the once thriving city of Ostia Antica 280.

DAY TRIPS

TIVOLI

FROM ROME: 40 MINUTES BY CAR

IN THE SHADOW OF ROME

The Roman Temple of Vesta.

Existing' in the shadow of Rome is difficult for all of the towns and villages that surround the most magnificent city in the world. However, Tivoli has become a wonder of its own, sort of 'the little village that could.'

A delightful town with a welcoming feel, Tivoli will entice you with its small-town Italian charm, its delectable food, and the locally-owned shops. In Tivoli, the chipped archaic walls whisper two millennia worth of the stories and secrets of those that came before.

Besides being home to the popular Villa d'Este (Tivoli Gardens) and Hadrian's wonder-filled archeological Villa, Tivoli has a few more secrets up her sleeve. **The Roman Temple of Vesta** stands bravely out on the tip of a cliff that hangs over the Aniene Valley. Archaeology buffs can visit **ancient Mausoleums** and even **Caligula's Aqueducts.**

The Villa Gregoriana is a public, heavily wooded park with picturesque waterfalls that peek out randomly and gush down to the Aniene River below. Alternate paths and trails lead to caverns, grottoes, and wooded vistas.

Rocca Pia, an overbearing fortress, bears the holy name of Pious Rock. But during the political battle between the Guelphs & the Ghibellines, the guelphs saw it as protection from their counterparts.

Most visitors come to Tivoli to see the Gardens *(Villa d'Este)*, and possibly Hadrian's Villa. But Tivoli is more than just those two sites. So much more.

Via delle Cascatelle

The Fortress of Rocca Pia

A stroll through the quaint and ancient streets of Tivoli will delight you every time you turn a corner to see her timeless and exquisite classical beauty.

DAY TRIPS

TIVOLI ~ VILLA D'ESTE

WATER & POWER

GREAT DAY TRIP! ~ WORLD HERITAGE SITE ~ TRULY STUNNING!

Must-See GEM! ~ PHOTO OPS

In ancient times, the ability to control water was synonymous with power. As populations around the world faded into oblivion caused by droughts, and diseased water decimated entire cultures, it becomes easy to understand that who ever controlled water, would be the most successful cultures in the world.

Rome was just such a culture. They had a seemingly other-worldly grasp on how to channel freshwater, how to distribute it, and how to luxuriate in it. They wanted everyone to know it: the aqueducts, the magnificent baths, the jillions of fountains that were placed over the entire Roman Empire. Water water everywhere, and you could drink it all. Whew ~ Talk about power!

As an individual during the Roman Empire, the more water you had on your property, the more powerful you were perceived to be. The more visible the water in your home, the more influence and authority you wielded.

Villa d'Este is a magnificent statement of the brandishing of that power. It is a stunning boast of liquid strength that will refresh your senses to the core.

Villa d'Este was a Benedictine convent before its ownership by Cardinal Ippolito II d'Este. A study in the glory of Renaissance symmetry, it was designed by Pirro Ligorio, a mid-1500s Mannerist architect. Cardinal d'Este, one of the most wealthy Cardinals of this period, was the grandson of Pope Alexander VI, Rodrigo Borgia.

The inside of the Villa itself is a masterwork of frescoes and sculptures. Cardinal d'Este commissioned a host of famous artists from the likes of Cellini to Bernini. A tour through the Villa will align you with a prime example of Renaissance art and architecture.

Today, the main attraction is its back yard exterior, giving it the qualifications to be a Unesco World Heritage site.

This is the marvelous garden of water. It features 51 fountains, 398 spouts, 364 water jets, 64 waterfalls, and 220 basins. These are all supplied by 875 canals, channels, and cascades. But here's the magic: all of this is supported *without pumps* ~ it uses only the force of gravity to operate!

Treat yourself to one of the most splendid sites in the area, then enjoy an exquisite lunch in the charming historic little town of Tivoli.

"Water" Music

The famous Hungarian composer Franz Liszt resided in Villa d'Este for 21 years until his death in 1886.

Author Patty Civalleri photographs a spectacular fountain in Tivoli Gardens.

DAY TRIPS

TIVOLI ~ HADRIAN'S VILLA

DAY TRIPS

GREAT DAY TRIP! · Must-See GEM! · UNESCO WORLD HERITAGE SITE · PHOTO OPS · TRULY STUNNING!

When Hadrian became emperor *(117ce)*, he felt that living outside Rome might be a bit safer for him. As an architect, he wanted to design his dream house, and nearby, Tivoli had ample available space.

Boy, did he dream big! This house consisted of over 30 buildings sitting on 250 acres. To give you an idea of just how big that is, the entire city of Pompeii was a mere 150 acres.

Hadrian's Villa included pools, baths, fountains, and canals. He decorated it with the themes of several favorite places from his travels. For example, there were 'Egyptian' pools, complete with crocodiles, sculptured, of course. His particular love for Athens is reflected in the architecture and in the Greek statues that were once quite abundant. Additionally, there were libraries, temples, stables, woods, and riding trails.

Toward the end of his reign, he moved the official business of running the Roman Empire to the Villa. The property had to accommodate hundreds of people, offices, sleeping rooms, kitchens, and a full staff of hundreds to manage it.

After his death, the Villa was used by Antoninus Pius, Marcus Aurelius, Caracalla, even the Queen of Palmyra *(Seria)*, among many others. After the Empire fell, Hadrian's Villa fell into disrepair.

During the Middle Ages, it was used as a warehouse where lime kilns would strip the lime from the marble to be used in other construction projects.

Nearly 800 years later, during the Renaissance, Cardinal d'Este removed much of the marble and sculptures to use in his new Villa d'Este or to sell.

1900 YEARS AGO

TODAY

DAY TRIPS

Canopus

Hall of Doric Pillars

South Stadium Garden

Vestibule Courtyard

279

DAY TRIPS

OSTIA ANTICA
VIALE DEI ROMAGNOLI, 717, 00119
ROMA RM, ITALY

COOL ARCHAEOLOGY!   Must-See GEM!   PHOTO OPS   Easy TRAIN Ride!

A mere 16-mile train ride from the historical center of Rome, lies the ancient port city of Ostia Antica (also known as 'Little Pompeii'), not to be confused with the modern-day Ostia.

During its ancient heyday, Ostia Antica bustled with ships, cargo, traders, cattle, and people. Lots of people. As the central Port City of Rome, it was where Rome-bound vessels from all over the world would dock to trade goods with the mightiest city on the planet. Products, ranging from grains to wines, from seafood to textiles, were brought into Ostia, given a catalog number, and were either warehoused for future usage or sent to the city of Rome for more immediate use.

The town began to grow during the first century when Emperor Augustus, and his right-hand man Agrippa, created projects to build it up. More and more massive warehouses were constructed; more shops lined the streets; residential areas sprang up during this time.

Many religions found a home here: there were 16 Mithra in Ostia, a Synagogue, and even places where tiny Christian cults could hold their secret meetings.

Pagan temples, public baths, and gathering places were added. Ostia had grown into a full-fledged flurry of trade with nearly one million citizens living and working here.

Ancient sculpture of Cupid & Psyche found in Ostia.

Sadly, as the city reached its peak, Emperor Trajan was well underway to creating a man-made port city nearby. This ceased growth, causing a decline in Ostia, as many traders began to prefer working through the newer port.

A slower-moving Ostia remained as a resort town for the wealthy before being covered over by sand for the next one thousand-plus years. Because the Tiber River has changed direction, today Ostia Antica is 4 kilometers from the coast.

The open Forum area is still semi-available for you to walk through. Note the marble that still exists on some of the columns as well as a few random structures.

This was the kitchen of a restaurant. Archaeologist Darius Arya and Roger Civalleri examine the ancient stoves that were used to keep the food moving through at a high rate.

Walk down the many streets in Ostia, nicknamed 'Little Pompeii.' Some of the structures are still fully enclosed, enabling you to enter and examine their way of life.

OSTIA ANTICA, Cont'd.

Ostia Antica began during the Regal period in the 600's bce by King Marzio as the official port city to Rome. When you visit here, you will go back in time, as far back as 2,600 years! Ostia remained populated and highly active for nearly 900 years. It is also known as 'Little Pompeii,' and is much easier to reach from Rome than is Pompeii. If you have only a half-day available and you want to see a real ancient city that does not boast of modern shops and restaurants and business buildings, Ostia Antica is within your reach, as it is a short train ride away from Rome.

Walk down the empty streets to see the homes of the working class and the wealthy alike. See how many homes had private baths, showers, and the public and private toilets (right). The shops, places of worship, and trading centers are all still quite identifiable to even the novice archaeologist.

The Wrong End of the Stick

Public restrooms (bottom photo) were common in ancient Rome, and were segregated by gender. They were not only public, but also a social gathering place. A 'user' would sit on the keyhole shaped bench, where water ran in a rivulet just below the floor level. When finished, a stick with a cloth tied around its end (like a large cotton swab) would be dunked in the clean running water below, and used to clean oneself. When finished, you would pass it to the next person to use. If you didn't like that person, you would pass him "The Wrong End of the Stick!"

MOSAICS OF OSTIA ANTICA

As you walk through the long line of ancient store fronts, you will find these mosaics were created as large welcome mats, both to greet their customers as well as to tell something about their businesses: a fishery, a shipping company, an African importer, etc. Can you guess what kind of business each of the markets offered?

Ostia Antica has the largest collection of intact mosaics remaining from the ancient world!

DAY TRIPS

BOMARZO AKA MONSTER PAR

GREAT FIND! · **Away From the HEAT!** · **EERIE!** · **PHOTO OPS**

Bomarzo *(bo-MART-zo)* is a little town that is approximately 68km *(1 hour)* north of Rome *(the travel time is the same via car or train)*. It is a crazy, mixed-up selection of fantasy, history, and imagination that will be a superb treat for the whole family. Dive into the woods and be startled as you round every tree, rock, and stream. Hidden throughout this park is an extensive collection of oddities that will amuse, amaze, and spook you.

Pack a lunch because this will be the coolest picnic you'll ever do!

In the 1500s, a Papal relative by the name of Pier Francesco Orsini owned this wooded parkland that was endowed with huge boulders strewn from end to end of his property. After his wife passed away, he decided to remodel his landscape and so he hired Mannerist architect Pirro Ligorio to design it. He, in turn, hired a sculptor to 'do something about these rocks.' Named Simone Moschino, the sculptor did

> In the central monster (right), the red writing around its mouth reads "OGNI PENSIERO VOLA" and translates to "Every Thought Flies."

as instructed and began sculpting figures from these giant rocks that randomly littered the Orsini grounds. Ligorio was the same fellow that design Tivoli Gardens, another highly recommended day-trip from Rome.

The park was considered to be grotesque at that time, but in today's world, it is simply fun! Visitors can climb on and through some of the sculptures, and kids will love the surprise they'll find around every turn in the trails.

The park has been known as Sacro Bosco ("Sacred Grove"), Park of the Monsters (Parco dei Mostri in Italian), and The Garden of Bomarzo.

DAY TRIPS

POMPEII

COOL ARCHAEOLOGY!

Easy TRAIN Ride!

A trip from Rome to Pompeii is doable in a single day round-trip train ride. But if time allows, I would recommend spending a night here, and a visit to Herculaneum as well. These are both fantastic - and huge - excavations that you will be happy to spend many hours visiting.

2,000 years ago, the ancient city of Pompeii, on Italy's west coast, was a popular destination for Wealthy vacationing Romans. They would pay top dollar for a pampered vacation in the seaside resort city of Pompeii.

In a single 24-hour period in 79ce, a catastrophic volcano in Mt. Vesuvius buried this luxurious city deep under of ash and lava, as much as 30 feet deep in some places. Today, it can be visited on foot thanks to over a century of archaeological excavations.

The Resort in the Shadow of a Time Bomb

The population of Pompeii was made up of mostly well-educated business people, teachers, skilled craftsmen, and artisans. They dressed in styles made from delicate fabrics and embellishments. Their homes were marbled and frescoed.

And their recreation would include lavish Roman baths, art galleries, theater performances, and of course the finest in exotic cuisine.

Mount Vesuvius had rumbled and grumbled for months. Residents in the wealthy city of Pompeii became quite used to the belching neighbor that regularly emitted rude noises and smoky plumes. So, they con-

Pompeii is an ancient, 150-acre city that was destroyed in a single day by the eruption of a volcano.

tinued to go about their daily business as usual.

It was a beautiful August morning in 79ce when it blew. Mt. Vesuvius unleashed a tranquility-shattering explosion causing a 360-degree apocalypse for miles around its base. The smoke and ash were so abrupt that people stopped in their tracks as they walked, bending in blinding fits of coughing and sputtering until they dropped where they stood. The Earth shook, and the sea brought wall after wall of home-shrouding waves in a blinding hot tsunami. Ash, mud, thick clouds of dust and fiery stones pummeled the city for nearly 24 hours. All that remained was a vast moonscape of dead scenery in the place of the town that was filled with laughter and glory only 25 hours earlier.

Over the next 2,000 years, the 30-feet of ash and mud hardened to stone. The citizens had been trapped on the first day and remained in that spot for the next two thousand years.

Haunted Excavations
In 1594, archaeologists undertook the painstakingly difficult task of excavating through the hardened ash and pumice in Pompeii to uncover her ancient secrets.   -->>

· · · · · · · · · · ·

A statue of Apollo held a bow and arrow in antiquity. However, today, he appears to be reaching out to a population that is no longer there.

287

POMPEII, Cont'd.

During the process of digging, they came upon large oddly-shaped spaces or 'bubbles' in the hard pumice. Later during the 1800s, an archaeologist named Giuseppe Fiorelli devised a smart way to understand these misshapen gaps. He filled the 'bubbles' with a plaster substance. After drying, Fiorelli removed the original outer pumice material from the hardened plaster. Doing so, he unveiled the most haunting site he had ever seen: the bubble was the mold of a human who had died in agony!

Fiorelli continued to fill more of these 'bubbles' and discovered the last moments of many of the Pompeiians as they took their final breath 2,000 years ago.

Villa of Mysteries
This villa has become famous because of the beautiful condition of its exquisite wall of frescoes. This type of art is instrumental in educating us about the life of the locals. In this scene, it appears that a religious cult is initiating a young girl, a point which is still argued by experts today.

All told, approximately 2,000 people lost their lives that fateful summer day. A small number of citizens survived because they managed to escape by various means. But the memories of too many lost souls have been preserved for us to remember for all time.

The boy in the workshop
This young man looks as though he futilely attempted to shield his eyes and nose from the onslaught.

Roman Baths *~ Because of the nearby Volcano, thermal baths were common in Pompeii. Unfortunately, the mountain that brought the naturally heated water and daily pleasure was also the instrument of their quick demise.*

Eye Witness Account

"In the darkness, you could hear the crying of women, the wailing of infants, and the shouting of men. Some prayed for help. Others wished for death. But still more imagined that there were no Gods left, and then the universe was plunged into eternal darkness."

~ Pliny the Younger, From "The Letters of Pliny the Younger: with observations on each letter"

No Exceptions
These children were found mercilessly robbed of breath at an early age. Children like these were found not just in Pompeii, but in many cities that surrounded Pompeii.

HERCULANEUM

EERIE!   PHOTO OPS   UNCROWDED!   COOL ARCHAEOLOGY!

DAY TRIPS

Herculaneum is considered to be the little sister to Pompeii. Eventually, when archaeologists uncover more of the city, it may match Pompeii in size. But today, however, only 25% of it has been properly excavated. But what a spectacular 25% it is!

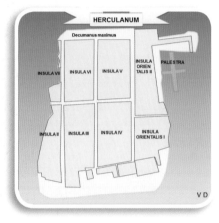

Victim to the same 79ce eruption of Mount Vesuvius as Pompeii, Herculaneum was a town with a higher tax bracket than Pompeii. Pompeii was a vacation town for the wealthy from Rome, and Herculaneum was where the local aristocrats lived. This makes finding priceless artifacts more prevalent in Herculaneum.

Several blocks have been beautifully excavated so far. Visitors can stroll up and down the streets, freely entering most of the old homes.

Because of the wealth of the former residents, architecture and art are incomparable. Some of the homes are multi-storied and beautifully decorated. Remnants of frescoes and mosaics are prevalent throughout the neighborhood, some in remarkable condition. Carved pillars and banisters decorate many homes. Restaurants are evident by the ovens and serving pots that still remain. The public baths were richly decorated.

Archaeologists have removed most of the movable artifacts, placing them in the on-site museum, as well as in the Naples Museum. Jewelry, coins, sculptures made of stone and bronze, everyday items such as silverware, dishes, and utensils have all been removed, cleaned, and displayed in the museums. An actual boat has been recovered, a rare find indeed!

The entire town seems to whisper their former happiness as you proceed down its streets. But as you approach the end of your visit, those whispers change to the silent screams of the people that perished on this day, so long ago.

The steep walls on the right of this photo did not exist before the eruption of Mt. Vesuvius in 79ce. The entire town was engulfed in this 30-40ft solidified wall. Archaeologists are digging the town out of the rock. The wet green area in front of the wall used to be the beach. The long series of arches were little ocean-front fishing boat garages. The town lies to the left, behind the old beach.

Looking down into the row of boat garages from the 30-40ft wall of hardened lava and ash, you can almost see the eeriness of what lies inside them. -->>

When they realised the volcano was going to consume their town, hundreds of people fled for shelter inside these garages. They all died instantly when the pyroclastic flows hit the town.

HERCULANEUM

Unlike Pompeii, which was hit unexpectedly, Herculaneum had some warning of the cataclysm that was bearing down upon them. Most of its residents were able to flee to safety. However, a few hundred citizens ran to the beach to take cover in the boat garages that faced the sea. And unlike Pompeii, whose people died from the inhalation of poison gases, our Herculaneans were hit by a scalding pyroclastic flow that cooked them in their garage tombs instantly. This is why skeletal remains were found here, rather than the human 'bubbles' that were found in Pompeii.

Many elaborate frescoes and wall mosaics remain in good condition. The inside walls of many of the homes were covered and decorated with frescoes, some as individual pieces of art as above, and others simply to add garnishments to both the interiors and the exteriors of their homes.

You can almost smell the aromas coming from these ancient restaurant serving pots.

This little inn featured a downstairs restaurant, and upstairs chambers for its guests.

DAY TRIPS

Fabulous mosaic tiled floors have been beautifully preserved in many of the homes and baths. The level of expertise required to create them in such exquisite detail is a reflection of the importance of artistic expression in their community, and their willingness to support it. During your visit, you will encounter many styles of mosaics all throughout Herculaneum.

As you can see, the modern town up on the right in this photo, was built over the remains of the ancient city of Herculaneum that has been dug out from beneath its basements. The biggest threat to ongoing excavations is the town itself that continues to grow over and around these ruins.

DAY TRIPS

LAKE NEMI

A picturesque little town, on a calm, blue, volcanic lake, is Nemi. A mere half-hour drive from Rome, Nemi is one of 15 connected villages that dot the foothills of the Castelli Area just southeast of Rome.

An excellent foray from the blisteringly hot city of Rome, the short drive out to Nemi will reward you with the cool, sweet breezes carrying the fresh aroma of the countryside.

Historically, Nemi, because of its easy access from Rome, was used as the country home for many Roman influencers. This included the most infamous Emperor, Caligula 104, who made a home, and he and kept his party barges *(opposite page)* there.

Additionally, a long-abandoned ruin of a Temple to Diana sits on the lakes edge. Once an ancient pilgrimage destination for those seeking to have children or to become pregnant, the Temple today is a partially-excavated ruin.

CALIGULA'S BOATS on LAKE NEMI

Lake Nemi is located approximately 19 miles southeast of Rome. Archaeologists found remnants of 2 ancient boats. They drained the lake to recover the pieces. During the restoration process, they verified that the 2 boats indeed belonged to Caligula **104**. However, use of the boats is largely speculative. A wonderful museum has since been created to protect the restored boats and their models, and is now open to the public.

It was nicknamed Caligula's Floating Palace and Caligula's Party Boat because of its extensive use of marble, and pieces of highly artistic mosaic flooring that were discovered.

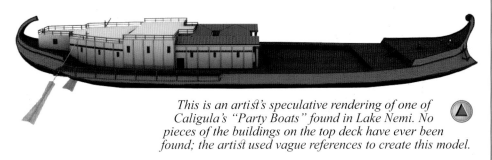

This is an artist's speculative rendering of one of Caligula's "Party Boats" found in Lake Nemi. No pieces of the buildings on the top deck have ever been found; the artist used vague references to create this model.

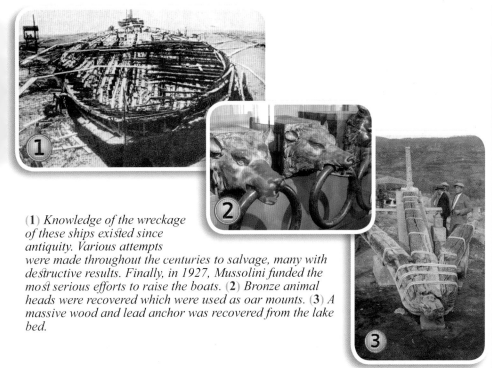

(**1**) *Knowledge of the wreckage of these ships existed since antiquity. Various attempts were made throughout the centuries to salvage, many with destructive results. Finally, in 1927, Mussolini funded the most serious efforts to raise the boats. (**2**) Bronze animal heads were recovered which were used as oar mounts. (**3**) A massive wood and lead anchor was recovered from the lake bed.*

ROME REBORN

The excellent works of the ROME REBORN project team has been an endless resource as I was researching for and writing this book. The ability to fling myself back in time to 320ce gave me a perspective that I didn't get by merely walking down the streets of Rome. Please take the time to go online and visit the RomeReborn.org site. If you happen to own a VR headset, you'll not only be able to see the ancient streets, but you'll be able to walk them, and enter some the buildings as they were in ancient times. Even Caesar would have been impressed!

If you could take a moment to leave a Review on Amazon, it would mean a WHOLE LOT to my business – and to me personally!

Thanks a Million!

To leave a review, visit
http://bit.ly/amazonPatty

Other books by Patty Civalleri

INDEX

PHOTO CREDITS

Our thanks and gratitude to all who contributed images for this book.